CORPORATE GOVERNANCE

Other books in The McGraw-Hill Executive MBA Series include:

CORPORATE STRATEGY
  by John L. Colley, Jr., Jacqueline L. Doyle, and Robert D. Hardie

ENTREPRENEURIAL MANAGEMENT
  by Robert J. Calvin

FINANCE AND ACCOUNTING FOR NONFINANCIAL MANAGERS
  by Samuel C. Weaver and J. Fred Weston

MANAGERIAL LEADERSHIP
  by Peter Topping

MERGERS AND ACQUISITIONS
  by J. Fred Weston and Samuel C. Weaver

SALES MANAGEMENT
  by Robert J. Calvin

STRATEGIC MARKETING MANAGEMENT
  by Mark E. Parry

CORPORATE GOVERNANCE

THE McGRAW-HILL
EXECUTIVE MBA SERIES

JOHN L. COLLEY, JR.
JACQUELINE L. DOYLE
GEORGE W. LOGAN
WALLACE STETTINIUS

McGraw-Hill

New York   Chicago   San Francisco   Lisbon   London
Madrid   Mexico City   Milan   New Delhi
San Juan   Seoul   Singapore
Sydney   Toronto

The McGraw·Hill Companies

Library of Congress Cataloging-in-Publication Data

Corporate governance / by John L. Colley, Jr. ... [et al.].
    p.   cm. — (The McGraw-Hill executive MBA series)
    ISBN 0-07-140346-9 (hardcover : alk. paper)
    1. Corporate governance.   I. Colley, John L., Jr.   II. Series.
HD2741 .C77462 2003
658.4—dc21

                                                    2002153991

3 4 5 6 7 8 9 0   DOC/DOC   0 9 8 7 6 5 4 (HC)

  4 5 6 7 8 9 0   DSH/DSH   0 1 0 9 (PBK)

ISBN 0-07-140346-9 (HC)

ISBN 0-07-146400-X (PBK)

This publication is designed to provide accurate and authoritative information in regard to the subject matter covered. It is sold with the understanding that the publisher is not engaged in rendering legal, accounting, or other professional service. If legal advice or other expert assistance is required, the services of a competent professional person should be sought.

—From a declaration of principles jointly adopted by a committee of the
American Bar Association and a committee of publishers.

McGraw-Hill books are available at special quantity discounts to use as premiums and sales promotions, or for use in corporate training programs. For more information, please write to the Director of Special Sales, Professional Publishing, McGraw-Hill, Two Penn Plaza, New York, NY 10121-2298. Or contact your local bookstore.

CONTENTS

Preface   vii

Acknowledgments   xii

Chapter 1   Capitalism, Free Enterprise, and the Corporation   1
Chapter 2   The Legal Obligations of Directors   13
Chapter 3   Board Organization   33
Chapter 4   Board Selection   55
Chapter 5   The Mystique of Board Meetings   83
Chapter 6   CEO Succession Planning, Selection, and Performance
              Appraisal   91
Chapter 7   CEO Compensation   109
Chapter 8   The Board-Management Relationship   133
Chapter 9   Corporate and Capital Structures   149
Chapter 10   Dealing with External Pressures   173
Chapter 11   How Directors Get into Trouble   187
Chapter 12   Not-for-Profit Organizations: The Differences   207
Chapter 13   Final Thoughts   227

Notes   247

Index   251

PREFACE

Frustrations with the performance of publicly traded corporations abound. Even before the Enron debacle and the other widely publicized scandals in 2002, there was a steadily increasing volume of criticism and complaints regarding the governance of many companies. Awareness of and new stories about dissatisfaction have only intensified over time as the complaints have continued to take many forms and address ever-broader issues. There is the perceived injustice of chief executive officers (CEOs) having made huge fortunes while company shareholders have lost significant portions of their investments and many employees have lost their jobs. Recent payoffs to underperforming CEOs have reached a level that is unacceptable to many people. CEOs whose unsatisfactory performance called for their dismissal have been able to leave with severance payments of $1 to $2 million per year for life. This tendency toward expansive severance payments is even more apparent in mergers. In one instance, the terms of the merger called for the CEO who was leaving to receive $5 million per year for life.

Both the public and regulatory authorities have been seriously misled by accounting irregularities and financial disclosure problems. In addition, a dot-com shell game has been played over the last 10 years or so as analysts hyped stocks whose prices found stratospheric levels from which they inexorably collapsed. There are also problems with the involvement of financial analysts in significant decision making within the firms they recommend. There is the practice of corporations guaranteeing loans to executives and the alleged use of corporate funds for executives' personal expenditures. This situation is compounded by the persistent public perception of corporate irresponsibility with regard to environmental issues. Add to all these problems the uneasy sense of big business' buying access to political influence in search of special-interest corporate subsidies, and we see a dark picture of senior corporate America indeed.

It is certainly tempting and easy for those of us in business to lay blame for this irresponsibility and greed at the feet of a few renegades. We like to think that the vast majority of businesspeople are honest and conscientious, trying to do the right thing. For the most part, this is fortunately true. Yet there seems to be entirely too many renegades in the corporate realm, and their indiscretions are damaging to us all. The pendulum apparently has swung too far toward the side of excess and willful nondisclosure, and our economic system has suffered as a result.

The collective problem of business today is coming to be seen as a failure of corporate governance, meaning that far too many boards are failing to execute their duties responsibly, both collectively and individually.

The critics are many. A number of reputable business-related publications have even begun to publish lists of the "worst corporate boards in the United States." Individual shareholders, investment fund managers, large state employee pension funds, lawmakers, government regulators, and a variety of activist groups are publicly and stridently questioning board judgments on a wide range of issues. These discontented critics invariably include employees who have invested portions of their 401(k) plans as well as other retirement assets in the shares of their employers.

Sustaining and fueling the criticism is the fact that investors have better access to more detailed information than ever before, enabling them to assess readily not only the performance of a company relative to its peers but also the lucrative agreements between boards and CEOs, conflicts of interest, and a host of other issues that historically have remained within the confines of the boardroom, largely unknown to the shareholder group. It is particularly in the absence of healthy corporate financial performance, however, that pressure is mounting against boards and their CEOs. In addition to scrutiny in the media, boards find themselves frequently facing questions from federal, state, and local governments, as well as federal and state regulatory agencies. The oversight of these groups reaches from the smallest company to the giants of our economy, many of which have felt the sting of legal and regulatory bodies. Consider the pressure brought to bear throughout the economy by the U.S. government's lawsuit to break up Microsoft, the successful effort by European regulators to halt the merger of GE and Honeywell in 2001, and the 2002 congressional investigations into Enron's collapse. According to the *Wall Street Journal*, the Securities and Exchange Commission (SEC) opened 570 investigations in 2001, which was more than in any year of the previous 10 years but, interestingly, just 10 more than in 1994.[1]

Adding further complexity, the laws and regulations governing business are by no means static over time. The rules of the game are in a state of constant revision, from Equal Employment Opportunity Commission (EEOC) regulations governing sexual harassment, equal employment opportunities, and age discrimination, to SEC regulations affecting corporate financial reporting and tax policies, to Environmental Protection Agency (EPA) environmental regulations and Occupational Safety and Health Administration (OSHA) safety rules. Parenthetically, these shifting standards have created a perpetual cottage industry for the legal and accounting professions both in the United States and abroad. This state of flux greatly complicates a board's best intentions to oversee completely ethical and legal operations. Some corporate actions that meet all contemporary regulatory requirements may be subject to critical scrutiny years later as a result of some event that focuses new attention on product safety or competitive standards.

These very public complaints about board performance have led many thoughtful people to a newly awakened interest in the subject of corporate governance and its critical importance to the U.S. and world economies. Likewise, such criticism has made corporate boards of directors more introspective. Many boards are rethinking their approaches to governing their corporations. The gradual increase in sophistication and power of financial analysts, large institutional investors, and other pressure groups also has forced boards to be far more sensitive to their firms' financial performance and its impact on stock prices. These pressures in the aggregate have prompted boards to wake up to the responsibilities for which they were elected, lest they find that events have outrun their ability to control them.

Despite growing interest, there is a general lack of understanding of the principles of effective corporate governance in most quarters, even those including many directors themselves. Evidence of this lack of understanding is the superficiality of the comments and analyses on the part of both the media and politicians with regard to the Enron scandal and other cases. For some parties, this lack of depth results from an absence of knowledge and/or experience. For others, it stems from a simplistic, single-issue focus on operations rather than governance. In any case, this lack of understanding can lead to poor policy decisions by boards and regulators alike, with potentially very adverse and unintended consequences. In extreme cases, complex issues become political, and passions overwhelm reason.

Consider the dilemma every company faces in determining a fair yet competitive level of compensation for its CEO. Few aspects of corporate governance are more likely to draw criticism from interested parties than the level of CEO compensation. Keep in mind that there is a free market for the services of CEOs and that at any specific time numerous companies are hard at work recruiting effective CEOs. For many years, CEO salaries had followed a pattern of steady increases, along with the costs of most goods and services, reflecting the competitive market for truly outstanding CEOs. The compensation for the majority of CEOs consists primarily of a salary, with an opportunity to earn bonuses for outstanding short- and long-term performance. While such salaries may appear large relative to that of a wage-earning person, these salaries are generally much lower than the compensation of small business owners/operators, professional athletes, actors, and media personalities. Yet CEOs of large companies are responsible for billions of dollars of shareholder assets and the livelihood of thousands of families of employees, and the effective ones can demonstrate that they make a difference in creating shareholder value in the hundreds of millions or even billions of dollars. In our opinion, the compensation of most good, effective CEOs is well earned.

We have observed the growing importance of corporate governance during many years of collective service on more than 70 public and private for-profit and not-for-profit boards. The ongoing immediacy of these governance issues and their importance to business managers, students, and investors confirmed for us the need for education on the subject of corporate governance. We are now in our fourth year of offering an elective MBA course at the Darden Graduate School of Business of the University of Virginia on the topic of corporate governance. The success of the course has been both rewarding and instructive. Through our own board experience and the experience of our teaching, we recognize that corporate governance decisions require analysis from several perspectives. These perspectives include

- *The legal issues.* What does the law require?
- *The ethics.* How does the organization define and fulfill its obligations to its constituencies or stakeholders in view of conflicting interests?
- *Effectiveness.* How does the board ensure that it and its management make effective decisions in an efficient and timely manner?
- *The board's relationships.* How does the board maintain effective relationships with its constituencies, particularly shareholders and management?
- *The group dynamics.* How well does the board function as a group or team?

We wrote this book with these multiple perspectives in mind. We also drew on our mutual experience base to fashion this book to address the many topics of primary import to current and future board members, as well as those who are likely to interact with boards of directors. These topics include the critical importance of the corporate form of business organization to our system of free enterprise and capitalism, the legal obligations of directors, the nuances of board selection, the most effective methods of board and corporate organization, and how boards could operate most effectively. We also have sought to provide a clear exposition of the methods employed for the selection, performance appraisal, compensation of, and succession planning for CEOs. We provide coverage of the board's role in strategy formulation, related business plans, and the means employed to finance a corporation and examine how the board should deal with external events, such as hostile takeover attempts, shareholder activism, proxy fights, and class-action lawsuits, to name a few. Additionally, we present a treatise on how directors get into trouble. Curiously, we have found a lack of coverage of this issue the most significant gap in the literature on governance. Finally, we consider the principles previously addressed for the context of the nonprofit or not-for-profit board.

Our goal has been to produce a book that would be informative for aspiring and active board members, managers, students of business, and individuals who want to understand the numerous facets of the governance process more clearly and are looking for useful insights into how they might do their work more effectively. This book focuses primarily on the governance of U.S. for-profit, publicly-owned companies, and as a result, we use the terms *shareholder* and *stockholder* throughout the book. Other names of constituencies would be appropriate for other forms of incorporation, such as *member* or *trustee*, for example, in the case of a mutual company.

In the end, we hope to contribute to raising the quality of the public debate surrounding corporate governance as we all strive to improve corporate performance.

John L. Colley, Jr.
Jacqueline L. Doyle
George W. Logan
Wallace Stettinius
Charlottesville, Virginia

ACKNOWLEDGMENTS

We are grateful to the University of Virginia, the Darden Graduate School of Business Administration, the Darden School Foundation, and the Batten Institute for their extensive support of this project.

It is a great pleasure for us to acknowledge the support and assistance of a number of administrators, faculty colleagues, and students without whose help this book could not have been completed. Dean Robert Harris of the Darden School, Associate Dean of the Faculty Jim Freeland, and the Darden School's Research Committee have been strong supporters of our effort. The Batten Institute, its executive director, Robert Bruner, and its director of research, Sankaran Venkataraman, provided valuable support. We also wish to thank our faithful assistant, Barbara Richards, for her extensive contributions to this effort. We are pleased to acknowledge the contributions of Jeff Gill and Tom Farrell to sections of this book dealing with the legal obligations of directors.

We are indebted to our esteemed colleague Ed Freeman, who has inspired us with his tireless dedication to his students, his colleagues, his research, his field of business ethics, and his family. He has broadened our thinking, especially regarding the important role of ethical behavior among directors, and in so doing has contributed to the betterment of this project.

We also wish to recognize a number of current and former students who assisted with various aspects of the book. We especially recognize the significant contributions of Kristin Hampton, Christopher Ling, and Allison Sewell Bridges. The following students also were instrumental in helping make this work possible: John Arendale, John (Jay) Evans, John Keppler, Evan Bates, Topher Fearey, Stuart Austin Marsh, James Bomar, Alexander Fraser, David Sadler, Charles (David) Cox, Keith Kaminsky, Seon Won, Linsley Craig, Matthew Kastantin, and Seok-Hwan Yoon.

We are grateful to the many students at the Darden School who have studied with us these past three years and to the numerous professional colleagues who have shared governance experiences with us over many years. We particularly and gratefully acknowledge the contributions of Warren Batts, who assisted us with the initiation of our course in corporate governance.

We also would like to thank our gracious colleagues at McGraw-Hill for their association and support. We are grateful to Laura Libretti for her superior professional administrative support. We are especially indebted to Kelli Christiansen for her unparalleled responsiveness and professionalism, her consistently constructive contributions, and her ever-optimistic support of this project.

Finally, we especially acknowledge the patience and support of our families, who have been silent partners in this effort.

Capitalism, Free Enterprise, and the Corporation

The societies of the developed countries of the twenty-first century live in unprecedented prosperity. These nations have produced the highest standard of living for the most people in the history of the world. How has this happened? We believe that the origin of this prosperity lies in the development of an economic system that embraces, for the most part, free enterprise, capitalism, and competition. Free enterprise brings to the economies of developed countries the sustained energy of competition, in which the creative minds of countless individuals are unleashed to pursue their individual best interests, the more unfettered by regulation the better. Adam Smith first wrote in 1776 that "an invisible hand of self-interest" moved to create a total environment in the best interests of "the many" when each of us acts to maximize our own individual interests.[1] The initial step in this amazing journey of economic development was thus the realization that the greater good would be served by each of us diligently seeking to optimize our own best interests. While counterintuitive in some respects, this remains an astonishing idea.

The concept of the efficacy of the invisible hand led logically to a second notion that as individuals attempt to pursue their separate interests, the intersections of their interests and objectives result in a natural state of competition. Specifically in the realm of business, we mean by this competition for raw materials, labor, customers, and investment capital. This competitive environment leads to a "survival of the fittest" regimen that, over time, weeds out the weakest competitors and promotes survival of the most successful. While some people may fear this relentless ferreting out of the less efficient, it is perhaps the most energizing aspect of our system of free enterprise and competition. The third key aspect of our economic system has been the development of modern capitalism, in which

1

the capital of many investors can be united to provide the large amounts of investment capital needed to fund extensive projects and massive enterprises. It is axiomatic that the greater the freedom of our corporate enterprises to compete in search of expansive returns, the greater is the inclination of individual and institutional investors to provide the capital sought. The three cornerstones of our economic system, therefore, are free enterprise, competition, and capitalism.

With the development of this economic system, enterprises of a size and complexity not previously thought possible flourished. The obvious question was, How could these enterprises be managed in the best interests of shareholders? Our premise in this book is that governance, as we know and practice it, has made the difference both at the macro levels—political, social, and economic—and at the level of the individual enterprise—corporate governance. Without an effective system of governance, there would be chaos in human affairs. It is governance that brings order out of the chaos. When individuals live together in communities, there must be rules and laws about how they relate to each other because conflict among individuals and groups is inherent in the human condition. Most of these conflicts result from different personalities and beliefs and from a natural competition for limited resources. Some have more serious moral implications, however, because they are rooted in a lack of respect and concern for the lives and property of others, inspired by the basest of human motives.

Moral conflict nakedly reveals the two sides of human nature—the good and the evil. We see the good in acts of love and selflessness, acts of courage, acts of genius in the arts and sciences, and acts of integrity, honor, and duty. We see the evil in acts of hate, greed, tyranny, oppression, cowardice, and dishonesty. Such struggles between the forces of good and evil have been at the core of the human drama since the beginning of time. The battle takes place within every individual of conscience, as well as between individuals and groups. We also see these conflicts playing out in the various forms of government prevalent around the world and, naturally, in the realm of modern business.

THE EVOLUTION OF GOVERNANCE

Early on in antiquity, the hard labor of subsistence living was transformed gradually by the invention of tools—the beginnings of technology. With the development of new sources of energy—first the steam engine and then electricity and the internal combustion engine—came machines that dramatically increased productivity. In the past 50 years technological advances in practically every field have exploded, nearly all traceable to the invention of the transistor. With the subsequent development of digital technology, we have seen revolutions in electronics, communications, transportation, medicine, and all forms of manufacturing, leveraged by an exponential increase in our ability to gather and disseminate information. A requisite driver of these evolutionary forces has been the advent of universal education. The breakthrough that made education more readily available to the masses was the invention of movable type by Gutenberg in 1438, and the evolution of printing that followed ushered in growing literacy that became the foundation for an educated populace. We recognize the impact of this innovation in the axiom, "We learn to read so that we can read to learn."

As widespread literacy spawned education that has driven technology, there has been a comparable evolution in how we govern our affairs. People have been living in groups from the beginning, first as hunters, gatherers, and fishermen and then in agricultural societies and eventually in industrial societies. From the outset, humankind has sought to discover the best ways to make decisions for its groups—to find ways to govern so as to resolve disputes, control destructive behavior, and achieve goals that advance the mutual welfare of the members of the society. The effectiveness of a given approach to governance has determined, to a large extent, the survival and prosperity of that society. In the beginning, groups of people were small, simple, and located in one place. Their governance processes could be equally simple. Over time, these groups have become large, complex, far-reaching organizations. Tribal and feudal fiefdoms have evolved into nation-states. Small, local proprietorships have evolved into large corporations. Their decision-making processes likewise have matured to reflect the more complex governance issues.

Among the seminal breakthroughs in this journey from simplicity to complexity in governance were the social revolutions of the eighteenth and nineteenth centuries—particularly the American and French revolutions and their accompanying periods of enlightenment. Prior to that time, as societies grew, they became progressively more stratified, with smaller ruling classes accumulating greater wealth generated by the labors of the subservient masses. Rich nations became ever more powerful and, by force, colonized weaker nations, particularly those endowed with an abundance of natural resources. For centuries, governance was exercised by a privileged few who had gained power over the many. The powerful ruled until they were overthrown by a revolt from within or defeated by a conqueror from outside. However, the nature of the society seldom changed; it was simply a case of one monarchy or dictatorship replacing another. Some were competent and benevolent, and the people benefited. More typically, there was incompetence, corruption, and oppression of the citizenry.

The prevailing system of governance resulted from the actions of individuals, not from the evolution of legal principles. As individuals gained power, however, they increasingly ruled by oppressive force, often creating a backlash of revolution. The social revolutions that followed were fueled by a hunger for individual freedom and by a sense of moral imperative of how people should treat one another. Out of these revolutions grew the modern concept of democracy—a rule of the people, by the people, and for the people—a concept implied in the Constitution of the United States and articulated in Lincoln's Gettysburg Address.

THE DEMOCRATIC EXPERIMENT

Government as we know it today in the United States actually had its beginning with the Greeks and Romans. Their examples influenced the development of the English rule of law, of which the Magna Carta, written in the thirteenth century, is surely the cornerstone, and most of American jurisprudence is rooted in English common law. During the Renaissance, the seeds for representative government were sown. They sprouted in the American Revolution in the eighteenth century and resulted in the Constitution that was painstakingly hammered out by our Founding Fathers to create a truly democratic form of government.

The evolution of democracy in the United States has been neither easy nor painless. Born of the idealism of the Declaration of Independence, it continued with the Articles of Confederation that lasted roughly a decade before they had to be discarded. Our democracy then came to life in a Constitution that had the near-fatal defect of tolerating slavery, in stark contradiction to the original concept in the Declaration of Independence that "all men are created equal." There was even confusion as to whether the Constitution created a nation. In fact, many preferred to think of it as a federation of sovereign states, thereby leaving unresolved the issue of federalism—the reaches and limits of the federal government (centralized authority) versus that of the states (decentralized authority). In the minds of some revolutionary leaders, the federal government actually was subordinate to the states, except in very limited and well-defined functions.

The Constitution obviously was not perfect when first written, and it was soon amended to include a Bill of Rights, which conferred a mix of individual rights, states' rights, and constraints on federal power. Those legal constructs acknowledged the potential for a tyranny of the majority and the need to protect the rights of minority groups. Even with its deficiencies, the

Constitution created a more representative government than had previously existed and clearly defined the separation and balance of power among the legislative, judicial, and executive branches of government. The process of amending the Constitution established early on that the document would be a work in progress, adapting to changing conditions and mores as times passed, as evidenced by its current 27 amendments.

Nonetheless, just 85 years from the founding of the Republic, one of the bloodiest civil wars in world history was fought to resolve two issues: to make the United States "one" rather than "many" (essentially to further define the rights of the states and the federal government) and to remove the blight of slavery that contradicted the basic premise of the Declaration of Independence that "all men are created equal." Another hundred years and the nonviolent civil rights movement were required to remove the legal barriers of segregation, which had resulted from a culture of white supremacy. On the way, as the new nation became, ultimately, a world power, it was forced to fight many wars to preserve freedom in the world, assuming the leadership role in defending and extending the democratic form of government. This great experiment in governance continues to this day as Americans struggle to harmonize the domestic differences of a pluralistic society and to live peacefully with their neighbors in an ever more tightly knit world community.

GOVERNANCE HAS MADE THE DIFFERENCE

The American experience with governance has been a great yet fragile experiment. It did not have to succeed. South America began its development into a number of individual countries (states) at about the same time as the United States. South America has had great difficulty establishing stable and democratic regimes, even to this day. The twentieth century also saw the growth and failure of totalitarian regimes in Germany, Japan, and Russia, with great personal suffering. The end of colonial rule in Africa following World War II has resulted in almost continuous political instability and bloodshed, as it has in other areas of the world. These experiments in self-governance around the world have not yet succeeded. It is worth noting that peace and prosperity in today's world tend to correlate with stable and democratic governments. Nations ruled by authoritarian regimes of one type or another appear to fall short of achieving both of these goals.

Thus in nation-states, governance indeed does make a difference in the success of a society, but good governance cannot be taken for granted. Without effective political and economic systems, it is virtually certain that no society can achieve sustained peace and prosperity.

CAPITALISM

A fundamental chapter in the evolution of governance was the concurrent development of a free-market economic system that spawned the prosperity that continues to this day. Democracy created a context in which this free-market economic system, called *capitalism*, could evolve. There is a clear and logical connection between the concept of individual political freedom and the freedom of individuals to pursue their economic self-interests. As mentioned earlier, Adam Smith, in his classic *Wealth of Nations*, written in 1776, described "the invisible hand of self-interest" as at the center of human behavior. Rather than seeing it negatively in moral terms, he saw it positively as the principal driving force for economic and social development.

A paradox resulting from the development of capitalism is that the collective pursuit of individual self-interest has created a prosperity that benefits us all. A concept that remains at issue, though, is "the tension between accumulating goods and cultivating goodness, which appeared early in the American experience and has lingered long."[2] The role of the economic system is to provide goods and services that meet the needs of the people and in the process provide the jobs that create the wealth with which people buy the needed and/or desired goods and services. In a poor economy, people are reduced to struggling for survival, often falling prey to disease and starvation. Surviving does not, by definition, create an attractive standard of living. Conversely, an economy that creates wealth does not necessarily meet high moral standards, depending on how the wealth is created, how it is distributed, and for what purposes it is used. Finding the right balance between "goods and goodness" is an ongoing debate. It is not our purpose here to resolve it, nor could we. However, we do want to acknowledge its importance and relevance to contemporary society. Most certainly, moral and ethical considerations must enter into the governance not only of nations but also of commercial enterprises, as we are sadly relearning as this is being written.

THE GAME

Businesses function in complex economic systems, each with its own characteristic ecology. We can view these systems using the analogy of a game, where participants typically compete within the rules of the game to get ahead. Such games have been played throughout recorded history and have developed in complexity and reach, with most changes having occurred within the past two centuries. Initially, though, the games were mostly local, confined to villages, townships, and small geographic regions. In the last several hundred years, they have expanded and grown to encompass whole nations. Currently, the games are becoming more global, with nations banding together to form economic unions. For the most part, though, the rules of the economic systems we describe are determined predominantly at the level of national governments, with trade restrictions eased or eliminated for member countries of economic alliances.

The nature of the game in each nation reflects a number of variables: the culture, the education of the population, the political system, the geography, and the available capital and natural resources. These attributes influence the creation of an infrastructure that supports the game. Of particular importance in this infrastructure are national defense and public safety, the nation's transportation system, and its legal system, both criminal and civil. The criminal system protects people and property and ensures domestic social order. Likewise, a strong military protects the nation from attack. The civil system arbitrates and enforces contracts and personal property rights. We find that within the context of the resulting organizational infrastructure, the game is influenced and substantially determined by three distinct institutions: the government, regulatory and law-enforcement agencies, and finally, those individuals or groups who choose or are forced to operate outside the rules of the game.

The Government and the Game

Federal, state, and local legislative bodies and various governmental agencies write, approve, and interpret the rules of the game. Governmental executives, particularly the president and state governors, also have a role in this process, primarily through the use of vetoes and executive orders. In a democracy, individual constituents as well as various interest groups try to influence the writing of the rules in their favor. Thus part of the game itself involves the efforts to modify the rules of the game.

The game's rules in the United States have centered on seven main goals:

- To maintain competitive markets via antitrust and fair-trade laws
- To regulate noncompetitive markets
- To maintain a balance of power between capital and labor
- To ensure orderly capital markets
- To protect consumers from unsafe products and fraud
- To ensure equal access to employment, education, housing, and public accommodations
- To protect the environment

The governance system can create rules that enhance prosperity or retard it. This is a complex topic that is the source of constant debate and considerable tension. Social conscience and populist politics push us toward a broad distribution of wealth, the logical extreme of which is a highly regulated socialistic system. Where these socialistic systems have been tried, however, they have failed repeatedly to produce a great deal of wealth for the masses. The reasons for this failure can be found in human nature. Such systems do not induce purposeful, productive behavior on the part of individuals. On the other hand, letting disproportionate wealth accrue to a very few individuals has been equally destructive of prosperity. The enduring challenge for this grand economic game is to find the balance between these extremes. What a society does with the largess of its output influences the health of its economic system and consequently, in a cyclical fashion, its future output.

Enforcement and the Game

While the legislative bodies and regulatory agencies in a democracy write the rules at the macro level, those rules are interpreted and enforced by regulatory agencies and the judicial system. Enforcement involves monitoring the actions of those playing the game to determine if rules have been or are about to be broken. In the United States, this attribute of enforcement has created a tension between privacy rights and police powers protecting the common good. The courts, which also represent an arm of rule enforcement, rule on these and all rule interpretation conflicts, negotiating often complex and delicate terrain.

Those Outside the Game

Most individuals and corporate entities participate in the game and operate within its rules. There are two groups, however, that are "not in the game." One of these groups is the underground economy, those who choose to play outside the rules. Ironically, underground economies are usually fostered by stringent rules of the game that create black-market opportunities. Such rules are usually intended to enforce morality, for example, attempting to limit the incursion of drugs, prostitution, gambling, and/or pornography, but they often produce negative, unintended consequences in the creation of underground economies for the illicit goods and services. A second group "not in the game" consists of those who are unable or unwilling to be part of the productive workforce. Welfare programs actually assisted in the creation of some members of this group until the related myths were exposed following the Welfare

Reform Act of 1996. Other members of this group simply do not have the requisite skills, training, or work ethic to earn a living in our increasingly complex environment. Additionally, over the years, many people have been excluded from effective participation in our economy because of prejudice.

Those not in the game, at a minimum, are a drag on it, but they also represent a latent threat to it. They can destroy the game if they become large enough to wield political power or desperate enough to revolt, as they have in many countries. In simple terms, if too many people are left behind and cannot participate fully in a capitalist system, the society will undergo a revolution promulgated by those left out. Consequently, it is in the best interests of those in the game to work diligently to bring in those who are not.

The result of the rule writing and enforcement, the governance process, is the competitive environment in which the game is played. This environment is either favorable or unfavorable for the creation of prosperity. In America, citizens have experienced in the preceding half-century the 50 most prosperous years in history. These were preceded by a worldwide depression and two world wars. The overriding challenge for those engaged in the national governance process is whether we can maintain (or improve) the current level of worldwide prosperity or whether we will repeat the history of severe economic cycles and the personal suffering that inevitably accompany them.

THE CORPORATION

Among the most important rules of the game that have evolved over the years are those addressing the form of governance for the business organization. We take the corporate form as a given today, but the corporation is a relatively new form of business organization, as noted below.

The nonbusiness corporation is an ancient form, originally used for towns, guilds, and colonies in Rome and, from the early Middle Ages, also for universities, religious orders, and other so-called benevolent organizations performing civic services and thus subject to government license and oversight. The Muscovy Company in 1555, the Spanish Company in 1577, and the East India Company in 1601 received history's first recorded business charters of incorporation during the reign of England's Queen Elizabeth I. The London Company, soon to be called the Virginia Company of London, followed in 1606.[3] Prior to the corporation, businesses were organized as proprietorships or partnerships.

The U.S. Supreme Court under Chief Justice John Marshall made corporations possible legally in the early nineteenth century. Marshall himself defined a corporation in *Dartmouth College v. Woodward* in the following terms:

> ... A corporation is an artificial being, invisible, intangible and existing only in the contemplation of the law. Being the mere creature of law, it possesses only three qualities which the charter of its creation confers upon it, either expressly or as incidental to its very existence ... [the most] important are immortality and, if the expression may be allowed, individuality; properties by which a perpetual succession of many persons are considered as the same, and may act as a single individual.[4]

In summary, the corporation is a creation of the law and has legal standing independent of its owners. Three features have made the corporation attractive—its unlimited life, the limited liability of the owners, and the divisibility of ownership that permits transfer of ownership interests without disrupting the structure of the organization. In recent years, tax considerations have become increasingly more problematic for standard or so-called C Corporations. The tax problems associated with corporations have been mitigated in recent years by the availability of Subchapter S as part of the Internal Revenue Service tax code and the limited-liability corporations (LLCs) created by state charters. LLCs have all the benefits of the corporate form, but their profits are taxed at the ownership level. This is in contrast to the traditional corporation, where the corporation itself, rather than the owners, pays taxes on profits. After its legal establishment, the corporation quickly became the preferred form of organization for larger enterprises. By 1919, corporations, while representing only 31.5 percent of the total number of businesses, employed 86 percent of the workforce and produced 87.7 percent of the total business output by value.[5]

THE TRUST

Another form of organization was experimented with around the turn of the twentieth century. J. P. Morgan, the financier, acted as an unofficial guide and lawmaker in the absence of strong federal regulation. Paul Johnson, in his exceptional book, *A History of the American People*, writes that J. P. Morgan believed that

> ... The tendency of economic activity in a free society was to produce primeval chaos, in which men fought savagely for supremacy and countless sins were committed. Freedom was needed for economic society to function efficiently, but the resulting chaos generated inefficiency as well as sin. He reasoned that some degree of order was needed, and that order could best be brought about by forms of economic concentration that imposed a degree of order without inhibiting freedom to the point where efficiency was again endangered. This valuable concentration was achieved by the corporation and the trust.[6]

The story of the trusts is a complicated one. During the Civil War, the United States followed a policy of high tariffs to protect its developing industries. Getting tariff protection required that independent corporations should band together to increase their collective political influence. Having learned to cooperate, a number of industries began to form trusts; sugar, tobacco, railroads, cattle, and oil are but a few examples. The trusts, of course, reduced competition and encouraged monopolies, a natural outcome. The courts began to step in, and by the panic of 1893, antitrust laws were in effect. This effort at organizing economic activity was no longer legal or, as time would prove, efficient.

THE ROLE OF CORPORATE GOVERNANCE

As with nations, governance matters profoundly in the success of individual commercial enterprises. An examination of businesses that have sustained success over long periods reveals boards that have governed the affairs of the business effectively. Likewise, with businesses that have performed poorly, it is rather commonplace to track the problems to boards that have not addressed the issues confronting their businesses effectively. The popular press reveals examples of the latter with regularity, whereas the business press less frequently highlights boards with strong performance.

The management of a corporation is usually accomplished under the leadership of a chief executive officer (CEO), who reports to the board of directors. While boards play a variety of roles, effective organizations acknowledge the board's role in selecting the CEO, advising on and consenting to the selection of businesses and strategies, and overseeing results.

The test of the effectiveness of governance is the degree to which any organization is achieving its purpose. While many of the principles we will discuss have application to organizations with a wide range of purposes, our focus is narrowed to address the governing of publicly owned businesses whose purpose is to create and serve customers, the reward for which, if done well, is profitability and a concomitant improvement in shareholder value.

An important distinction between publicly owned businesses and privately owned businesses is that privately owned businesses tend to be owner-managed. Because the owners of private businesses are typically directly involved in their enterprises, they are better informed about the affairs of the business and can reasonably represent their own interests. They have not delegated control to a representative board of directors. Thus the potential conflicts of interest that exist between investors and those who have been hired to run the business are not as relevant. Even so, many of the governance principles that apply to publicly owned businesses are also applicable to privately owned businesses.

Thus the board of directors of the publicly owned corporation is the focus of our interest in corporate governance in this book. We begin our discussion of this entity in Chapter 2 with an examination of common forms of board and corporate organization, along with the bylaws that embody the standards and limits of the board's dealings.

REVIEW QUESTIONS

1. How does the free-enterprise system create the environment within which modern corporations flourish?
2. What is the role of governance in our system of free enterprise, capitalism, and competition?
3. How does competition promote the continuous strengthening of our economic system?
4. Could our economic system flourish if the corporate form of business organization did not exist?

CHAPTER 2

The Legal Obligations of Directors

When individuals own and manage a business, we presume that they will act in their own self-interest, making managerial decisions to support the achievement of their short- and long-term goals, whatever they may be. There is no opportunity for a conflict of interest. When individuals serve as directors of businesses, they represent the interests of the other owners. In this situation, the potential for conflicts of interest indeed exists. The elected director assumes the obligation to represent the interests of those owners who cannot represent themselves, undertaking a serious fiduciary responsibility. Effective representation, however, requires more than integrity. It also requires the competence to make sound decisions. Good directors know their limits and turn to more expert advisers when their judgment so dictates. Directors who are "dumb but honest" fail to fulfill their obligations. In fact, legislators need to keep in mind as they write laws and regulations that well-intentioned incompetence can be as dangerous as dishonesty.

Even when competent individuals act with the best of intentions in the role of director, business setbacks and failures may occur. In cases of unsatisfactory results, shareholders may scrutinize the causal actions of the directors with the advantage of hindsight. They particularly seek answers to questions of whether the directors acted responsibly in fulfilling their obligations. At issue, though, is how "fulfilling their obligations" is defined.

The purpose of this chapter is to provide an overview of laws that define the legal obligations of directors. These laws are primarily state laws, as opposed to federal laws, because, with only a few minor exceptions, states grant and administer corporate charters through their laws and regulations. Some banks and other federally regulated entities may not be incorporated in a state.

Corporate laws vary by state. The state most influential in setting corporate legal standards has been Delaware, where more than 50 percent of publicly owned U.S. companies are incorporated.[1] The State of Virginia passed a new set of statutes in 1985 (Virginia Code Annotated, paragraph 13.1–690) that stipulates the very popular *business judgment rule*. This rule has been held up in the courts as being very favorable to directors. While all states have the same business judgment rule as a concept, Virginia courts have given its construction a much different meaning than it has in many other states. In states other than Virginia, the business judgment rule does not supplant the other fiduciary duties of a director, but as construed in Virginia, it appears that the business judgment rule can exonerate a director who may not have exercised any judgment at all or whose business judgment was lacking.

In this chapter our discussion of legal standards for directors will focus on these two states—Delaware and Virginia—as examples of how states approach such issues. We will note substantial similarities and differences because the codes of these two states, to a large degree, define the legal spectrum across most states. All directors must recognize, however, their critical responsibility to understand the laws of the state in which the corporation on whose board they sit is chartered.

In addition to state laws, there are federal laws and regulations that relate to the activities of corporations. Among these are securities laws addressing the issues of full disclosure and insider trading that are most relevant to directors. These laws are highly technical, but every director must be familiar with them. Because they are not actually matters of governance, however, we have chosen not to address them or other similar corporate laws in this book. Ensuring that a corporation is complying with them is a governance issue, though. Such compliance is imbedded in the duties of directors that are the focus of our discussion.

We have drawn on descriptions from the American Law Institute's *Principles of Corporate Governance: Analysis and Recommendations*, published in 1992, to provide a general overview of managerial duties that approximate the business laws in place throughout the United States. The questions below and their accompanying responses highlight the most important elements of a director's responsibilities.

WHO IS RESPONSIBLE FOR GOVERNING THE AFFAIRS OF A CORPORATION?

The classic corporate law 101 answer to the question of who is responsible for governing the affairs of a corporation is the board of directors. The board's powers are derived from the shareholders whom they represent and are articulated in the corporation's governing documents, which include

- The articles of incorporation
- The bylaws
- Shareholder agreements

We discuss these documents in detail in Chapter 3, which addresses board organization. When confronted with a corporate governance legal issue, directors should first check the corporation's governing documents and subsequently the applicable state laws and case precedents.

State law dictates the establishment of boards of directors for most corporations. For example, the Delaware General Corporation Law Code [paragraph 141(a)] states: "The business and affairs of every corporation organized under this chapter shall be managed by or under the direction of a Board of Directors, except as may be otherwise provided in this chapter or in its certificate of incorporation." The Commonwealth of Virginia has similar language in paragraph 13.1–673(B) of its code, which states, "All corporate powers shall be exercised by or under the authority of, and the business and affairs of the corporation managed under the direction of, its board of directors, subject to any limitations set forth in the articles of incorporation or in a . . . [shareholder's agreement]."

While every state has a similar statute empowering the board of directors to govern and manage the affairs of the corporation, the shareholders ultimately control the affairs of the corporation because they elect and can replace the board of directors. The shareholders of a corporation also have the statutory right in most states to approve major transactions or decisions, such as mergers, the sale of assets, or dissolution of the company. They also may reserve other rights in the governing documents of the corporation. In situations where the majority of stockholders of a corporation disagree with a significant action or actions of the board, the stockholders *almost always* win, but it may take some time, particularly if the matter has to be litigated to reach a resolution. Such situations may involve the board's refusal to accept an offer for the sale of the company, the board's approval of actions leading to a drastic decline in financial performance, or the board's choice of a controversial chief executive officer (CEO).

As a matter of practice, the board of directors delegates most decisions to management, either formally or informally. Consequently, senior management typically has the authority to make day-to-day decisions in running the business. The relationship between the board and management is a critical one, both practically in terms of how well the business is run and legally in terms of who is accountable for the actions and results of the corporation. We will spend a great deal of time in subsequent chapters discussing this relationship from a variety of perspectives. In brief, we find that most boards perform the following actions: hiring, evaluating, and firing the CEO; exercising oversight of CEO actions; advising on and consenting to major decisions and policies, typically developed by the CEO; and reviewing results. In matters of litigation, senior management *always* loses in a conflict with the board of directors, provided the board is truly independent of management influence.

WHAT ARE THE RESPONSIBILITIES OF DIRECTORS?

All states define the roles of directors in terms of duties. As we will note, Delaware and Virginia differ in how those duties are interpreted and articulated. In addition, in publicly owned companies, the Securities and Exchange Commission (SEC) imposes regulatory requirements on the corporation and hence the board, particularly with regard to full and timely disclosure of information and insider stock trading. The stock exchanges also have rules that prescribe certain responsibilities, enforced through the standards required for listing on each exchange.

The legal obligations of directors can be broadly summarized by the managerial duties that the law prescribes for directors. The major duties of directors are

- The fiduciary duty
- The duty of loyalty and the duty of fair dealing
- The duty of care
- The duty not to entrench
- The duty of supervision

Let us examine these duties in turn.

The Fiduciary Duty

Central to the role of a director is the fiduciary role—being trustworthy in acting in the best interests of those whom the director represents. This duty has, as we have discussed, the elements of both integrity and competence. What is the duty? It begins with understanding the objective of the corporation.

Paragraph 2.01 of the *Principles of Corporate Governance: Analysis and Recommendations*, assembled by the American Law Institute in 1992, provides the following discourse regarding "The Objective and Conduct of the Corporation"[2]:

(a) Subject to the provisions of Subsection (b) and Paragraph 6.02 (Actions of Directors . . . That Have the Foreseeable Effect of Blocking Unsolicited Tender Offers), a corporation should have as its objective the conduct of business activities with a view to enhancing corporate profit and shareholder gain.

(b) Even if corporate profit and shareholder gain are not thereby enhanced, the corporation, in the conduct of its business:

   (1) Is obliged, to the same extent as a natural person, to act within the boundaries set by law;

   (2) May take into account ethical considerations that are reasonably regarded as appropriate to the responsible conduct of business; and

   (3) May devote a reasonable amount of resources to public welfare, humanitarian, educational, and philanthropic purposes.

The director's challenge is how he or she should interpret this fiduciary obligation to pursue the objectives of the business in any given situation. Many corporate governance issues involve subtle questions with regard to specific facts and circumstances.

Paragraph (a) states the economic objective of enhancing profits and shareholder value. This sounds simple but, in fact, involves a fair amount of complexity. Profit is difficult to measure as well as predict. Peter Drucker has written, "Profit, it cannot be said often enough, is an accounting illusion."[3]

As Drucker points out, there are two dimensions to the reported profit in any period—that which is a result of current period activities harvesting prior periods' investments and the future profits that will result from the current period's investing. In theory, we might try to measure the amount invested in the future but generally do not do so because it is very difficult. The difficulty arises because it is so tied to the effectiveness of current operations—the maintenance of equipment and facilities, the development of improved processes for efficiency and quality, the building of customer relationships and brand strength, and the growing of effective human resources, as well as more visible research and development (R&D) efforts or the expansion of capacity. In short, there is not only an amount of profit but also a quality attribute of profit that reflects the efforts to generate future profits. Because the two perspectives are so closely intertwined in the operation of a business, it is very difficult, if not impossible, to account for them separately with any meaningful accuracy. What is impossible in the short run is to measure, in any finite way, how well the resources have been spent. In addition, while a company may be profitable as defined by accounting rules, its profits may or may not cover the cost of its employed capital.

In fulfilling a fiduciary duty, directors must consider that the objective of the corporation also includes enhancing *stockholder gain*. This is a broad-er term that implies everything that contributes to strengthening the eco-nomic efforts and value of the corporation. While profit may be the legal objective of the corporation, profit is a result of how well the corporation is functioning. Therefore, in order to create profit as going concerns, corpora-tions also must have the objectives of creating customers and meeting their needs efficiently and effectively in a competitive environment, which requires capital resources and investments, as well as human resources in the form of motivated, competent, and committed people. These objectives support not only the creation of profit but also the enhancement of stock-holder gain. There is a cause and effect at work that must be understood. This, too, allows much room for well-intended interpretation.

Because corporations, their customers, and their employees exist in the greater society, how well that society functions has a direct impact on the profitability of a business. Reflecting this concept, paragraph (b) addresses social responsibilities. This paragraph allows that corporations may devote resources to social causes even if doing so does not enhance profit or shareholder gain. Taking a long view, though, we may see that fulfilling social responsibilities enhances society, which benefits cus-tomers, employees, and shareholders alike, and thus contributes to the future profitability of the business to the degree that it facilitates creation of a more stable and prosperous society.

The law generally gives boards of directors the latitude to consider the long view in determining the best interests of the corporation, as well as ethics, legality, and the interests of all stakeholders in the fulfilling of their fiduciary duty. Vignette 2-1 discusses the relationship between a director's responsibility to shareholders and other societal interests.

VIGNETTE 2-1

BALANCING RESPONSIBILITY TO SHAREHOLDERS WITH INTEREST IN SOCIAL CAUSES

THE ISSUE

What is the obligation of a corporation to its shareholders versus its obligations to other stakeholders and to society in general? Is there an inherent conflict, or does fulfilling social obligations somehow fulfill long-term profit goals? While many people agree that corpo-rations have a social obligation, there remains wide disagreement on what these obligations are and how they should be fulfilled.

Continued

Continued

THE SITUATION

Two entrepreneurs who were very interested in various social causes founded a company to produce a premium consumer product in a state generally favorable toward such businesses. These interests of the founders were public knowledge from the very founding of the company. A percentage of the company's profits were committed to the support of various social and environmental concerns. This publicly stated intent, no doubt, generated a lot of public interest and support and aided in the strong and rapid growth of the company over a period of several years. All was well for several years until the founders decided to take the company public. While the public knew of the personal values and inclinations of the owners, the act of going public created a new dynamic.

The founders still owned a significant amount of the outstanding shares, although they did not retain outright majority control of the company. Initially, there were no problems. Over time, however, the profit performance of the company declined, and there were mounting pressures from shareholders for greater attention to the company's share price. The board continued to reflect the interests of the founders in community and social issues, with a heavy emphasis on directors with social responsibility connections and far fewer with business backgrounds.

In the struggle to resolve the conflicting values, the company was able to obtain the passage of a state law that allowed directors to consider whether a sale of a company was in the best interests of its employees, its suppliers, and the economy of the state. The enactment of this provision was intended to strengthen the ability of the company to remain an independent company headquartered in its state of incorporation and to pursue its philanthropic practices. This legislation had not been tested in court.

Subsequently, one potential acquirer made an offer to buy the firm. It was reported that the company's insiders were split on taking the offer. The founders and some of their friends were worried about whether the offering group shared the company's interests in social issues. After the offer became public knowledge, several other interested parties stepped in with increasingly more favorable offers, raising the stakes and precipitating an auction. As the controversy continued, the pressures from various interested parties escalated on Web sites set up to favor or oppose the sale.

Continued

Concluded

This situation pitted the duty of the individual directors on the board to represent faithfully the interests of the shareholders against an implied, but not necessarily legal, requirement to consider the interests of other stakeholders. With the offers having reached a level significantly greater than the share price when this process started, the board had to consider the various offers on their merits.

THE BOARD'S ACTION

After carefully considering its legal responsibilities, the board accepted the bid deemed most favorable for shareholders. This led to loud protests about the abandonment of one of the company's original missions.

THE POINT

Interested parties have concluded that as long as the organization's intentions are widely and publicly known, investors should be personally accountable for any consequences of investing in the company. It is also evident that not-for-profit organizations and private companies could best carry out activities aimed at advancing social and community interests. The owners of a private company obviously can carry out any legal activities in which they are interested because the investment in the company is theirs alone. The rules change, however, when a company becomes a public entity.

The Duty of Loyalty and the Duty of Fair Dealing

By assuming his or her office, the corporate director commits allegiance to the enterprise and acknowledges that the best interests of the corporation and the shareholders must prevail over any individual director's interest. The basic principle of this duty of loyalty is that the director should not use his or her corporate position to make a personal profit or gain other personal advantages.[4]

The duty of fair dealing can be viewed as a component of the duty of loyalty, requiring that all transactions with the corporation be handled in a forthright and open manner that is fair to the interests of the corporation. Specifics of these duties are provided below.

Paragraph 5.05 of the *Principles of Corporate Governance: Analysis and Recommendations* provides the following discussion regarding "Taking Corporate Opportunities by Directors or Senior Executives"[5]:

General Rule: A director or senior executive may not take advantage of a corporate opportunity [to be defined below] unless:

(1) The director or senior executive first offers the corporate opportunity to the corporation and makes disclosure concerning the conflict of interest and the corporate opportunity.

(2) The corporate opportunity is rejected by the corporation; and

(3) Either

   (a) The rejection of the opportunity is fair to the corporation;

   (b) The opportunity is rejected in advance, following such disclosure, by the disinterested directors, or, in the case of a senior executive who is not a director, by a disinterested superior, in a manner that satisfies the standards of the business judgment rule [details of this rule are provided with the discussion of the duty of care]; or

   (c) The rejection is authorized in advance or ratified, following such disclosure, by disinterested shareholders, and the rejection is not equivalent to a waste of corporate assets.

Definition of a Corporate Opportunity: For purposes of this section, a corporate opportunity means:

(1) Any opportunity to engage in a business activity of which a director or senior executive becomes aware, either:

   (a) In connection with the performance of functions as a director or senior executive, or under circumstances that should reasonably lead the director or senior executive to believe that the person offering the opportunity expects it to be offered to the corporation; or

   (b) Through the use of corporate information or property, if the resulting opportunity is one that the director or senior executive should reasonably be expected to believe would be of interest to the corporation; or

(2) Any opportunity to engage in a business activity of which a senior executive becomes aware and knows is closely related to a business in which the corporation is engaged or expects to engage. . . .

Thus, in general, a corporate opportunity is an opportunity to engage in business of which a director learns and believes would be of interest to the corporation. A director may not take advantage of such opportunities unless he or she first offers the opportunity to the corporation, revealing a personal interest, and the corporation rejects the opportunity.

Paragraph 5.06 of the *Principles of Corporate Governance: Analysis and Recommendations* provides the following discussion related to "Competition with the Corporation"[6]:

General Rule: Directors and senior executives many not advance their pecuniary interests by engaging in competition with the corporation unless either:

(1) Any reasonably foreseeable harm to the corporation from such competition is outweighed by the benefit the corporation may reasonably be expected to derive from allowing the competition to take place, or there is no reasonably foreseeable harm to the corporation from such competition;

(2) The competition is authorized in advance or ratified, following disclosures concerning the conflict of interest and the competition, by disinterested directors, or in the case of a senior executive who is not a director, is authorized in advance by a disinterested superior, in a manner that satisfies the standards of the business judgment rule (paragraph 4.01); or

(3) The competition is authorized in advance or ratified, following such disclosure, by disinterested shareholders, and the shareholders' action is not equivalent to a waste of corporate assets. . . .

Similar to the situation of business opportunities, directors in general may not seek monetary gain by engaging in competition with the corporation. This stipulation may be altered if the predicted benefits to the corporation outweigh the foreseeable harm, as determined by the corporation, or if the corporation authorizes the competition after the director reveals his or her personal interest.

Duty of Care

It is incumbent on directors to act carefully in carrying out their responsibilities. This is only common sense, but it is a legal requirement as well.

Paragraph 4.01 of *Principles of Corporate Governance: Analysis and Recommendations* provides the following discussion related to the duty of care[7]:

A director or officer has a duty to the corporation to perform the director's or officer's functions in good faith, in a manner that he or she reasonably believes to be in the best interests of the corporation, and with the care that an ordinarily prudent person would reasonably be expected to exercise in a like position and under similar circumstances. This Subsection (a) is subject to the provisions of Subsection (c) (the business judgment rule) where applicable.

(1) The duty in Subsection (a) includes the obligation to make, or cause to be made, an inquiry when, but only when, the circumstances would alert a reasonable director or officer to the need therefore. The extent of such inquiry shall be as the director or officer reasonably believes to be necessary.

(2) In performing any of his or her functions (including oversight functions) a director or officer is entitled to rely on materials, and persons

in accordance with 4.02 and 4.03 (reliance on directors, officers, employees, experts, other persons, and committees of the board).

(a) Except as otherwise provided by statute or by a standard of the corporation and subject to the board's ultimate responsibility for oversight, in performing its functions (including oversight functions), the board may delegate, formally or informally by course of conduct, any function (including the function of identifying matters requiring the attention of the board) to committees of the board or to directors, officers, employees, experts, or other persons; a director may rely on such committees and persons in fulfilling the duty under this Section with respect to any delegated function if the reliance is in accordance with paragraphs 4.02 and 4.03.

(b) A director or officer who makes a business judgment in good faith fulfills the duty under this section if the director or officer:

(1) Is not interested in the subject of the business judgment.

(2) Is informed with respect to the subject of the business judgment to the extent the director or officer reasonably believes to be appropriate under the circumstances, and

(3) Rationally believes that the business judgment is in the best interests of the corporation

(c) A person challenging the conduct of a director or officer under this Section has the burden of proving a breach of duty of care, including the inapplicability of the provisions as to the fulfillment of duty under Subsection (b) or (c), and, in a damage action, the burden of proving that the breach was the legal cause of damage suffered by the corporation.

In summary, the duty of care, in general, requires a director to act in the best interests of the corporation and with the care reasonably expected of "an ordinary prudent person." The director also has the duty to be informed and to make necessary inquiries to arrive at this state. This duty, however, allows the board to delegate functions to and rely on others, including other directors, officers, employees, experts, and board committees. Such delegation and reliance do not negate the board's ultimate responsibility for oversight, however.

What is being addressed is the reality that a director cannot know everything nor be totally expert in every facet of a business. While they have the duty to be very careful in determining the facts, directors can rely on management and experts for information they do not have and judgments about which they are not expert. This raises the question of what they should know—when they can claim ignorance as a defense. The answer, as usual, is that it depends on the situation. One of the key skills of an effective director is to understand what is relevant and to persistently seek that information, particularly when he or she has or should have a feeling of discomfort with the situation. It also emphasizes the importance of having competent and trustworthy managers and advisers, which is one more aspect of the duty of care—choosing these people well.

The Duty Not to Entrench

There is some evidence that the Delaware courts are in the process of creating and imposing on directors another fiduciary duty, a "duty not to entrench." There is a body of opinion that if a corporation is not performing well, changes should be made in management. If the problem can be tracked beyond management to a board that is not fulfilling its responsibilities, changes need to be made there as well. There are many examples of companies with poor performance where the board and management continue in place without successfully addressing the issues—in effect, they become entrenched. It emerges as an issue when a board attempts to block a change-of-control transaction either through the sale of the company or in a proxy fight where dissident shareholders attempt to elect a new slate of directors.

Not all opposition to change of control, however, is evidence of entrenchment. Many times, directors think that the motives of the other party or parties attempting to force change do not represent the best interests of the shareholders as a whole, and as a result, the directors are duty bound to oppose the effort. In many cases they are correct in doing so. Fulfilling the duty not to entrench depends more on following good business practices in evaluating the corporate performance and the performance of management and the board than on complying with the law.

Some observers advocate term limits to avoid entrenchment. This assumes that all directors are motivated to entrench themselves and that a board is incapable or unwilling to deal with poor performers—which is not a universally valid assumption. Further, it ignores the value of continuity and experience. While it does ensure against entrenchment, it deprives boards that are working well of effective directors at a time when getting good directors is not an easy task.

The Duty of Supervision

The duty of supervision is an element of the duty of care; it deals with the effectiveness with which directors exercise their oversight responsibilities. The duty of supervision addresses what directors should know about the operations of management, how they should come to know it, and what they should do when there is an issue or problem requiring attention.

As an initial step in fulfilling this duty, the board must establish policies of ethics and disclosure that set the standards for behavior of directors and senior executives. The board also must ensure that there are internal controls in place to provide accurate reporting of what is going on in the corporation. This control function is generally the responsibility of the Audit Committee of the board. The board also must establish policies addressing which decisions require board approval and what information the board should regularly receive about the performance of the corporation and its various entities.

Perhaps the most important task associated with the duty of supervision is the regular meeting of the board to discuss the performance of the organization and to ask penetrating questions of management. One of the critical skills for a director is the intuitive sense of what needs to be questioned and the willingness to be persistent in pressing for access to relevant information. Directors must know what they need to know and insist that it be provided.

Dealing with Hostile Takeover Offers

Dealing with hostile offers for the company is another particularly important and difficult responsibility. Because such offers happen very infrequently, directors are often not well informed on this topic. An additional complicating factor is the tendency for hostile offers to end up in litigation as a result of their very high visibility with shareholders.

Paragraph 6.02 of *Principles of Corporate Governance: Analysis and Recommendations* presents the following discussion of "Action of Directors That Has the Foreseeable Effect of Blocking Unsolicited Tender Offers"[8]:

(a) The board of directors may take an action that has the foreseeable effect of blocking an unsolicited tender offer, if the action is a reasonable response to the offer.

(b) In considering whether its action is a reasonable response to the offer:

    (1) The board may take into account all factors relevant to the best interests of the corporation and shareholders, including, among other things, questions of legality and whether the offer, if successful, would threaten the corporation's essential economic prospects; and

    (2) The board may, in addition to the analysis under 6.02 (b)(1), have regard for interests or groups (other than shareholders) with respect to which the corporation has a legitimate concern if to do so would not significantly disfavor the long term interests of the shareholders.

(c) A person who challenges an action of the board on the ground that it fails to satisfy the standards of Subsection (a) has the burden of proof that the board's action is an unreasonable response to the offer.

(d) An action that does not meet the standards of Subsection (a) may be enjoined or set aside, but the directors who authorize such an action are not subject to liability for damages if their conduct meets the standard of the business judgment rule [paragraph 4.01(c)].

In summary, boards may act to block hostile takeover bids for the corporation when, after having considered carefully what is in the best interest of the corporation and shareholders, they make the judgment that the takeover may jeopardize the viability of the corporation. This means that they can consider the impact on groups other than the shareholders, as well as other factors that they consider relevant.

WHAT STANDARD DETERMINES IF DIRECTORS HAVE MET THEIR RESPONSIBILITIES?

In the United States, the laws of the states and the regulations of a number of government agencies, at both the state and federal levels, spell out the duties and responsibilities of directors and establish the standards of performance for directors that define their obligations. Certain court rulings provide insight into these standards of performance for directors.

Legal challenges to decisions of a board of directors typically come from stockholders who feel that the board that has been chosen to represent their interests has somehow failed in its duties. Courts traditionally have been extremely reluctant to overturn or second-guess decisions made by a board of directors. This sentiment is captured in the following opinion from a Delaware court issued in 1988 in the *J. P. Stevens & Co. Shareholders Litigation* case:

> Because businessmen and women are correctly perceived as possessing skills, information and judgment not possessed by reviewing courts and because there is a great social utility in encouraging the allocation of assets and the evaluation and assumption of economic risk by those with such skill and information, courts have long been reluctant to second-guess such decisions when they appear to have been made in good faith.

As a result of this traditional reluctance of courts to become involved in corporate governance and decision making, the business judgment rule developed. The business judgment rule, which also was presented earlier in this chapter in the citing of paragraph 4.01(c) of *Principles of Corporate Governance: Analysis and Recommendations*, is expressed in another Delaware court ruling in the case of *Aronson v. Lewis* in 1984:

> Under the general business judgment rule, there is a "presumption that in making a business decision the directors of a corporation acted on an informed basis, in good faith and in the honest belief that the action was in the best interests of the company."

Regarding the Delaware ruling, a *presumption* means that the conclusion is drawn unless there is evidence to the contrary and that the burden of proof is on the party asserting the claim, not on the board of directors defending its action. As a practical matter, if a court determines that the business judgment rule applies in a given case, the decision of the board of directors will be upheld. The business judgment rule does not apply if the challenging stockholder(s) can convince the court that in reaching its decision, the board of directors violated one of its fiduciary duties, traditionally the duty of care or the duty of loyalty.

The business judgment rule is alive and well in most states. The Delaware courts, however, have become increasingly assertive in recent years, and the health of the business judgment rule is not as certain there. In *Brehm v. Eisner* in 2000, a Delaware court held

> Thus, directors' decisions will be respected by courts unless the directors are interested or lack independence relative to the decision, do not act in good faith, act in a manner that cannot be attributed to any rational business purpose or reach their decision by a grossly negligent process that includes the failure to consider all material facts reasonably available.

What the court is saying is that it is going to look very carefully at the presumption that directors have fulfilled their duties. If there is sufficient evidence, the failure to fulfill other duties can override the business judgment rule. If the directors have violated the duty of care, for instance, or did not act in good faith, they cannot get protection under the business judgment rule.

The traditional business judgment rule presumption does not apply at all in Delaware to decisions of a board of directors relating to takeover defenses or change-in-control matters, a position that was taken in the famous *Unocal Corp.* case in 1983:

> Because of the omnipresent specter that a board may be acting primarily in its own interests, rather than those of the corporation and its shareholders, there is an enhanced duty which calls for judicial examination at the threshold before the protection of the business judgment rule can be conferred. . . .
> In the face of inherent conflict, directors must show that they had *reasonable grounds* for believing that a danger to corporate policy and effectiveness existed because of another person's stock ownership.

It is not yet clear whether this more activist stance taken by the Delaware courts will remain generally confined to Delaware or will spread to other states. Even in Delaware, the courts are mainly reviewing and challenging the processes and methods a board employs to reach a challenged decision and are still generally reluctant to attack or overturn a board's decision on substantive grounds.

In Virginia, the standard for how directors are required to discharge their fiduciary duties is found in Virginia Code Section 13.1–690 as follows:

> A director shall discharge his duties as a director, including his duties as a member of a committee, in accordance with his good faith business judgment of the best interests of the corporation.

What is unusual about Virginia is that the Virginia courts have interpreted this section simply to require a board of directors to follow a good process in reaching its decision. If a good process is followed, the Virginia courts will not review the substance, reasonableness, or even the rationality of a board's decision under Section 13.1–690.

INTERPRETATION OF THE DUTY OF CARE

As stated earlier, the duty of care requires a board of directors to act in good faith and to make *informed* business decisions. As we have pointed out, the consequences of breaching the duty of care are severe because the business judgment rule does not apply, and the board of directors must establish the "entire fairness" of its decision. *Entire fairness* means that the shareholders have been, when all things are considered, treated fairly—that the result is fair without regard to how the board arrived at its decision.

Prior to 1985, courts generally assumed that a board of directors satisfied its duty of care in reaching a decision. A board had to go out of its way to breach its duty of care. In 1985, a Delaware court held in *Smith v. Van Gorkom* that "the duty of care includes a duty to inform themselves, prior to making a business decision, of all material information reasonably available to them."

The facts in *Van Gorkom* are instructive and include

- The board of directors had no advance notice that a board meeting was to include consideration of the sale of the company.
- The board agreed to sell the company after a 2-hour meeting.
- The board had no information as to valuation of the company or alternatives such as other potential buyers.
- In effect, a strong-willed chairman rammed through a sale of the company without many questions from or involvement on the part of the other directors.

The Delaware law has evolved to an *objective* "reasonable person" test: Have the directors acted in good faith and with the degree of care that the ordinarily prudent person would have exercised? To satisfy the duty of care in Delaware, directors must consider all material information reasonably available.

Virginia law is very different. Duty of care for a Virginia corporation is reviewed under a *subjective* good faith standard. In *WLR Foods* in 1995, a Virginia court held

> A director shall discharge his duties as a director, including his duties as a member of a committee, in accordance with his good faith business judgment of the best interests of the corporation. Good faith is measured by the directors' use of an informed decision-making process and the procedural soundness of the decision-making process, and not by a substantive evaluation of the directors' conduct or by the rationality of the decision made.

As noted earlier, the emphasis in Virginia is on the process employed rather than on the attributes of the decision itself.

Duty of Care Commandments

In order to ensure proper execution of their duty of care, directors should abide by the following "commandments," or rules of guidance. Conscientious boards likely adhere to these in all substantial decision-making matters.

The board is likely to have met its duty of care if it

- Engages experienced legal counsel to design and manage the governance process and maintain appropriate records of the proceedings.
- Does not rush important decisions; at least not unnecessarily.
- Gives board members adequate prior notice of important business to be conducted at a meeting.
- Distributes major documents or position papers to board members well in advance of meetings.
- If possible, has one or more informational meetings, follows up with distribution of additional information in response to questions, and convenes subsequent discussion and action meetings.
- Provides board members with adequate information to make an informed decision, including
  - Access to opinions of expert advisers
  - Management analysis and recommendations

- Identification of and information on alternatives
- Fairness opinions
- Does not submit to the pressures of a domineering CEO and/or others who clearly have committed to a decision prior to the board's discussions.

If the board follows a sound process, courts in Virginia and, to some degree, in most other states will not overturn a decision on substance in duty-of-care cases.

THE DUTY OF LOYALTY IN PRACTICE

Consequences of breaching the duty of loyalty are also severe. Again, the business judgment rule does not apply, and the board of directors must establish that the challenged transaction was fair.

As with the duty of care, there are certain "commandments" that establish a list of required behaviors for conscientious boards. If these directives are followed, problems with the duty of loyalty are typically easily avoided.

The duty of loyalty includes the following:

- An interested director must fully disclose any conflict of interest and the basis for it when the issue arises and in advance of related discussions and decisions.
- The interested director must not unduly influence discussion of the transaction, may need to leave the discussion, and almost certainly should abstain from voting on the issue.
- The proposed issue must be resolved by a majority of the disinterested directors.

INDEMNIFICATION OF DIRECTORS

It is a general practice for corporations to indemnify directors against liability for their legal actions. This means that the directors are not personally liable for any damages that may result from legal acts of the board to the extent that there are corporate assets to cover any awards to plaintiffs. Most corporations purchase directors and officers liability insurance (D&O coverage) as part of their indemnity program. Certain behaviors are, by statute, excluded from indemnification. These matters are covered in more detail in Chapter 11.

SUMMARY

Clearly, a director individually and a board of directors as a whole must act in accordance with legal standards spelled out by the state in which the business is incorporated. These laws are complex. While no layperson can expect to fully understand them, it is essential that each director has a working knowledge of them and knows how and when to seek competent legal advice. Of particular importance are the duties of being a director. At one level, they are simply common sense. However, in particular situations, they create technical compliance issues that may go beyond common sense. Directors need to follow the laws and build records of what they have done to protect themselves from challenges that have the advantage of hindsight.

In Chapter 3 we will look at how boards organize and function to carry out their duties.

REVIEW QUESTIONS

1. What is the basic role of the board of directors in the governance of a corporation?
2. What are the basic duties of the board and individual directors as they go about governing a company?
3. What is the responsibility of the board in balancing the interests of shareholders with those of other stakeholders or social causes?
4. What are the special responsibilities of the board in responding to hostile takeover offers?
5. What is the purpose of indemnification for the corporation and for the members of the board?

CHAPTER 3

Board Organization

State laws, as noted in Chapter 2, prescribe the duties of directors in representing the interests of shareholders. State laws also allow for the chartering and incorporation of the vast majority of businesses in the United States. This chapter describes the process by which a corporation is formed under the provisions and statutes of a given state and how a board of directors is generally organized to oversee the management of the corporation.

The state of incorporation selected by a corporation is critically important because most legal actions related to the activities of the corporation will be conducted under the laws of that state. Normally, the state corporation commission or the office of the secretary of state authorizes the use of the name of the corporation and issues the charter for the formation of the corporation. The articles of incorporation and the bylaws of the corporation become the basic, binding set of rules, procedures, and conditions under which the corporation will be governed. This chapter outlines representative contents of these governing documents as well as their importance to the management of the corporation.

THE STATE OF INCORPORATION

The first governance choice to be made is the selection of the state in which the business is to be incorporated and, consequently, the state law and judicial system under which the firm will operate. Most companies are incorporated in the state in which the business is domiciled. If the corporation is to engage in interstate commerce, it may consider selecting another state that might be seen as more business friendly.

Jay Lorsch, in a review of American corporate boards, provides the following brief history related to corporate location:

> As commerce expanded in the eighteenth and early nineteenth centuries, various states vied to have companies domiciled in their jurisdictions, courting them through the creation of the most liberal laws applying to

directors. In this context, "liberal" meant that directors would not be held to the same tight standards as trustees, the so-called prudent man rule. Instead, directors were expected to exercise the "duty of loyalty" and the "duty of care," and their conduct was judged according to the "business judgment doctrine." In spite of the evolution of corporate law and legal variations among the states, these principles still remain at the heart of the directors' responsibilities in all jurisdictions.[1]

Delaware has been the most successful of the states in attracting publicly owned corporations and reportedly has incorporated some 50 percent of all such corporations.[2] The State of Virginia adopted what many claim to be a model corporate code in 1985.

THE ARTICLES OF INCORPORATION

Corporations are created by a state charter on the application of one or more individuals acting as the incorporators. Corporations are governed by articles of incorporation, adopted at the time of incorporation, and modified by the acts of the shareholders from time to time. They are filed with the state in which the company is to be incorporated, usually in the secretary of state's office or with a state corporation commission. The articles of incorporation can be thought of as a broad constitution that defines the purpose of the organization and the limits that the shareholders may place on its operations. The articles of incorporation can be changed only with shareholder approval. A number of articles customarily contained in a firm's articles of incorporation are described below.

Article I: Corporate Name

This article merely specifies the name of the corporation. Naming a corporation can be as simple as using the founder's name or the name of the place where the corporation is going to operate, often combined with a descriptor of the nature of the business, for example, Jones Auto Supply or Town Auto Supply. The use of geographic descriptors can be too limiting if the business plans on expanding to other areas, although a number of national chains retain a geographic reference in the firm's name as a description of the regional flair of their products. Naming the corporation also can be a major marketing decision if the name is to be the basis for a brand. When this is the case, the name must be distinctive and work phonetically and graphically. The corporation must clear the proposed name with each state in which it is to be employed to avoid the use of a name that is already taken, as well as to avoid issues of copyright and/or trademark infringement.

Article II: Purpose

A second article of incorporation describes the purpose of the organization. The organizers of the corporation may choose to make the purpose very broad, for example, "To engage in any lawful act or activity for which a corporation may be organized under the laws of the State of [name]." Or the organizers may choose to be very narrow in describing the purpose, restricting the corporation to a specific business or location. Most organizers opt for the broader definition to give the corporation the widest possible latitude in its operations. A more narrow definition is used when the organizers expressly want to restrict the activities of the business to their intentions at the time of incorporation.

Article III: Registered Office or Agent

This article names the address of the corporation's initial registered office in the state of incorporation and the name of the registered agent at that address. The registered agent is the person responsible for filing all required documents and for receiving all legal notices served on the corporation. Usually the registered agent is the organization's lawyer or its corporate secretary. If a corporation fails to maintain a registered agent at the registered office, it will affect the company's ability to do business in the state, cause corporate contracts to become void, and can result in personal penalties or fines for the officers and directors of the corporation.

Article IV: Authorized Capital Stock

This article deals with the classes of stocks and the number of shares to be authorized, along with the par value of each share. Every corporation will have at least one class of common stock, which represents the ownership of the corporation. Common stockholders take all the risk, maintain all the control, and receive all the income in proportion to the shares owned, unless they create other classes of stocks or debt that shifts some portion of risk, control, or income to the other stock classes or creditors. Other classes of stock may have preferred positions on income and/or liquidation with less risk; or they may receive preferred distributions of earnings. Other classes of stock also can be created to provide for voting rights disproportionate to the capital contributed, often characterized as class A or class B common stock.

It is important to note that it is shares owned, not capital contributed, that determines how income, risk, and control are allocated. At the time of incorporation, most shareholders will pay the same price per share, although a discount to the price or an outright grant of shares may be provided to key managers. Over time, as new shares are issued, they will reflect the value at the time of the stock offering.

Article V: Bylaws

This article states that the provision for the regulation of the internal affairs of the corporation will be set forth in the bylaws. Any limitations on the bylaws would be articulated in this article.

Article VI: Duration

Corporations generally have a perpetual duration, and this is stated in this article unless some termination date or event is selected. An example of a corporation with a termination date would be a joint venture between a mining company and the owners of a property. Since a mining site has a definite lifespan, it would make sense to tie the life of the corporation to the depletion of the site's natural resources.

Article VII: Board of Directors

The number of initial directors is specified in this article. Generally, the number of directors is also identified in the bylaws and can be altered by changing the bylaws. Usually, the state requires the names and addresses of the members of the initial board of directors.

THE BYLAWS

The bylaws stipulate how frequently the board must meet and how the agenda will be prepared and by whom. Any special arrangements with regard to directors' voting will be detailed in the bylaws. The bylaws also specify the rules by which individuals standing for election will be ratified by the shareholders. Commonly, such elections occur after the names of nominees for election (or reelection) to the board are forwarded from the nominating committee. The bylaws also indicate the procedures for selecting board and corporate officers and may spell out the terms under which the services of board members may be terminated. These might include term limits, a mandatory retirement age, or the conditions under which a director could be removed "for cause." In one company with which we are familiar, directors who missed two consecutive board meetings were considered to have resigned. Other examples of causes for which a director could be removed might include a change in the director's status (for example, when a chief executive officer of another company resigns that post) or the commission of some reprehensible or illegal act that would bring discredit on the corporation.

The bylaws may specify the level of compensation for directors for their services, including, for instance, annual retainer fees, fees for attending board and committee meetings, restricted stock and stock-option awards, insurance, and perhaps transportation expenses for travel on behalf of the company.

The bylaws may cover additional structural and operational details, such as

- The number of directors who will sit on the board
- The number of "insiders" and "outsiders"
- The length of terms of directors
- The various board committees and their charges
- Details about the annual meeting of shareholders
- The conditions under which proxy statements will be issued to the shareholders
- How directors will vote and how the votes will be counted
- The election and duties of corporate and board officers

The ideal number of directors who should be elected to represent the shareholders is the subject of debate. Some boards function effectively with as few as 7 or 8 directors, whereas others have more than 20 directors. There is a semblance of a consensus that some number between 12 and 15 is most effective for many organizations. Many people feel that fewer than 12 directors can allow a small group to control the board, whereas more than 15 directors renders the board unwieldy. This is one of the many judgments that those setting up a new corporation have to make.

The bylaws normally can be changed by a majority vote of the board of directors, except in cases that are subject to shareholder vote, as required by a specific state statute. The incorporators should give careful consideration to the bylaws. In addition to setting up orderly governance processes, the bylaws can come into play when conflicts of governance arise.

The annual shareholders' meeting is a major event for public corporations. These meetings are scheduled routinely at a convenient time after the close of business at the end of the corporation's fiscal year and following the availability of audited financial statements. The chairman of the board presents the results of the year's operations and takes questions from the shareholders and others in attendance. The degree of harmony or discord at these meetings invariably reflects the perception by the attendees of the soundness and attractiveness of the corporation's operating results.

The board must communicate with the company's shareholders when shareholder approval is required for certain actions of the board and management. These communications are achieved through the mailing of proxy statements to each shareholder. The proxy statements (often referred to as *proxies*) advise the shareholders of the board's position on one or more issues for which the shareholders' opinions must be gathered in the form of votes. Thus the proxy statement outlines such issues as a slate of candidates for election as directors, approval for a sale of major assets, or a merger or sale of the company. The board is also required to provide certain details in the proxy statement about executive compensation, including salaries, bonuses, and stock options or restricted stock awards. The proxy statement normally includes a ballot in the form of a card or letter on which the shareholder can indicate his or her approval or disapproval of management's proposals. These proxies are returned to the company, often to the company secretary, allowing management or the board to vote for a shareholder's preferences in the event that the shareholder cannot attend the annual meeting of shareholders in person. Occasionally, proxies are tallied by independent organizations hired solely for this purpose. Hence the term *giving someone a person's proxy* refers to the act of entitling the holder of the proxy to vote instead of the absentee.

Major Considerations Relative to the Bylaws

A major question for the incorporators drafting the bylaws of a firm is how much flexibility should be given to the shareholders to call special shareholder meetings and to present proposals for voting. For example, the bylaws would stipulate how much advance notice would be required to call such a meeting. On the one hand, the shareholders own the business and should be given ample opportunity to express their views and to vote on the issues they think are important. On the other hand, corporations frequently must deal with vocal minorities who push agendas that may not be shared by the majority of shareholders. Such proposals often reflect a political or social agenda, or they may come from individuals attempting to gain control of the majority of the shares of the corporation at a low value in order to pursue their own interests. In many cases, these rogue proposals are not considered to be in the best interests of most shareholders.

It is important, however, not to generalize about the motives or competence of either the board of directors or of the dissident shareholders. History provides us many examples of irresponsible or illegal behavior in each camp. What is important is that there be an orderly set of rules to ensure that the interests of all shareholders are protected while the dissenting voices can be heard. Vignette 3-1 provides an interesting example of the use of the bylaws to maintain control of a company.

VIGNETTE 3-1

BYLAWS MATTER

THE ISSUE

Bylaws are the rules that govern the operation of a board. In routine times, they are followed as a matter of practice and have little impact on decisions. In fact, there may be very little awareness of them. However, when there is conflict, bylaws can play a major role in which party prevails.

THE SITUATION

In one company there was a bitter disagreement over whether the chairman and chief executive officer (CEO) should continue in his role. There were 12 members on the board, and they were evenly split on the issue. As they were negotiating a resolution to the dispute, one of the members opposed to the chairman had a debilitating stroke and was no longer able to function. This created a potential six-to-five vote in favor of the chairman.

The bylaws stated that the chairman could call an official meeting without stating the subject to be discussed as long as a quorum, defined as a majority of the directors or in this case seven, were present. This meant that the six directors favoring reelection of the chairman would need at least one director opposing his reelection to be present to take a vote.

BOARD ACTION: THE MEETING

The chairman chose to call the meeting, and prior to its occurrence, the chairman's supporters requested that a relative of the ill director use his power of attorney to submit the director's resignation from the board, creating an opening. The opposing side did not know of

Continued

Concluded

this proposed action until the meeting began, at which time the resignation was submitted and accepted.

The chairman's supporters then immediately elected a replacement director who was friendly to the chairman on a vote of six to five. The individual who was elected then joined the meeting, creating a seven-to-five majority. The opposing side could have disrupted this process by walking out and destroying the quorum; however, because they were caught by surprise, they did not think to do this at the time.

To negate the possibility of quorum issues at future meetings, the majority also proposed to immediately amend the bylaws to add 2 additional directors. This would bring the total number of directors to 14 and the quorum requirement to 8. On passing the amendment, the majority immediately elected the 2 additional directors and attained a working majority of 9 who favored the chairman versus the 5 who did not.

THE POINT

One side of the described dispute understood the bylaws and used them to design a process that settled the dispute. The other side did not think to use the bylaws strategically to their own advantage, and their lack of understanding played out in their defeat.

Defensive Measures

During the 1980s, there was a period during which hostile takeovers occurred frequently. Buyers, often referred to as *raiders*, were characteristically either strategic buyers, usually meaning a competitor, or financial buyers, meaning individuals or groups looking for a bargain. The target companies were as a rule perceived to be underperforming, demonstrating attractively low market valuations, often having substantial liquid assets, and sometimes having business units that could be sold off. The raiders would use a variety of financial instruments, including high-yield "junk" bonds and/or a company's own assets to finance a hostile takeover offer. The practice of hostile takeovers was justified as a way of removing entrenched management and unlocking the value of the business for the shareholders, and in some instances, this was the case. In many cases, however, the raiders were attempting to gain control of the company at a substantial discount. Often raiders did not want to purchase the whole company but instead only enough shares to gain control. If the raiders were successful in gaining control of a firm, the remaining minority shareholders were left in the unenviable position of having little or no voice in the ongoing governance of the firm.

Defensive measures were developed in response to the practice of hostile takeovers, and critics remain divided on their utility. Some claim that defensive measures serve to protect entrenched management and boards of nonperforming companies at the expense of shareholders. Those with an alternate view contend that the measures are not designed to protect management, but instead the shareholders, by allowing the board to maintain control of any transaction process. This situation, the supporters of defensive measures believe, ensures that shareholders would get the best possible price if the company were to be sold.

Both arguments have merit. Certainly there are entrenched, underperforming managers and boards, and the threat of a hostile takeover could make them more responsive to shareholder interests. Alternatively, the raiders are not always "good guys" looking out for the shareholders' interests. A determination of which side actually represents the best interests of the shareholders can only be made on a case-by-case basis and often only after the fact.

Defensive measures commonly used by corporations when under hostile attack include

- Limitations on special meetings
- Staggered terms
- "Poison pills"

We describe each of these briefly below.

Limitations on Special Meetings
The bylaws typically state the types of decisions that require shareholder approval, and universally, one of these decisions is the consideration of a tender offer or offers. The ability to call special meetings and set agenda topics is a powerful tool that can be used when a firm is a takeover target. The board of directors empowered to call special meetings and/or set their agendas could keep a takeover attempt at bay by delaying shareholder meetings or by controlling the agenda so that raiders could not present their proposals to the other shareholders.

Staggered Terms
Before the times of prevalent hostile bids, boards historically had been elected at the annual stockholders meeting for a yearly term or until their successors were elected. This last phrase is a technical term often included

in bylaws to ensure that the board would not be reduced to an unworkable extent by the failure to elect new candidates. Under this election protocol, raiders found that they could get an entirely new board elected with a simple majority vote, and as a result, they could control a corporation with just 51 percent of the outstanding shares.

In order to make it more difficult for anyone or any group to gain control of the board, many public corporations now employ staggered terms for directors. The members are split into a number of classes, usually three or four, much like graduation classes. The classes for a given board contain approximately the same number of directors, and they are elected to 3- or 4-year terms. If 3-year terms were employed, it would take 2 years for a takeover group to gain control of the board and 3 or perhaps 4 years for it to install a total slate of board members. The process of extending the time interval required and making the battle more difficult gives the shareholders a better handle on the issues at stake and the motives of the dissident groups.

The "Poison Pill"

The "poison pill" is a very complicated way of dealing with potential hostile takeovers. The pill is so effective that one has never been triggered. Further, it has been litigated successfully in a number of court challenges. The poison pill is a plan whereby the board issues existing shareholders the "right" to purchase additional shares at a very low price, say, 1 cent per share. These rights would be triggered if a hostile purchaser were to accumulate more than a predetermined percentage of the outstanding shares, usually in the range of 10 to 20 percent of the outstanding shares. The new shares issued to preexisting shareholders would dilute the shares of the hostile pursuer dramatically.

The intent of putting the poison pill in readiness is not to prevent a transaction from taking place but rather to ensure that the board is in control of the process. Several studies indicate that companies with poison pill provisions get a higher price for a sales transaction (in the event of a sale of the company) than those without one, the obvious reason being the mere existence of the poison pill threat.

PROCEDURE GUIDELINES

In addition to the bylaws, many corporations have formal board procedure guidelines that expound on how the board is to function. For example, the procedure guidelines used by one major industrial corporation provide the basis for the discussion of guideline elements below.

Corporate Officers

State statutes generally require that a corporation have a president and a secretary, with other officers optional.

The Chairman of the Board and the CEO

The major governance issue with regard to officers is whether to have a CEO who is also the chairman of the board or to separate the two positions. Clearly, there are two jobs: one manages the affairs of the business, and the other supervises the work of the board in overseeing the affairs of the business. The majority of public corporations over the last several decades have combined the two jobs, primarily on the theory that the organization needs a strong leader. This move has been motivated by a fear that a strong chairman would become a rival to the CEO and undercut his or her stature. Many interested observers, however, feel strongly that these jobs constitute a distinct conflict of interest for anyone holding both positions. Given that the board (and especially the chairman) must evaluate the performance of the CEO, a person holding both positions is necessarily called on to evaluate himself or herself. Consequently, there has been a slowly emerging trend to use a nonemployee chairman of the board who works closely with the CEO in managing the board's work. A very good alternative is to have a lead director, who often serves as chairman of a committee of outside directors, one of whose primary tasks is the evaluation of the CEO's performance.

A related issue is whether to have executive officers, in addition to the CEO, on the board as inside directors. When there are insiders on the board, the outside directors come to know management better and get a broader exposure to the inner workings of the company. One danger related to this arrangement, however, is that the managers who are subordinate to the CEO will have great difficulty disagreeing with their boss. If this is not the case, the alternative danger is that the inside directors could undercut the leadership of the CEO, particularly if they differ with him or her on some important issues. In any case, it is critically important that there be more outside directors than inside directors in order to have a board that is independent of management when judgments about management performance are made. If there are inside directors, an effective and active committee of outside directors facilitates the performance of functions requiring independence.

The committee of outside directors is somewhat similar to the European two-tiered model of governance, in which there is a supervisory board and an executive board. The supervisory board is usually composed of outsiders who represent the employees and shareholders. It appoints and oversees the activities of the executive board and is broadly responsible for what the law terms "the well-being of the company." The executive board, on the other hand, is composed of senior managers, the insiders, and is responsible for running the company.

Board Committees

A board of directors normally conducts its business through a well-organized committee structure that partitions the work of the board and allows directors to make maximum use of their expertise. Many issues are too complicated to be dealt with by the entire board. It is a matter of time and efficiency as well as expertise. The board can delegate certain policy or issue decisions to the relevant committee or can ask the committee to complete a detailed study of the issues and come back to the entire board with recommendations. Each committee should have a clear charge, or set of duties, and their reports become part of the board's minutes as they report at appropriate board meetings.

Most boards have the following standing committees in some form:

- Committee of outside directors
- Executive committee
- Compensation committee
- Audit committee
- Nominating and governance committee

Boards also may have other committees that reflect their specific industry or circumstances. Each of the listed committees is described briefly below.

The Committee of Outside Directors

This committee was described previously. The chairperson of this committee is elected by the other directors and commonly serves as the lead director. The office of the CEO ideally provides staff support for this committee, and the company's general counsel often advises this committee, particularly when there are issues that have legal implications.

The Executive Committee

The executive committee can be used in three distinct ways:

- It may provide a backup mechanism that acts for the board when time or circumstances make it difficult to bring the entire board together. Members are chosen, among other criteria, on their ability to be available on short notice.

- It may be composed of the chairs of the other standing committees and may be the means for coordinating their activities.
- It may be a senior board to which all issues are presented before going to the whole board. This is usually found when there is a very large or oversized board that does not meet as frequently as the situation requires. In past years, banks that preferred large boards, primarily for marketing benefits, used a senior board. One disadvantage of this arrangement is that it may create an "in group" and an "out group."

The Compensation Committee

The compensation committee deals with the compensation and benefits of executives. The senior human resources officer provides staff support, and frequently the committee employs outside compensation advisers. The committee obviously should be composed of outside directors. In some companies, the management of retirement investments is also a responsibility of this committee. When this situation is not the case, the function of managing retirement benefits is delegated to a separate committee composed of individual directors who have investment expertise.

The Audit Committee

The audit committee is a critical committee and must, by Securities and Exchange Commission (SEC) regulation, be composed of independent directors. Independence means not only that the members should not be in management but also that no one with close family or business ties to management or who has been part of management in the last 5 years should be a member of the audit committee. The chief financial officer (CFO) of the company provides staff assistance for this committee, along with senior accounting managers. This committee works closely with the external auditing firm and generally meets quarterly with its representatives to review the company's 10-Q form, which must be filed quarterly with the SEC. Management is generally absent from these external auditor review sessions.

The audit committee's traditional responsibility has been to know what is in the financial statements and to ensure that they are accurate and reported properly to those outside the firm. Over the years, the audit committee's function has expanded into oversight of financial controls, often using an internal audit staff. More recently, these responsibilities have tended to expand to overseeing processes that monitor compliance with laws, regulations, and the corporate code of conduct and to conducting special investigations.

A few companies have begun to use the internal audit staff as consultants to review the effectiveness of operations and transfer best practices between or among corporate entities. A growing area of audit committee concern is risk management. Traditionally, this has been interpreted to mean management of the insurance program. It is beginning to extend into an understanding of all the risks the company faces and how they can best be managed, such as the risks inherent in interest-rate swaps and hedges.

Appendix 3-1 summarizes in more detail the functions of and current thinking about the crucial role of audit committees.

The Nominating and Governance Committee

The nominating committee identifies and recruits new members of the board when openings occur, with staff support provided by the CEO. In many companies, this committee has begun to manage the process of evaluation of individual board members, as well as the board as a whole. This has led to its being responsible for much of the governance process. The committee is also usually responsible for the procedure guidelines.

Other Standing Committees

There are a number of other committees that might be appropriate in specific situations. Some companies use a strategy or planning committee. Some will have a finance committee to manage the capital structure and related financial instruments. There also may be a committee on the environment.

Special Committees

From time to time, the board may appoint an ad hoc committee to deal with a specific issue. The special committees are directed to study and report on novel issues facing the corporation or urgent issues not covered by other standing committees. These special committees usually dissolve upon the completion of the assignment.

SUMMARY

This chapter has described and provided examples of the nuts-and-bolts actions and procedures that provide for the governance of public corporations. Many of the same precepts also apply to private companies. Unfortunately, too many managers and even members of boards of directors have less than a requisite understanding of these important governance procedures. The fiduciary responsibility that goes with serving on a board of directors as the custodians of the shareholders' interests, however, requires that the company's structural underpinnings be well understood. Numerous examples throughout the remaining chapters illustrate the pitfalls associated with a failure to understand the rules and conventions of corporate governance.

We now move on in Chapter 4 to the process of selecting directors.

REVIEW QUESTIONS

1. What important facets of a corporation are covered in the articles of incorporation?
2. What important aspects of the board's organization and operation are covered in the bylaws?
3. Why is it essential that every director know the bylaws in detail?
4. What are the advantages and disadvantages of having one person hold the offices of chairman of the board and CEO?
5. How does the board use committees to further its work?

GUIDE FOR AUDIT COMMITTEES

Audit committees play a critical role in today's corporate governance. In a period of what seems like rampant corporate scandal, this committee of corporate boards has been drawing the critical eye of American regulators, legislators, and investors—and understandably so. As noted in this chapter, the traditional duty of the audit committee has been to be knowledgeable about the content of the firm's financial statements and to guarantee their accuracy and proper reporting. When corporate giants plunge with startling speed to the brink of bankruptcy because of misleading, if not fraudulent, reporting of financial results and structures, the entire business community and its oversight agencies rightfully should seek answers as to how such shocking events were able to occur. In pursuing their investigations, they should turn to the firms' audit committees.

We recognize that the foundation of American business was built on the notion of capable people doing an honest job. This foundation to a large degree remains, although perhaps with the amendment of capable people doing an honest job within the law. It is the job of the audit committee to ensure, as far as it is able, the accuracy of financial statements. The committee is hampered when it is fed information from dishonest executives acting outside or on the very edge of the law. In any case, the members of this committee must be wise, insightful, and thorough in carrying out their duties. The job they commit to perform has widespread ramifications in publicly traded firms and should not be entered into lightly.

Because of the crucial nature of the work of audit committees, we have assembled a guide providing numerous details and suggestions regarding its responsibilities, requirements, and organization. This guide, mostly in outline form, is presented below.

Guiding Principles

An audit committee should

- Encourage a strong operating culture that conveys basic values of integrity and the expectation of legal compliance, forthright financial reporting, and strong financial controls

- Have a written charter, approved by the board, that describes its mission, organization, roles and responsibilities, and policies and practices
- Have members who are intellectually independent, qualified, and diligent
- Be properly informed by and have open and candid communications with management
- Have direct, independent communications with both the external and internal auditors
- Make it unequivocally clear that the ultimate accountability of both internal and external auditors is to the audit committee and the full board
- Guarantee compliance with generally accepted accounting principles (GAAP) and insist on full, accurate, and timely disclosure of all relevant information to the public

The Charter

The charter of the audit committee defines the role of the committee and the responsibilities delegated to it by the board of directors. The board must approve the charter.

The Mission

The mission of the audit committee should include the following:

- Assist the board of directors in fulfilling its oversight responsibilities by reviewing
  - The financial reporting process
  - The system of internal controls
  - The audit process
  - The company's process for monitoring compliance with laws and regulations and its code of conduct
  - The company's risk-management initiatives
- Ensure internal and external auditor independence
- Maintain effective working relationships with
  - The board of directors
  - Management
  - The internal and external auditors

The members of the committee should possess individually, as well as collectively, a full understanding of the responsibilities of the committee and the company's business, operations, and risks.

Organization and Actions

Audit Committee Membership

- *Committee size.* The audit committee should comprise at least three members (preferably no more than six, with some exceptions made for small businesses).
- *Member independence.* Members of the audit committee should demonstrate the following attributes of independence by
  - Not having been employed by the company, an affiliate, or a current parent or predecessor within the past 5 years
  - Not having been a member of the immediate family of a current executive officer of the company or an affiliate within the past 5 years
  - Not being or having been an executive of another business organization where any of the company's executives serve on that organization's compensation committee
  - Not having or having been a partner, controlling shareholder, or executive officer of a business organization that has a material business relationship with the company
  - A singular exception to the rules of independence can be made for one committee member if the board of directors determines it is in the best interests of the company, but only for one.
- *Member qualifications.* At least one member of the committee must have accounting or related financial skills and experience defined as
  - The ability to read and understand financial statements, including a company's balance sheet, income statement, and statement of cash flows or
  - The predisposition and commitment to gain such expertise within a reasonable period of time after joining the committee
  - Holding the qualification of certified public accountant or having comparable experience or background, which results in financial sophistication, including being or having been a CEO, a CFO, or other senior officer with financial oversight responsibilities in an unaffiliated enterprise
- *Member characteristics.* All members should demonstrate the following characteristics:
  - Integrity and a willingness to accept accountability

- Informed judgment
- Mature confidence
- Objectivity and intellectual honesty
- *Chairperson.* The chair should
  - Be a proactive leader
  - Fully understand the committee's functions
  - Be able to lead constructive dialogue with management, auditors, and the board
  - Have strong financial literacy skills
  - Have time available
  - Have a naturally skeptical eye and ear
  - Have tenacity and courage
- *Resources.* The committee requires access to the administrative support, management, and consultants as appropriate to fulfill its responsibilities.

Roles and Responsibilities

The roles and responsibilities of the audit committee include

- Ensuring that there is a well-defined, well-written, and well-communicated code of ethical standards and guidelines for acceptable behavior, on which a climate of integrity is built and well established
- Ensuring the adequacy of internal control policies, systems, and practices that promote the effectiveness and efficiency of operations, reliability of financial reporting, and compliance with applicable laws and regulations
- Selecting, evaluating, and replacing the independent auditor subject to board and/or stockholder approval
- Reviewing in a timely manner all annual and interim financial statements; including the management's discussion and analysis, auditor's comments and suggestions, and any significant accounting or reporting issues
- Reviewing the process for compliance with all laws and any legal matters that could have a significant impact on financial statements
- Ensuring that business risks are identified and that appropriate actions are taken to monitor them and minimize exposure to them

Policies and Practices

A number of important policies and practices of the audit committee are listed below.

- Meetings
  - *Frequency.* The committee should meet at least quarterly and as needed when there are major issues; in any event, the committee should meet frequently enough to fulfill its responsibilities.
  - *Participants.* The members, senior management (CEO, CFO, and controller), the internal auditor, the external auditors, and any others who are familiar with or responsible for topics on the agenda.
  - *Agenda.* A written agenda covering
    - Minutes of the previous meeting.
    - A review of current financial statements, including comments by the auditors, encompassing an assessment of whether the financial statements are complete and consistent with the information known to the committee members and management and reflect appropriate accounting principles. Particular emphasis should be paid to complex or unusual transactions and judgmental areas involving the valuation of assets, liabilities, and reserves.
    - A report by auditors (internal and external), as appropriate, on the audit scope and plan or audit findings, generally on a quarterly basis.
      - Any current issues or briefings on a selected topic.
      - Private meetings with the internal auditor, external auditor, and perhaps management as appropriate.
      - Executive sessions when needed.
- Working with management and the internal auditor
  - Effective oversight requires the committee to have significant interaction with management, to ask difficult questions, and to obtain reasonable answers. To do this, the members must have a solid understanding of the company's business and operations.
  - Senior management should systematically brief the committee on its control practices and any related issues as they arise, especially any risks or problems as they develop. Open and candid communications are essential.
  - The CFO and the internal auditor should have direct access to the committee, both formally and informally.

- The committee must have a clear understanding of the internal audit process and its findings.
- Working with the external auditor. The audit committee should
  - Ensure the independence of the external auditor, including the monitoring of any nonaudit services and related fees
  - Understand and approve the proposed audit scope, approach, and fees
  - Understand the audit findings and ensure that management addresses any problems in a timely and effective manner, particularly if there is a qualified opinion
  - Be readily available to the external auditor for any formal or informal comments
  - Receive and review required communications
  - Evaluate the performance of the external auditor
- Reporting responsibilities
  - *The board of directors.* The chairperson of the committee should make regular reports to the board of the committee's activities and findings, usually at regularly scheduled board meetings.
  - *Shareholders.* Review all interim and annual reports to the shareholders. Provide an annual statement that describes the committee's responsibilities and how they were discharged. This report is generally found in the annual proxy statement.
- *Self-assessment.* The committee should review its effectiveness annually to determine how well it is meeting its responsibilities and following its prescribed policies and practices.

How Audit Committees Get into Trouble

Audit committees may find themselves in trouble with regulators and shareholders for a variety of reasons. These reasons typically relate to the failure of the committee to perform its duties diligently. Studies have shown that there are some situations in which fraud is more apt to occur than others. They include situations where

- A majority of overall boards of directors are insiders and inexperienced
- There are weak controls over top management, since it is very difficult to have major fraud without the collusion of either or both the CEO and the CFO
- There is no audit committee, or the audit committee functions infrequently and/or ineffectively

CHAPTER 4

Board Selection

Because shareholders in a publicly held corporation cannot represent themselves, they must select others to perform that function for them. How, then, should shareholders choose (elect) a specified number of qualified and respected people to represent their interests as members of a corporation's board of directors? This chapter describes the various processes by which directors are chosen and elected. The strength of any board correlates with the aggregate abilities of the directors and with their individual capacities for independent action. The latter is difficult to quantify, whereas the former is generally apparent, based on the nominees' career experience and specific skills. The more diverse the backgrounds and skill sets of nominees, the greater is the likelihood of effective aggregate ability. Logic, however, must govern the nomination process. For example, it is quite unlikely that an airplane manufacturer would benefit from the experience of a professor of linguistics.

Thus, at the macro level, the board must, in aggregate, contain a proper mix of individual director attributes relevant to the mission of the company. For instance, the board of an independent bank in a medium-sized city should include the kinds of high-profile community leaders who can substantially contribute to its success. In a similar way, the board of a state-oriented health insurance company would need a mix of members that includes the points of view of its constituents, including the medical community (doctors), hospitals, employers (who provide the insurance and pay the premiums), and the employees and their families who are covered by the insurance. On top of these divergent points of view would be the need for a presence from each geographic area of the state. A large national public company would best be represented by a board that includes chief executive officers (CEOs) of other companies and people with industry-specific experience and general business and financial acumen, along with a general orientation representative of national and international interests. Finally, not-for-profit boards need to be structured to provide the greatest confidence for donors regarding the integrity and mission orientation of the agency. Regardless of the type of organization, the board must, as a total group, provide the necessary mix of skills and experience to support effectively the achievement of the company's goals and objectives.

It is always necessary to understand and deal with tradeoffs that will have to be made to fit the individual directors to the larger purpose of the organization. First and foremost, candidates for the board must have unquestioned integrity. Because shareholders entrust directors with complete authority to act on their behalf, the shareholders must be confident that the candidates are of the highest character and adhere to lofty ethical standards. Individual directors should bring needed expertise to the board, which could be related to the industry, customers, financial matters, or general management skills and experience. The stronger the individual members of the board, the stronger the board will be. Finally, it is essential that individual directors, regardless of their other attributes, be capable of playing effectively on a team and engaging in no-fault confrontation. They must also be willing to express contrary views when they are called for.

THE CONVENTIONAL WISDOM ON BOARD STRUCTURE

A great deal of the literature on corporate governance is appropriately aimed at commenting on the most effective structure for boards. Numerous articles in the press and in business periodicals, relevant books, and statements by CEOs, pundits, and shareholder activists generally embrace a few very basic ideas about the role of the board's structure in the effectiveness of corporate governance. First, many people believe that boards should be small, with 10 members or fewer, and should be dominated by outsiders. This view embraces the belief that a small board has a better chance of building internal trust and acting quickly and decisively when necessary. For the board to be effective with a small number of members, there is no room for the dead weight of incompetent or uncommitted directors. Most interest groups (shareholders, activists, and financial analysts) are deeply distrustful of the appointment of individuals solely because they bring a "diverse" viewpoint or diversity itself in some form to the board. These constituents are equally wary of nepotism and of the appointment of cronies of current board members. They feel that every member of the board should be selected for his or her experience, integrity, and demonstrated performance in fields related to the company's business.

A Study of Typical Board Structures

We report here certain results from a study of some representative boards. We chose to analyze various aspects of the board structure of the 30 companies that constituted the Dow-Jones Industrials in 2000, and we compared the results with those from a systematic sample of the companies that made up the Standard and Poor's 500 (S&P 500) Index in 2000. Appendix 4-1 provides a detailed description of the process used to arrive at a sample of 25 firms from the S&P 500. The appendix also presents lists of the S&P sample companies as well as the 30 firms of the Dow.

The Dow list provides a group of widely recognized, very large companies that literally have come to represent the mainstream of the population of large U.S. companies. The systematic sample from the list of S&P 500 companies includes nearly the full range of the sizes of the 500 firms, which was much broader than the size range of the Dow firms. Collecting data for both groups of firms allowed us to study the extent to which the board demographics varied, whether between the two groups or within either group.

Reviewing the overall size of the boards, we found somewhat similar ranges for each of the two groups of companies. Although there were a few boards with fewer than 10 or greater than 18 members in each group, the majority of the boards in both samples fell between 9 and 16 members. The S&P 500 sample demonstrated greater variability (dispersion) across the group than did the Dow companies. Exhibit 4-1 shows the distribution of board sizes of the Dow companies and the S&P 500 sample.

In addition to the size of the boards in our two samples, we gathered data on the guaranteed compensation (board fees) for the companies in each sample. Exhibit 4-2 shows the contrast in board fees between the two samples. We see that the average board fees for the directors of Dow companies were more than 60 percent higher than the average of the sample of S&P 500 companies.

ORGANIZING THE BOARD FOR SUCCESS

After a talented team has been put in place, the board must manage its collective affairs based on a few simple principles. One action among the board's most important responsibilities is to attract and retain talented management (read CEO) and hold him or her accountable for executing the company's agreed-upon strategy and achieving outstanding results compared with peer companies. Performance, however, should not be judged quarter by quarter but instead should be linked to the appreciation of the company's

Exhibit 4-1

Number of Members on Dow 30 and S&P 500 Sample Company Boards of Directors: Year 2000

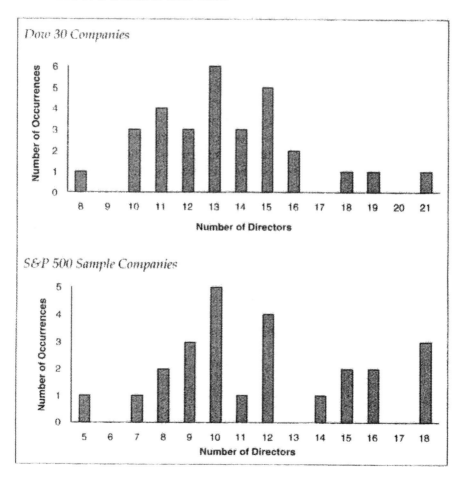

value (market value or capitalization) over some longer time frame. Board members seeking solid performance from the management team should, in most cases, expect appreciation in market capitalization to exceed the rate of appreciation of other firms in the company's industry. In order to judge the performance of the leadership team adequately, the board should meet regularly without the inside board members to evaluate performance.

Second to the obvious need to attract the most talented management team possible, another critical responsibility of the board is to decide how

E x h i b i t   4-2

Annual Guaranteed Individual Compensation for Directors of Dow 30 and S&P 500 Sample Companies: Year 2000

	Dow 30 Companies	S&P 500 Sample Companies
Minimum	$8,000	$20,000
Average	$61,233	$37,409
Maximum	$125,000	$100,000

the firm's available capital is to be allocated between reinvestments in the company and distributions to the shareholders. In nearly all other matters, the board should stay out of the management details and let the management team run the company.

Independence of Board Members

Effective boards should, in our view, be composed of a majority of nonmanagement directors. Because the first duty of any board is to protect the interests of the shareholders, the composite independence of the board should not be in question. Members of management, so-called inside directors, while professing fealty to their shareholders, are invariably influenced by the benefits of their positions. Having a solid majority of the board, at least two-thirds, composed of nonmanagement directors removes the potential for conflict between management and shareholders. *Independence*, however, may be defined more broadly than "nonmanagement." According to corporate governance standards proposed by the New York Stock Exchange (NYSE) in 2002, directors with immediate family members who have worked for the firm in the preceding 5 years may not be considered independent. (The definition of *immediate family member* had yet to be fully delineated at the time of writing.) Many firms already have similar standards in place.

Exhibit 4-3 shows the distributions of the proportions of inside directors on the boards of the Dow 30 companies and the sample of 25 S&P 500 companies, respectively. We can see from the figures that there is little substantive difference between the attributes of the two samples, perhaps indicating that this element of board structure is similar over a wide range of sizes of companies.

E x h i b i t 4 - 3

Proportion of Insiders on Dow 30 and S&P 500 Sample Company Boards of Directors: Year 2000

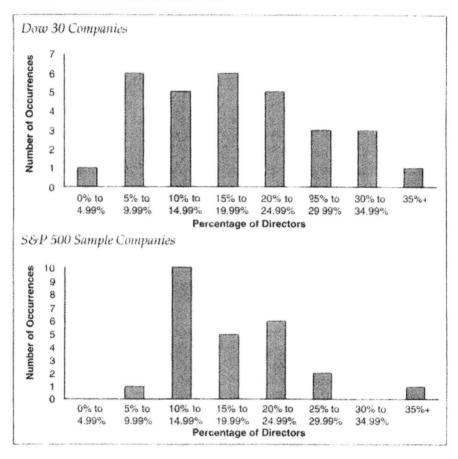

Exhibit 4-4 shows the minimum, maximum, and average numerical data for the proportion of inside directors for each set of companies. As shown, the average percentage of inside directors is 17 percent for both groups of companies. One also may see from the extremes (maxima) of Exhibits 4-3 and 4-4 that only one firm in each sample demonstrated a proportion of insiders greater than the suggested one-third insiders. This is good news for investors.

The independence of the board is tested in a number of ways: through the effectiveness of its auditing function, the administration of

E x h i b i t   4 - 4

Proportion of Insiders on Dow 30 and S&P 500 Sample Company
Boards of Directors: Year 2000

	Dow 30 Companies	S&P 500 Sample Companies
Minimum	5 percent	9 percent
Average	17 percent	17 percent
Maximum	38 percent	43 percent

CEO and executive performance appraisals and compensation, and its
willingness to question and, if necessary, overrule management recommendations. For example, in the case of an acquisition or of being
acquired, board independence of action is critical. In the event of a possible acquisition, senior management often will be too close to the circumstances surrounding the target, potentially overlooking the practical
downside risks inherent in the deal. Conversely, if the board's company is
the target, senior management can present a seemingly endless series of
objections to the proposed deal if their status and comfort levels are likely to be altered materially. These objections may or may not coincide with
the interests of shareholders. The best decision—that is, a decision in the
best interests of the shareholders—can only be made through applied
objectivity, exercised by truly independent directors.

THE DIRECTOR'S STAKE IN THE GAME

A major issue in selecting outside directors is the company's view toward
ownership. Donald Hambrick and Eric Johnson reviewed this issue and
provide the following comment on their findings: "The majority of outside directors of major American companies have modest shareholdings
in the companies they govern. This reflects an implicit long-held belief
that directors are fully motivated to act conscientiously and vigorously by
forces other than a financial stake in the firm: their sense of professionalism, concern for their reputations and stature, and the threat of lawsuits."[1]

There is a growing view, however, that directors need to own significant amounts of equity in a firm to motivate them to become fully
engaged. Competent directors are usually extremely busy with many
demands on their time. Thus, unless they are willing to make substantial

investments relative to their net worth in a business, they are implicitly revealing that they are allocating their resources elsewhere. It seems that these directors, then, are likely to put their time and energies where their personal funds are invested. This logic suggests that all directors should be required to make a substantial investment in the company's shares when elected to the board and that a major part of their compensation as a director should be in the form of stock in the corporation. We discuss the importance of directors owning a substantial number of shares in the company again in Chapter 11.

THE RETIRING CEO

Another policy issue that deals, at least in part, with the question of independence is whether a CEO should remain on the board after he or she retires. The advantages of retaining former CEOs include their knowledge of the business and the strong likelihood of their having a major stake in it. The disadvantage of their retention is the lack of independence arising from their ties to management. Moreover, a former CEO may create problems for the new CEO, particularly if the new CEO wants to make major changes. It would be difficult for a retired CEO to openly oppose the recommendations or actions of the new CEO without creating unfortunate tension for the other directors.

The conventional wisdom is that a retiring CEO should leave the board. His or her departure may occur after a short transition period (a year or so), and in certain situations, there may even be reason to make exceptions to this rule. Retaining a retired CEO on the board, however, should occur only after careful consideration of the potential implications of doing so. In situations where the retiring CEO is a major shareholder and has a long record of success and good personal chemistry with the new CEO, a board may lean toward making an exception, but even under these circumstances, it is a risky practice.

THE REELECTION OF INCUMBENT DIRECTORS

Among the traditions of many boards, there is an assumption that lacking specific term limits in the bylaws, sitting directors customarily should be reelected unless they are removed for cause. The term *for cause* commonly arises from the legal interpretation of some action or inaction that most often involves a conflict of interest, the commitment of some illegal act, or behavior that constitutes an embarrassment to the firm. In the absence of cause, boards should perform or commission a regular review of the contributions and performance of individual directors and of the board as a whole. The circumstances of a business and those of individual directors change over time, and as a result, a person who was once an excellent director may no longer fit the company's contemporary situation. Alternatively, individual performance issues may suggest that it is time for a given director to move off the board. In either case, a periodic review of board and director performance should identify such situations for deliberation and action. Obtaining the evaluation, however, is likely to require some effort.

It is difficult for a governing body to conduct objective self-evaluations and peer evaluations without creating political tensions within its ranks. One alternative to the approach of using evaluation to identify poorly fitting directors is the use of term limits. With term limits, though, the good directors rotate off the board with the poor ones because there is no discrimination. The loss of good directors is costly, and strong replacements are not easy to find, particularly when it is hoped that they will invest heavily in the business. Also lost is the continuity of in-depth knowledge of the business, as well as the value of that knowledge itself. Even good new directors take a year or more to get fully acclimated to a business. A practical solution to maintaining an effective board without term limits is to have a universal agreement among all the directors that reelection is not automatic. The board then should employ a meaningful process to regularly evaluate the performance of the board as a collective body and of incumbent directors by their peers, taking into account the current needs of the corporation. These reviews should be annual, formal, and thorough. The results should be discussed with each director and with the entire board.

Problems with the effectiveness of the overall board can be addressed through the selection, recruitment, and election of more effective individual directors. Individual directors who are ineffective should be given the opportunity to resign from the board before the nominating committee withholds its renomination at the end of their terms.

Most boards do have mandatory retirement ages, usually somewhere between 70 and 75 years of age. This is generally regarded as a good policy. Many boards also require that a director submit his or her resignation on a change in primary employment circumstances. The resignation may or may not be accepted by the board, depending on how the fellow directors perceive the change in status will influence the director's ability to function effectively.

THE SELECTION PROCESS FOR NEW DIRECTORS

As we move on to the mechanics of director selection and recruiting, it bears repeating that in order to be truly independent and to act first and last in the interests of shareholders, a board must be composed of directors whose overriding loyalty is to the shareholders. If a board does not establish a genuinely objective selection process, it risks allowing a persuasive and personally dominant CEO to irresistibly wield an invisible hand over the nomination process. The outcome of such an occurrence would reveal an apparently independent majority that, in practice, takes its cues from senior management. The end result is a board whose conduct is functionally that of insiders. Corporate governance thus may be cloaked in the appearance of independence, yet its substance is one of dependence, lying within the orbit of senior management. Consequently, the establishment of a genuinely objective process is critical for corporate boards. The nominating committee carries out the largest part of the selection process for most boards.

Ideally, every board should have a nominating committee, the majority of which is composed of outside directors. The CEO also should be a member of the board's nominating committee. This committee, also known as the *governance committee* in some cases, is responsible for the identification and selection of prospective board nominees. In the absence of such a committee, the board's executive committee generally performs this duty. Except for the audit committee, no other board committee is charged with as sensitive a task as is the nominating committee. The effectiveness of a board and the quality of its decisions are linked directly to the caliber of its members.

The Board Profile

The first step for the nominating committee in identifying candidates is to create a profile of the types of skills and experience needed on the board. This list of desirable attributes would depend on the business or businesses in which the company engages and the strategy it expects to employ. It also would include necessary functional expertise such as accounting, finance, marketing, operations management, industry expertise, and demographic diversity, along with general business experience applicable to the activities of the firm. For instance, if the nominating committee felt that the board should include the CEOs of four other companies, ideally, they would come from different industries.

After the nominating committee has clearly identified the desired skills and experience of board members, it should compare its ideal attributes with the characteristics and experience of the returning board members and identify any apparent gaps. The committee would then search for candidates who could complete the ideal profile of the board. The committee should heed the wisdom that it is important for individual directors to bring to the board a diverse set of skills and experience. If too many members have similar backgrounds, discussions will tend to take on a predictable pattern, and the effectiveness of the decision-making process will be impaired. Vignette 4-1 describes how a board must change, adjust, and adapt itself as a company grows and prospers.

VIGNETTE 4-1

EVOLUTION OF A HIGH-TECH BOARD

THE ISSUE

The preferred attributes of individual directors and a board as a whole do not remain constant over the life of a company. Instead, the composition of the board necessarily should change as the company evolves from a startup company, through the initial public offering (IPO), and finally, to a large, public multinational corporation. Boards inevitably must change, adjust, and evolve as their companies move ahead.

THE BEGINNINGS

A team of scientists from a major research university started a high-tech company. These scientists were fortunate to find themselves with a major technological breakthrough coupled with a strong vision and an accompanying business model. They decided to leave their academic careers and seriously pursue their business dreams. The first challenge faced by the business founders was to finance their enterprise. They approached a number of venture capitalists with regard to financing their venture and succeeded in launching their business on very favorable terms. Having secured valid patents on several key aspects of their technologies, they were in a position to choose from among several available financiers, all of whom structured major personal stakes in the company for the founders. The original board consisted of three members representing the scientific team and five representing the financial backers. This distribution of board memberships roughly represented the proportional shareholdings of the two parties. Thus the board, from the beginning, drew its technical capabilities from the founding scientific team and its business acumen from the venture capital group.

Continued

Continued

RAPID GROWTH

This simple board structure served the company and its shareholders well in the early stages of the company's history. The company had to move its products from the development stage into production, establish sales representatives and distributors, and determine the channels through which the products would be sold. Ultimately, the management team had to manage its finances carefully until it reached an adequate scale and sufficient profit margins to become cash self-sufficient. Management also had to develop the product, marketing, and pricing strategies that would provide a basis for sustained growth, and it also had to have the capacity in place in anticipation of an expanding market for its products. As the company successfully maneuvered through these challenges, its continued research and development efforts produced a series of new and differentiated products that gave it market supremacy in a rapidly growing high-technology field. Its products were synonymous with quality and reliability, and the firm dominated its market segments. This placed the firm in a strong position to cement its dominance through the acquisition of competitors and small startup firms with new technologies or strengths in technology niches.

At this point, the board decided to take the firm public through an IPO. The board reasoned that the IPO would bring many advantages to the firm, including raising a large amount of capital to fund the company's further expansion; creating a currency to fund acquisitions through the use of the very valuable shares of company stock, which was expected to maintain a high share-price-to-earnings multiple; providing liquidity for some shareholders who would like to exit years after having financed the company at startup; and establishing a discipline for the board and management as the company continued to grow. In preparation for the IPO, the board was expanded and the profiles of its members broadened to include more general business skills, two CEOs of other public companies, three directors with experience in other high-growth, high-technology companies, and other skills and experience thought valuable to a firm competing for capital and investors on a now national basis. This series of strategic and operational moves carried the company for some years after the IPO until sales reached $1 billion per year.

Continued

Concluded

EXPLOSIVE FURTHER GROWTH

Over the next 10 years, the company grew rapidly to an annual sales level of more than $20 billion through impressive organic (internal) growth and through dozens of acquisitions of firms with key technologies. As the firm grew, its share price skyrocketed, reflecting a strong respect for the company on the part of financial analysts, institutional investors, and individual investors. Along with this explosive growth, the board continued to broaden the skills and experience of its membership to provide representation consistent with the growing international powerhouse the company was becoming. Additional CEOs of other companies were added, directors with broad name recognition were elected, and steps were made to bring more diverse points of view to the board's deliberations. In addition, the board continually adjusted its internal organization and committee structure to reflect the latest reasoned ideas about corporate governance.

THE POINT

We should note the continuous evolution of this company's board and its strategies as the firm grew relentlessly from a small startup with a strong technology base to an international technology company. It was thus essential for the board to adapt and restructure itself to meet the needs of the growing concern. As time went by, the talents brought to the board by certain directors were no longer needed, and these directors were replaced with new directors whose talents, skills, and experience more closely reflected the needs of the firm going forward. This high-technology firm, whose board began as a group of scientists and venture capitalists, managed this process handily, continually matching board endowments with the needs of the firm. This consistent alignment undoubtedly contributed to the organization's ongoing success.

The Search and Screening Processes

After the nominating committee has identified the needs and desires of the board regarding new members, its next step is to begin looking for appropriate candidates. A few companies use professional search firms for this task, but most will ask existing board members to put forward the names of potential candidates. The board also may seek suggestions from other groups or individuals familiar with the firm, such as investment bankers, lawyers, and customers. After a list of potential candidates has been compiled, the nominating committee should perform an initial screening. This typically involves gathering reported information about the individual candidates and their credentials.

This sequence of identifying potential candidates for board service may vary for those nominees who own or represent large shareholdings, such as the family of the company's founder or a representative of a nonprofit foundation with a large equity position in the company. While their nomination to the board may be more of a formality, it is important for such candidates to recognize that if elected, they must represent the interests of all shareholders, not just those of their special interest group. Even though logic would assume these interests to be symmetrical, often they are not. As a part of director orientation, all new board members should be educated to recognize this primary duty to represent the interests of all shareholders.

The last step in this private phase of identifying candidates for board service is to arrive at some priority ordering of the potential candidates. This ordering may be done across the entire list or in categories representing the skills or experience needed for the board. The nominating committee then should analyze the entire list in order to decide which candidates best fit the needs of the board and the company in its contemporary circumstances. This step, like all the steps that precede it, should be a board-confidential activity. When the board moves on to researching and recruiting new members, the curtain of privacy surrounding the process will be pulled back.

DUE DILIGENCE

The next step for the nominating committee would be to conduct its due diligence, meaning really getting to know the individual candidates and their reputations. After determining that the preferred individuals might be interested in joining the board, several members of the committee, perhaps joined by other members of the board or the CEO, should meet with the candidates individually. References also should be checked thoroughly. Because people of the required stature are normally well known to the public, it is usually rather straightforward to find out what the committee needs to know to determine whether there would be good chemistry between the candidate and the other members of the board and whether the individual has the time and interest to make the necessary commitment to join the board. It is essential that the individual demonstrate an interest and desire to be on the board and that he or she not have prior commitments that would conflict with this service. The due diligence process morphs into recruitment when the committee has decided that it wants the individual. In fact, the due diligence and recruitment processes actually may proceed virtually simultaneously.

Recruitment

The actual recruitment of prospective nominees can take a variety of approaches, but the most common is recruitment through a personal relationship with one or more existing board members. It may involve visits to the company facilities, meetings with key managers, and social occasions with existing directors. At such gatherings, the board is usually attempting to impress the candidate with the attractiveness of the opportunity to serve on the board and the effectiveness of the board and management. Board members also should emphasize the contribution the recruit might make to the board and the company.

The Nominee's Decision to Serve

After being approached by a current board member, a candidate for board service should perform some research before agreeing to stand for election. It is incumbent on the prospective nominee to determine precisely what a director's full responsibilities are and to judge his or her individual ability to fulfill them. It is also the task of the prospective nominee to be absolutely certain that no real or perceived conflicts of interest exist. Such conflicts can assume a variety of forms in addition to competitive conflicts, and a nominee should explore them fully. Due diligence is an important process for the nominee as well as the company.

Election of Directors

The election of directors takes place at the annual meeting of shareholders. The shareholders elect directors, who will be legally charged with representing their interests. In the case of interim vacancies, the board generally is empowered through the bylaws to fill the vacancies for the balance of the unexpired terms or until the next annual meeting. Normally, the number of nominees is identical to the number of vacant seats. If not, the directors can change the bylaws to create the proper number of openings. It is important to note that directors are elected for a term of usually 1 to 3 years. Terms begin and expire on the date of the annual meeting of shareholders. The removal of a serving director is next to impossible, lacking some cause that could lead to his or her resignation. This rigidity in the matter of board service puts a high premium on a thorough process of identification, recruitment, and election of directors. Vignette 4-2 describes how a successful process was conducted in putting together a new board for a startup community bank.

VIGNETTE 4-2

STRUCTURING A NEW BOARD FOR SUCCESS—AND ENSURING AGAINST FAILURE

THE ISSUE

Two entrepreneurs who decided to start a new community bank set about structuring the board for the new enterprise in a way to provide a high degree of likelihood for success.

THE SITUATION

In February 1995, the Office of the Comptroller of the Currency (OCC) granted a charter to Mountain Bank, a one-bank holding company in Pinnacle, Virginia. The bank opened in May 1995, with an initial capitalization of $9 million and by year-end 2001 had assets of $200 million and after-tax earnings of $1.6 million, despite its having opened five additional branches in the intervening 5 years. Unlike many community banks, Mountain Bank had avoided all the factors that traditionally exposed new community banks to mediocre performance, regulatory problems, and even outright failure. How did this happen?

The answer lies in the process by which its board of directors was formed. In September 1992, an out-of-state superregional bank acquired Commerce Bank, Pinnacle's only locally headquartered bank and holder of the largest market share, roughly 43 percent. Pinnacle thus became the largest city south of Portland, Maine, north of Jacksonville, Florida, and east of the Mississippi River without a community bank. This fact acquired significance given that historically 20 percent of any market would migrate over time to a well-managed community bank, provided this alternative were available. This asset migration, oddly enough, is not the marginal bottom 20 percent of the market in desirability but rather the top 20

Continued

Continued

percent. In 1992, the Pinnacle market had approximately $3.2 billion in deposits, indicating that a $500 to $600 million long-term opportunity existed. Furthermore, the market's deposit base had been growing consistently 2 to 3 percent per year for over 30 years.

In the fall of 1993, a senior Commerce Bank executive who was cast off from its merger met with a well-known business and civic leader in Pinnacle to first discuss the possibility of founding a new community bank in that year. Their specific interests and concerns were why such banks succeeded and, equally, why they failed. They identified the following factors. Community banks succeeded when

- The organizers/directors were well known within the market.
- No other well-capitalized or aggressive community bank(s) existed.
- Individual organizers did not themselves need a lending institution.
- High-caliber management was available.
- The organizers/directors believed that the community was entitled to a locally controlled and focused lending institution.

Conversely, community banks failed or delivered mediocre performance when

- They were undercapitalized.
- They suffered from marginally talented management.
- The organizers had limited community profiles.
- One or more of the organizers needed a lending institution.
- The organizers as a group funded less than 20 percent of the initial capitalization.
- The organizers' lack of a strong spirit of collegiality that led to factional decision making on difficult issues.

Success, therefore, was rooted in the profile of the organizing group, the availability of quality management, and the level of initial capitalization. Failure or mediocre performance lay in the absence of these attributes. The challenge was managing the formation process for success while avoiding a negative or marginal result.

Continued

Continued

TAKING ACTION

The two organizers first outlined the personal and collective profiles of ideal members of an organizer group: well known within the community but not socially stratified, possessing assets to make a significant ($200,000+) equity contribution, not in need of a lending institution, a composition reflective of the community, a strong desire for community economic development, and a common belief in the principle of retaking local control of lending decisions.

Based on these profiles, the original two organizers next identified 30 prospective additional organizers. Early on, they determined that they would approach each prospective organizer collectively, meaning that each successive organizer who joined the group would then become part of the whole, which would then, in turn, subject the next prospect to the same election standards. Thus the first two organizers recruited the third, the three then recruited the fourth, and so on until there were 14 organizers, including the proposed CEO. One of the original two organizers was designated chief operating officer (COO), and the other became the chairman of the organizing group. Therefore, the organizing group (which traditionally becomes the board on the OCCs granting of a charter) was composed of 12 outside and 2 inside directors. Throughout the process, each successively recruited organizer had veto power over the next prospective organizer, as opposed to selecting by a majority vote.

THE RESULT

The end result of the careful selection process was a board possessing a profound commonality of interest in the success of the institution. Private agendas had been identified and vetoed. In 1997, when significant weaknesses were revealed in the CEO, he was replaced by a unanimous board decision, and the senior lender was promoted to CEO and elected a director. Such conflicts often fracture a board, creating divisive groups within it as individual directors take sides. To the contrary, this transition was seamless and done with the blessing of the OCC, which traditionally is skeptical of such a radical change early on in the formation of a new bank. Moreover,

Continued

Concluded

over the 6½-year life of the bank, only $24,000 of loans had to be written off, which was a strikingly small figure considering a current loan portfolio of $150 million and a total turnover of loan takeouts and paydowns of over $1 billion. Additionally, there had never been pressure on management from individual directors to make uncreditworthy loans, which could cause the institution to face unacceptable credit risks as a result of the influence of an individual director.

THE POINT

Independence of thought and collegiality of action ruled the conduct of this board. Its selection process guaranteed it, and the results continued to validate it. Earnings in the first quarter of 2002 were 41 percent ahead of the first quarter of 2001.

MAINTAINING BOARD EFFECTIVENESS OVER THE LONG TERM

We must remind ourselves of the very long time frame within which corporations function. Many continue on for decades, requiring an orderly series of transitions in both boards and CEOs. It is therefore important to take an equally long-term view in the processes of board selection. The fact that a board is especially effective at one point in time does not mean that shareholders can relax and expect continuity. Boards do not suddenly become exceptional or troubled. Lists of the 10 worst boards and the 10 best boards are published regularly in the business press. The movement of these boards to excellence or ridicule took place gradually over an extended period of time, hardly overnight. As terms expired, the relative effectiveness of the entire board was shaped by each sequential selection decision.

Strong boards evolve from a culture that includes a strong, independent set of directors and a well-functioning nominating committee charged with identifying, recruiting, and obtaining the election of people meeting the criteria described earlier. Weak boards, on the other hand, almost invariably emanate from a dominant CEO who is able to control the nominating process to the extent that his or her cronies come to dominate the board. The CEO then has total control, and the board no longer represents the best interests of the shareholders in the sense intended by statute and in the company's bylaws. Thus the selection process by which the board is formed must ensure that each appointment of a new director moves the total board further in the direction of excellence with regard to all the criteria by which the interested parties measure the effectiveness of boards.

It is often virtually impossible to determine the true degree of a board's objectivity, especially when many of its decisions in the ordinary course of business would be identical, regardless of composition. Given that the initial selection process is accurately characterized by objectivity, it is primarily in the areas of senior management compensation, auditing, and structural equity shifts, such as acquiring other companies or being acquired, that a board meets or fails the litmus test of independence.

ATTRIBUTES OF DIRECTORS OF MATURE VERSUS GROWTH COMPANIES

We report here the results of a study comparing the boards and governance processes of a set of more mature companies with a selection of fast-growth companies regardless of their size. The lists of 20 mature and fast-growth companies were identified on Fortune.com in February 2001. The samples were the top 20 companies drawn from the Fortune 500 list (representing the 500 largest U.S. firms and considered here a universe of mature companies) and the list of the Fortune 500 growth companies (considered here a population of growth companies). The sample list of mature companies included General Motors, Wal-Mart, IBM, Citigroup, and Hewlett-Packard. The sample of fast-growth companies included Siebel Systems, Salton, Stericycle, and Mercury Interactive. No company was on both lists. The data gathered included the market capitalization of the companies, the sizes and composition of their boards, the frequency of board meetings, facts about the CEO, and the companies' stock performance relative to the S&P 500 Index. Exhibit 4-5 summarizes some of the comparative results of the study.

Conclusions

Some general conclusions regarding the differences between mature and fast-growth companies based on the samples examined include

- On average, boards of mature companies are
  - Larger and more diverse.
  - Less insider-oriented.
  - Less industry-biased.
- CEOs of mature companies tend to be equal in age to directors; CEOs of growth companies tend to be younger than directors, on average.

E x h i b i t   4 - 5

Governance Comparative Overview: Mature versus Fast-Growth
Companies

Metric	Mature	Growth
Average market capitalization	$132 billion	$4 billion
Average number of directors	14	7
Percentage of insiders on board	19 percent	36 percent
Diversity (gender, race)	Medium	Low
Average age of directors	60 years	52 years
Average tenure of directors (length of service on the board)	9 years	6 years
Average annual board fees paid to directors	$60,000	$10,000
Typical number of board committees	5	2.5
Bias for directors from same industry	Low	High
Frequency of board meetings	9 per year	6.5 per year
Frequency of committee meetings	4 per year	2.5 per year
Annual cash compensation of CEO	$10.3 million	$970,000
CEO relation to chairman	75 percent same	80 percent same
Average age of CEO	59 years	48 years

- Directors and CEOs at mature companies are paid more on average than directors and CEOs at growth companies.
- Directors at mature companies are older and more experienced in board service than are directors at growth companies.

As described in Vignette 4-1, governance structures evolve as companies become more mature. Directors become older and more diverse, and boards become larger with more committees and, concomitantly, more formal operating structures. Mature companies appear to value diversity among their directors, whereas growth companies value focus and industry insight among their directors. Growth companies seem driven, at least in part, by younger CEOs and boards who share an insider vision of their industries. Growth companies tend to be focused on younger leadership both in the corporate office and in the boardroom.

THE DOMINANT PERSONALITY

There is a final, intangible aspect of board structure and performance. It can best be described as the dilemma of the dominant personality. We are all familiar with the larger-than-life corporate leaders whose names become synonymous with their companies' names. Given that there are some 5000 public companies whose shares are traded on the major stock exchanges in the United States and that the average tenure of a CEO is about 7 years, the expectation would be that some 700 of these CEO positions would turn over each year. Such a rate of turnover would require the selection and appointment of approximately 14 new CEOs a week, or almost 3 per working day. The vast majority of these CEOs remain anonymous, known only to those with whom they work and interact in their businesses and a small circle of competitors, suppliers, financial analysts, and bankers. Most do a credible job of running their companies and move through their tenures with little controversy or notoriety. The performance of their companies is more or less in line with that of their industry peers or generally accepted performance norms.

A very small number are found to be dishonest or suffer from character flaws that lead to their dismissal, after which the company moves on under new leadership, provided it survived the flawed leadership of the CEO. Another very small number of CEOs achieve a celebrity status that transcends the business they are running. They may become well known for a variety of reasons: superior performance over a number of years, some major event of a positive or negative nature, very poor performance over a protracted period, or even their adeptness at public relations. Most Americans recognize the names of Jack Welch (GE), Michael Eisner (Disney), Roberto Goizueto (Coca Cola), and Warren Buffett (Berkshire Hathaway). For a variety of reasons, these CEOs have achieved a personal celebrity that overshadows the normal role of a CEO. Some produce long-term results so outstanding that they achieve almost total control over their boards, since results are the primary preoccupation of the board. As a result, these CEOs may enjoy little direction from their boards with regard to major strategic moves, such as acquisitions or divestitures or in planning for their succession.

OTHER AVENUES BY WHICH CEOS HAVE OR GAIN CONTROL

Other CEOs gradually gain control over their boards by a process of ensuring the appointment of friends or supporters on whom they can depend for favorable consideration of their initiatives. In these situations, the less-than-desirable level of CEO control can persist for long periods of time, to the detriment of helpless shareholders. Under the governance system in place in the United States, it is perfectly legal for such a situation to continue indefinitely, since there is no simple method to displace enough directors to effect change. The only mechanisms available for dealing with this phenomenon are shareholder lawsuits or hostile takeover bids as the firm's value drops to levels attractive to potential acquirers. As we described in Chapter 3, various "poison pill" measures have virtually eliminated the ability of outsiders to effect hostile takeovers. This leaves the unhappy shareholder the nonnegotiable option to sell his or her shares.

Let us now consider several additional ways in which a dominant CEO may come to have gained control over the board. We understand clearly the difference between so-called public and private companies. There are, however, numerous firms that we choose to describe as quasi-public companies. We use the term *quasi-public company* to mean a firm that is effectively controlled as a private company but has the reporting requirements of a public company. One way in which such firms come to exist derives from a private company that chooses to go public through an IPO in which a minority portion of the company's shares is sold to the public. This produces a public company that is, in effect, controlled by a small group of shareholders who own a majority of the company's shares. Yet another method is for a much larger private company to merge into a smaller, already listed public company and in the process become a public entity, but one firmly controlled by the shareholders of the previously private entity.

A quasi-public company also can come about through the process called *entrenchment*, in which a number of elections to the board are controlled by the CEO to such an extent that, in effect, the CEO and his or her cronies control the company. This is despite the fact that the company is a public company, subject to all the attendant reporting requirements. The control of the company by the entrenched board is just as firm as that of a group that decides to take a company public by selling a minority of its shares to the public.

There are some readily apparent contradictions between the conventional wisdom about board structure and the way many such quasi-public companies operate. Small boards (less than 10 directors) that are clearly dominated by insiders represent the shareholders of many prominent companies. One highly respected company's board includes 7 members, of which only 2 are truly outsiders. It is often the case in such situations that the activities of the board and the company appear to revolve too heavily around one person (frequently a major shareholder or the CEO) for the board to be truly independent. In all other respects, however, the boards of such companies may be models for their structure, organization, and even long-term financial results. Each board member may be a substantial long-term shareholder, which serves to align his or her interests with the long-term success of the firm. Cash compensation may be minimal by normal standards, and stock options may not be awarded to the directors. For directors who may already be wealthy, such forms of compensation may be viewed as short-term incentives that might detract from the longer-term goals of value creation espoused by the major shareholders.

CONCLUSIONS ABOUT BOARD STRUCTURE

Mainstream corporate American thinking is captured in the following list of norms regarding board structure and organization.

- The best boards consist of directors who are also substantial, as opposed to nominal, shareholders.
- The best boards emphasize the long-term creation of shareholder value and, as a result, are more concerned with the strength of the company than with short-term fluctuations of the share price.
- The board may hold businesses indefinitely, or it may sell a business when restructuring is deemed important for the future of the firm, but it never trades in and out based on short-term market conditions. These behaviors engender strong trust and stability on the part of management teams.
- Talented management should be recruited to the firm, and management interests should be aligned with those of the board through the purchase of substantial amounts of stock, not through grants of stock options, which are risk-free to the recipient and not a conclusive indicator of alignment.
- Capital allocation and performance reviews are the major periodic governance issues routinely undertaken by the boards.

It is interesting that the governance structures of successful firms are closely aligned with shareholder interests, leading to handsome financial returns over time. Public ownership complicates governance issues, but an appropriate mix of simplicity, rigorous adherence to goals and mission, and the alignment of management and governance interests with shareholder interests would improve the results of most public and quasi-public corporations.

THE BOTTOM LINE: CONTROL AND POWER

Board control and power effectively are determined on two levels. The first level is entirely practical and overtly rooted in the company's bylaws, which, for example, dictate the number of directors, those specific items requiring board approval, and whether a simple- or a super-majority vote is required for passage. The second level is characterized by great subtlety. Who influences whom? Are there shifting coalitions driven by topic or perceived self-interest? Do one or more directors, whether they would be characterized as inside or outside, effectively exercise control through force of personality or through the granting or withholding of favor? Such dynamics are beyond elementary board politics, which are self-evident in most group situations. These subtle aspects of board construction and operation determine, in the end, how effective the board is in fulfilling its role as the legal representative of the shareholders.

In Chapter 5 we move on to more routine actions of boards of directors. That chapter will provide some insights into typical board meetings.

REVIEW QUESTIONS

1. What are the norms as to board size and the split between inside and outside directors?
2. What is the role of independence in directors carrying out their duties?
3. What is the role of a preferred profile in the selection of new directors?
4. How does a board adapt itself to a corporation's changing circumstances?
5. How does a CEO gain control over the board?

APPENDIX 4-1:

DETAILS OF THE STUDY OF REPRESENTATIVE BOARDS

Sample Selection

As a first step in identifying a representative sample of the S&P 500 companies, any firm with a fiscal year-end other than December was removed from the pool. This action left 366 firms from which the sample would be drawn. This initial step was taken to ensure that the data represented identical periods in a time of pronounced economic and market fluctuations, including the dot-com collapse and the disruption of September 11, 2001. The S&P 500 firms were then rank ordered by their market capitalization as of November 30, 2001, using data from the Compustat database.

A random number generator was used to determine the starting point for selecting the sample, with the goal of the selection process being a sample of 25 firms. The random number generator produced a value of 3, which resulted in the third firm on the list (beginning with the largest market capitalization) being chosen as the initial firm and starting point for selection of the systematic sample. Thereafter, each fifteenth firm was chosen (thus the firm with the eighteenth largest market capitalization was selected as the second firm in the sample) and so forth until the sample of 25 S&P 500 companies was complete. Complete lists of the firms in the Dow-Jones Industrials and the sample of 25 from the S&P 500 are shown below.

Firms in the Dow 30 and Sample from the S&P 500

Complete List of Dow 30 Companies

Alcoa, Inc.
Coca-Cola Co.
General Motors Corp.
International Paper Co.
Minnesota Mining & Manufacturing
American Express Co.
Disney (Walt) Co.

Hewlett-Packard Co.
J. P. Morgan Chase & Co.
Philip Morris Co.
AT & T Corp.
Du Pont (EI) de Nemours
Home Depot, Inc.
Johnson & Johnson
Procter & Gamble Co.
Boeing Co.
Eastman Kodak Co.
Honeywell International
McDonald's Corp.
SBC Communications
Caterpillar, Inc.
Exxon Mobil Corp.
Intel Corp.
Merck & Co., Inc.
United Technologies
Citigroup, Inc.
General Electric Co.
International Business Machines
Microsoft Corp.
Wal-Mart Stores, Inc.

List of Sample S&P 500 Companies

AES Corp.
Chubb Corp.
First Data
NICOR
State Street
Allegheny Energy
Constellation Energy Group
Gillette
Northrup Grumman
Stilwell Financial
Aon Corp.

Dynegy
Goodrich
Sears Roebuck
TECO Energy
Avery Dennison
Exxon Mobil Corp.
Inco, Ltd
Sprint
Tribune
ChevronTexaco
Federal Home Loan Mortgage
Louisiana-Pacific
St. Jude Medical
Waters Corp.

CHAPTER 5

The Mystique of
Board Meetings

In most corporate cultures, the board meeting is viewed with some awe. To those on the outside, the corporate board is seen as some sort of omnipotent body making profound decisions that are shrouded in mystique and secrecy. The outsiders metaphorically wait for the white smoke to emanate from the chimney, signaling some great pronouncement. What actually goes on in the boardroom seldom justifies this kind of reverence. After all, directors are fallible human beings trying to communicate with and influence each other as they wrestle with issues that are sometimes quite complex. Board meetings can be chaotic and complicated, especially when there are difficult questions to address, compounded by conflicting views and interests. As in any deliberative body, passion can and sometimes does override reason. Many of a board's subtle behaviors, however, are devoid of passion, including such mundane activities as the predilection of many board members to sit in precisely the same seat at the boardroom table, meeting after meeting, year after year. In this way, board members can become creatures of habit.

The most likely barrier to conducting an effective board meeting is the basic asymmetry in the amount of information available to members of management versus nonmanagement board members. When a considerable disparity occurs, which happens frequently, discussions become one-sided. This situation persists unless an effort is made to close this gap and provide all the directors with equal amounts of information.

It is difficult to characterize a typical board meeting; they vary with a company's circumstances and the personalities of the directors. They can be very short and informal or just the opposite, lengthy and ceremonial. Board meetings can be friendly and relaxed or adversarial and tense, efficient and no-nonsense, or rambling with a great deal of irrelevant discussion. Probably the single most influential variable contributing to the tone of a meeting is the personality of the leader or leaders. When there is a dominating leader or clique present among the board, the meeting will reflect the leadership's style and agenda, and often, decisions will have been made prior to the actual meeting. In this type of situation, other directors are expected to act as a rubber stamp, for to do otherwise would be seen as disruptive. Consequently, the meetings themselves are mere formalities, fulfilling the legal requirements as quickly and efficiently as possible.

One is left to wonder why directors will submit to this kind of dictatorial leadership, but it happens regularly in many of our best-known large corporations. Some directors may be on the board for the money (fees and stock options) or prestige. Others may hold the leader in awe because of his or her perceived superior knowledge, or they actually may be intimidated by a leader's behavior. This kind of subservience does not create problems when the leader is, in fact, exceptional, honest, and totally concerned about the interests of shareholders and other constituencies. Problems arise when the leader is not so wise or honest or has an agenda that is contrary to the interests of shareholders.

At the other end of the spectrum of board operations is the truly deliberative body, in which the directors individually and as a group take their responsibilities seriously. Here the leadership is less concerned about control and more concerned about a rule of reason. The leader wants orderly processes that tap into the diverse abilities of the directors and make it easy for each member to participate in and contribute to the discussions.

Another variable in a board's effectiveness is its perspective. There is a tendency to spend a great deal of time reviewing the past because this is the easy part of governance. The past is important in that there are lessons to be learned, and the board must identify and deal with any issues that have emerged. The board, however, must put most of its energies into where the business is going in the future. Too much emphasis on the past is similar to driving down the road looking in the rear view mirror. Focusing on the future is, of course, much more difficult work for the board, but it is precisely here that its intrinsic value to shareholders resides.

Just as a board needs to be future-oriented, it also must avoid too much emphasis on the administrative and the trivial. Some of this administrative work is legally necessary, but too frequently, boards will lose sight of the important larger picture by focusing on inconsequential details. Finding an appropriate balance is important to a board's effectiveness and is often a keen indicator of the board's leadership quality.

In summary, effective board meetings are most likely to take place when a board is a truly deliberative body focused on the substantive and the future. As we move forward with the topic of board meetings, we will describe typical procedures and activities for such a board.

PREPARATION FOR THE MEETING

Effective board meetings are made possible by careful preparation. Some argue, though, that the time required for management to prepare for board meetings could be better used running the business. This may be true if board meetings are elaborate show-and-tell events. Good management, however, already would be concentrating on items of deep interest to the board, so reporting on their plans and results should require minimal additional effort. The discipline of pausing periodically to reflect and summarize its plans has its own benefits for a management team. Preparing for and responding to probing questions about results or plans serve to sharpen thinking, confirm understanding, and identify shortcomings in reasoning, to the benefit of all parties involved.

The Importance of Effective Staff Work

A prerequisite for a productive meeting is to have good staff work that provides relevant information, frames issues, and preferably offers reasoned recommendations that are supported by analyses. Ideally, the material should be distributed to the board sufficiently in advance so that members may study it carefully, become comfortable with the topics to be considered, and arrive at the board meeting prepared with questions or informed positions on the topics of discussion.

It is of critical importance that management presentations be balanced and fairly present the pros and cons of the viable alternatives that have been identified. Directors should not be subjected to a "sales pitch" for management's recommendation. It is often readily apparent when members of management have stopped analyzing and started selling, which can damage their credibility with the board.

The Importance of Good Committee Work

Unless the board is very small (fewer than five or six persons), it generally does the bulk of its work in committees. The members are assigned to committees based on their individual expertise, thereby bringing the board's best minds to bear on any given topic. Board committees must have access to key managers in their areas of responsibility, as well as to outside experts when needed. They should have time to delve into the issues being studied in appropriate detail and to consider carefully all the viable alternatives. Since committees are smaller subgroups of the board, full participation by their members in fruitful discussion is easier to achieve. Such engagement by all directors strengthens the board's cohesiveness and effectiveness.

Committee exposure to managers other than the chief executive officer (CEO) has multiple benefits to both the managers and the directors. Close exposure to the directors can broaden the perspective of the managers. Conversely, the directors have a chance to see the managers dealing with real issues. Directors get a much better feel for the managers, as well as a close look at the unvarnished reality of the business situation.

Provided that the committees do their work effectively and are consistent with their responsibilities delegated by the board, they should be able to bring recommendations to the board with sufficient logic and supporting documentation to have wide credibility. If board members not on a particular committee disagree with the committee's recommendation, they are free—and actually obligated—to express their views in the board meeting and to vote their convictions. Boards that fall into the habit of routinely attempting to redo committee work in full session, however, usually become inefficient and have difficulty reaching a consensus on any issue.

WORKING AS A TEAM

An effective board approaches governance much as a sports team would approach a game. All members must have confidence in all other members, and each should be focused on contributing to an effective, working consensus. When there is a controlling individual bent on having his or her way or who does not have confidence in the other members, decision making can become very difficult. In fact, there are some very competent entrepreneurial individuals whose strong personalities do not permit them to function very well on boards.

THE MECHANICS OF MEETINGS

The frequency of board meetings varies from company to company and within a company depending on the company's circumstances. The maximum amount of time between meetings in order to have a properly functioning board is probably 3 months (quarterly meetings), with a fifth annual or planning meeting often added to reinforce the importance of looking ahead. At the other end of the spectrum, a few boards meet monthly. The choice of frequency of meeting has to do with the complexity of the situation—either in the size of the company, the issues being confronted, or the dynamics of the competitive situation.

The geographic location and the other commitments of the directors are also factors. If most of the directors are located near the corporate headquarters, it is possible to have more frequent, shorter meetings. If they have to travel a long way to meet, this generally means fewer, longer meetings.

Board meetings, depending on their frequency, can last from a couple of hours to a couple of days. When the directors live at a distance, the committee meetings are usually held the day before or on the morning of the board meetings. If the directors are local, the committee meetings can be held at times other than the board meetings. Quarterly meetings generally range from one-half to three-quarters of a day, frequently preceded by a dinner the night before.

There is a growing tendency to have meetings via teleconferences, sometimes with video, in lieu of investing the time and expense required for directors to travel long distances. Such arrangements often can seem to be efficient, but typically they are not as effective as having everyone in the same room. Moreover, teleconferencing sometimes proves more expensive than traveling.

EFFICIENCY AND FORMALITY

The efficiency with which meetings are conducted varies quite widely, as would be expected. Some boards are very informal, and the discussions can ramble. Some boards may require many hours of discussion to conclude what other boards can resolve in 30 minutes or less. On these boards, the discussion often may tend to expand to fill the time available. Other board meetings are very focused and task-oriented. They follow formal procedures—to the point of following parliamentary rules of order. Most boards operate somewhere in between these two extremes. They will meet with an agenda that they generally follow, and decisions will be made by means of voting on a formal motion, after a second, followed by discussion. However, the recognition of each speaker is usually more informal, unless there is a strong controversy with heated debate.

ATTENDEES

In addition to the directors, there is frequently a corporate secretary in attendance who takes the minutes of the meeting. Many boards find that it is useful to have someone with legal experience in this role because the minutes are an important part of the company's records. Most companies will bring in key managers from time to time to make presentations on operations or proposals. As noted earlier, this is an excellent opportunity for the board to see managers in action, as well as for the managers to gain a broader perspective of the governance of the corporation. Some companies have key managers sit in on the entire board meeting to answer questions and observe the proceedings. This practice, however, is not recommended. It works fine when there is no controversy, but it can inhibit the candid probing of the CEO. While it may appear awkward to ask people to leave, it is common practice in many boards that people who attend for some special reason understand that they are expected to leave after their business with the board is concluded. Some boards will have the legal counsel in the room at all times as an observer, whereas others do not think that this is necessary.

THE AGENDA

The chairman of the board prepares the agenda in collaboration with the CEO if separate people hold the two positions. If the CEO is also the chairman, he or she will consult with the lead director or chairman of the committee of outside directors (if either is in place) to set the agenda. If there is no director with whom to consult, the CEO is well advised to check with key directors to be sure that the agenda is appropriate, especially if there is any doubt as to the issues that should come before the board. Exhibit 5-1 shows the topics the agenda often includes for a regular meeting.

THE MINUTES OF THE MEETINGS

The board's secretary should prepare careful minutes of the proceedings of each meeting. The minutes record all the official actions of the board, including the votes, noting any directors casting negative votes or abstaining from voting by name. The minutes also may include brief descriptions of topics discussed and divergent points of view, if any surfaced. Between board meetings, the minutes should be transcribed and formalized. They may be approved by a mail or fax vote or saved for presentation and board approval at the next regular meeting of the board. Directors should read the minutes carefully, with the understanding that once they are approved, they become the official record of all deliberations and actions of the board. These become very important if serious concerns or differences of opinion develop regarding board activities or the effectiveness of its oversight.

THE BOARD'S CALENDAR

A board typically meets after the end of an operating period for which results are prepared, such as a quarter. The board may meet more frequently if it chooses, and special meetings may be called to deal with unusual opportunities or problems. As part of their routine, many boards

Exhibit 5-1

Sample Board Meeting Agenda

Item	Discussion
Quorum	There must be a quorum to have an official meeting.
Approval of the agenda	Some boards will give the directors a chance to modify the agenda.
Approval of the minutes of prior meetings	Most bylaws require the approval of minutes before they are official. These are generally mailed out in advance, preferably reasonably close to the completion of the prior meeting, while its substance is still fresh in the participants' minds.
Consent items	Some boards will address routine action items that require no discussion at this point. Examples might be the approval of minutes, declaration of the regular dividend and annual meeting notices. Related material should be mailed in advance of the meeting so that no briefing is required. Directors can, of course, ask for discussion, but in general, this is an efficient way of disposing of administrative items.
Committee reports and actions	Typically, the chair of each committee will report to the board on the outcome of committee meetings, including major issues discussed, actions taken, and recommendations for board action.
Current operations reports	The CEO reports on results of the last period and near-term prospects. The CFO may give a financial report, and the CEOs or presidents of major divisions or subsidiaries may also report.
Briefings or proposals	At this point, management may brief the board on topics or issues of interest or bring proposals to the board for action. Major capital investment decisions are also presented at this time. In the case of a major proposal, such as the acquisition of another company, the entire board meeting might be devoted to the single topic.
Executive session	Many boards go into a routine executive session at the end of each meeting. Management and the CEO are asked to leave, and the directors are given an opportunity to privately discuss issues of interest or concern. The chairman or lead director may be instructed to take messages to the CEO, or the CEO may be asked to return to the room to participate in the discussion.

have a regular cycle through the year to deal with planning topics. The annual budget customarily is approved near the beginning of the fiscal year. If the company generates a longer-term plan, it commonly would be reviewed several months in advance of the annual plan in order to create a proper context for discussion of the annual plan (budget). In the first half of the year, the strategy of the company should be assessed and refined or changed as appropriate. This kind of orderly cycle enables the board to be a routine participant in the strategic management process.

Board members also maintain a calendar for the meetings of the committees of which they are members. As noted previously, committee meetings are often, but not always, held the day before board meetings.

SUMMARY

Board meetings are the means by which the directors meet their responsibility to oversee the operations of the company on behalf of shareholders. Formality at these meetings tends to benefit the organization because the responsibilities to which the directors have committed themselves are serious. Consequently, the meetings should be planned, organized, and conducted with due consideration for the importance of the occasion.

Among the regular tasks of the board of directors is the evaluation of the performance of the CEO, and occasionally, the board must choose a successor for a departing CEO. These principal duties of the board are addressed in detail in Chapter 6.

REVIEW QUESTIONS

1. Is there a "typical" board meeting?
2. What activities prior to the board meeting enhance the effectiveness of the actual meeting?
3. What are the mechanics of an effective board meeting?

CEO Succession Planning, Selection, and Performance Appraisal

The selection of the chief executive officer (CEO) has a profound impact on the success of the enterprise and is the exclusive responsibility of the board of directors. When seeking a new CEO, the board must fully understand the prevailing dynamics of the company's situation and objectively assess how well the personal attributes of each CEO candidate meet the requirements of the role. The eventual marriage of personal attributes and role requirements is best executed following a significant courtship. Naturally, this objective is met more easily when the candidate has risen through the ranks of the enterprise.

Because corporations evolve as their competitive environments change, the leading candidate for the CEO position at one stage in the life cycle of the enterprise may well be ill-suited at another stage. If the board fails to grasp how these changes affect the role requirements, it may make a seemingly obvious selection that in fact fails to serve the requirements of the position. Similarly, the level of objectivity with which the board approaches selection of a new CEO often suffers because of a long association with the presumptive heir apparent. The selection of a new CEO, therefore, should constitute a stand-alone, discrete process. Except for the initial selection of the CEO for a startup company, CEO selection is always in the context of choosing a successor. For going concerns that have reached steady-state operations, succession planning should constitute the first step in the process of CEO selection.

THE ROLE OF THE CEO IN SUCCESSION PLANNING

The outgoing CEO normally will be involved in the process of choosing his or her successor—unless there is some discord or a mutual understanding between the CEO and the board or its committees. Some CEOs do not want the responsibility of choosing their successors, preferring to leave that task to the board. In most cases, though, the CEO will have developed a succession plan and will have groomed a successor within the company. If the board is pleased with the company's performance, its competitive position, and its long-term prospects, the board will be predisposed to respect the CEO's succession plan, and a smooth transition will be the expectation.

Special problems and opportunities accompany succession planning following a powerful, successful CEO. It is almost axiomatic that strong, dynamic leaders are often less than spectacular judges of the leadership capabilities of others, especially their subordinates. These hard-charging CEOs become enamored with their own ideas and successes and are most comfortable with people who think as they do. These are also the strong leaders whose boards are least likely to confront them by insisting on an independent search for a new CEO.

This default in succession planning has led to disastrous results in numerous companies. It is not that boards should ignore the ideas of their outgoing stars, but it is their explicit duty to select and govern the leadership of the corporation. Leaving the task of choosing the next generation to the predecessor often results in "yes people" being appointed to positions that require the most courage and character for success. There are those who believe that it is nearly impossible for a board to overrule such powerful and successful leaders, but strong boards find a way.

INSIDERS VERSUS OUTSIDERS

The question invariably arises as to whether the board should focus on so-called internal candidates, usually loyal and diligent long-term employees who naturally might feel that they should be considered for the top job in the companies. Undoubtedly, these executives will have demonstrated an ability to work effectively as a member of the team of the outgoing CEO. The better the performance results of the company, including the most recent trends in performance, the more likely the board is to seriously consider the best of the internal candidates as very viable candidates for CEO. Insiders actually may have an edge in competing for the job in such cases.

Consider, however, an alternative setting in which the board is not especially enamored of the performance of the CEO and the company. The board may question the CEO's strategy. Alternatively, the board may feel that strategy is not the problem but that the management team has one or more weak members. A company with strong market positions, perhaps protected by patents or outstanding research and development capabilities that led to proprietary products, may have stagnated. In some cases, strong market positions and their concomitant financial results may have carried the enterprise for years despite weak managers.

Perceptive board members may realize that the CEO and the current management team have been "coasting" on a broad base of strengths provided by previous management teams. Another performance pattern that may lead the board to choose an outsider results from a clear, longer-term history of weak performance. If the company has endured a crisis, or if performance has been in a slow decline, perhaps leading to a steep drop in share price, the board may be galvanized into action to turn around the performance in the best interests of shareholders and to protect its image as an effective board.

In these situations, the board will feel that significant changes are in order and that going outside in the search for a successor gives the company and its shareholders a better chance for greater long-term success. We do not minimize the confrontational nature of the board's looking outside the immediate management group. In some respects this is an acid test of board independence. As we will discuss in Chapter 7, it is logical to assume that the level and components of total compensation required to dislodge a successful external executive from a position of strength tends to be greater and perhaps more varied than that required for an insider.

There is another factor that leads boards to seek a new CEO from the outside. Otherwise well-meaning directors may have a tendency to look at the management of competitors, companies considered peers, and the industry in general, with the view that somehow executives at the other companies are better than the insiders. It may just be a notion that somewhere in the competitive world there has to be a better manager than the firm's internal candidates. When such a mood persists, it is almost impossible to placate the board, and the company is very likely to bring in the most attractive outsider that can be lured to take the CEO position.

It is also quite prevalent that the board and the rest of the organization will discover the new, outside CEO's flaws in due course because it is very difficult to obtain straightforward negative feedback on potential candidates. Our litigious society has come to the point that few are willing to state for the record, or even off the record, what they really think are the negative attributes of anyone. Thus the board will know the inherent weaknesses of internal candidates, who are then compared with an outside candidate or candidates whose problems are not well understood. It is no wonder that the outsider is often chosen, with the board and employees at all levels finding out soon enough that the new CEO is sometimes deeply flawed.

The tendency for a board to hire an outside manager as CEO is also enhanced by the steady growth in the use of executive search firms or headhunters. These organizations are professional firms that exist to identify, arrange interviews for, and represent candidates available for consideration for the CEO position and other management positions. The headhunters, of course, command handsome fees for their services, often equal to a year's total compensation for the executive position being filled. When board members are inclined to check outside, perhaps just to be certain that they are not overlooking a strong candidate, they often and unwittingly set in motion a process that inevitably will lead to the appointment of an outsider. Consequently, boards should not test the outside market unless they are reasonably sure that the insiders at hand are not adequate to fill the role.

The Pros and Cons of an Inside Candidate

The issue of management succession is normally the responsibility of the board's human resources (HR) committee, its executive committee, or a special committee. Regardless of the venue, the related choice of insider or outsider remains the same, except for some presumptive ability of an HR committee to deal with personnel questions with greater insight and effectiveness than a headhunter. An inside candidate has the advantages of

- Being well known to the decision makers
- Having probably managed his or her career path with the top spot in mind
- Being generally predictable in behavior and attitude toward others
- Having been groomed to some degree by his or her predecessors
- Possessing substantial knowledge of the inner workings of the enterprise

Nonetheless, the insider is also saddled with certain disadvantages, including

- Having his or her weaknesses likewise well known to the selection group
- The inevitable presence of adversaries within the organization who may work subtly to tarnish the performance of the new CEO

- Automatically creating one or more losers should there be multiple inside candidates for the job, which could remain a residual problem
- A more narrow perspective on marketplace possibilities than a pure outsider may have
- The distinct possibility that, on succession, his or her mantra would be business as usual
- The potential to cause a substantial lack of collegiality and dissention among board members when a board is not in uniform agreement about the succession decision. In the case of the insider candidate, such friction is measurably more visceral because the successor is well known to all and early on may not be given the benefit of the doubt generally enjoyed by an outside successor.

The Pros and Cons of an Outside Candidate

Outside candidates likewise bring their own set of advantages and disadvantages. These are not simply the inverses of those of the insider candidate, although certainly they apply. With the outside candidate, the dynamics are not so straightforward.

The outside candidate generally has the advantages of

- A reputation and perhaps mystique built entirely independently of the enterprise
- Standards of performance that are discrete and inevitably differ from, though not necessarily in conflict with, those of the prospective employer, yielding the possibility of a fresh standard for success
- Enhanced opportunity for a genuinely arm's-length, objective relationship with his or her new board, provided there exists a broad consensus about the CEO's selection
- Entering into an atmosphere of optimism and hope to capitalize strongly on the opportunity at hand

Conversely, the outside candidate is burdened as well with inherent disadvantages, such as

- Initial board skepticism of the candidate's ability to lead the enterprise as a result of the new CEO's lack of understanding and appreciation of the subtleties of its history and culture
- In many cases the absence of strong relationships with both major vendors and customers and perhaps a narrow window within which to build them

- Board friction and potential factionalism should there be an inside contender, plus the potential that the insider's benefit to the enterprise could be lost through resignation
- Shareholder disillusionment with the board's choice of an outsider, an unfamiliar and consequently unsettling event, especially among larger institutional shareholders comfortable with the status quo
- The element of risk, regardless of the intensity of the due-diligence effort, that invariably accompanies the shift of leadership to an outside candidate

Boards of directors must weigh carefully all the nuances that surround the insider versus outsider succession issue. The essence of these deliberations, for most firms, is the fundamental question of whether the firm needs a change agent or should stay with the status quo. It is possible to find change agents inside (such as Jack Welch at General Electric) or outside (such as Lou Gerstner in a sequence of high-profile positions); thus the need for a change in direction alone does not necessarily lead the board to go outside for the new CEO. It does mean that the board, as it considers all candidates, must assess their strengths and weaknesses relevant to the intended direction sought for the firm. Vignette 6-1 relates a set of unintended consequences that resulted from the hiring of an outsider as CEO when he and the board had different notions about the best long-term strategy for the company.

VIGNETTE 6-1

UNINTENDED CONSEQUENCES OF CHOOSING AN OUTSIDER AS CEO

THE ISSUE

There is a strong risk of unintended consequences for the board in every choice of CEO, whether it is an inside or outside choice. This risk is probably greater among outside choices simply because the inside candidate may have built up many years of loyalty to the company, whereas the outside candidate brings no such predisposition to stay the company's course. The sudden appearance of unintended consequences in connection with a transition in CEOs has occurred in numerous public companies in recent years.

Continued

Continued

THE SITUATION

The board of a well-known public company, for whatever reason, chose to bring in an outside candidate to replace a retiring CEO. The board felt that the company was well positioned in its markets, had strong brand recognition, possessed a healthy balance sheet, and was generally well managed. The board, lacking special enthusiasm for any of the available internal candidates, sought outside candidates, conducted thorough due diligence, selected the strongest candidate who seemed to fit the company's needs best, and subsequently hired him as CEO. In order to provide strong incentives for the new CEO to align his interests with those of the shareholders, the board, with the approval of the shareholders, granted an expansive set of stock options to the newcomer, along with a customary "package" of base salary, bonuses, and grants of restricted stock. The restricted stock and the stock options would vest gradually, over a 10-year period, providing strong incentives to align the CEO's long-term objectives with those of the shareholders.

While the board had one view of this compensation package, it soon became apparent that the CEO had an alternative view. Less than a year after taking the job, the CEO brought to the board a "deal" he had negotiated to merge the company with (that is, sell the company to) another large public company for a substantial premium over the current market price of the company's shares. This turn of events left the board with very limited options. Because such information rarely can by kept confidential, word would soon leak out that the company was "in play," which might incite other bidders for the company to come forward, thus precipitating an auction for the company. It would be very difficult for the board to control this process. The board could reject the offer or even terminate the CEO in the process, but then it would be faced with beginning a new search for a CEO very soon after just having completed one, an expensive and risky process from any point of view. This would not be a preferred tack. The board was thus left with a choice of undesirable alternatives, brought on by the sudden shift in strategy by the new CEO.

Underlying this huge dilemma was the compensation package the board had provided for the new CEO, including the grants of restricted stock and stock options that were intended to vest gradually over 10 years, providing strong performance incentives for the

Continued

Concluded

CEO. It is customary in almost all plans for granting restricted stock or stock options that in the event of a change in control of the company, these instruments vest immediately. It was thus clear that the CEO had a strong, personal conflict of interest in this situation. In fact, he stood to benefit from merging or selling the company to the extent of more than $25 million, all for less than 2 years' work, by the closing of the deal. This largesse would be in addition to his other salary, bonus, severance, and retirement benefits, all of which were substantial. In addition, the acquiring company had agreed for him to continue in the new company as vice chairman, with the expectation that he would assist in the integration of the two companies. This likely meant that he would have a new set of financial incentives of the same sort in the acquiring company, amounting to a classic "double dip."

THE BOARD'S ACTION

Given this set of circumstances, the board had scant room for any action except to approve the offer to merge or sell the company. The board learned the hard way of the bitter unintended consequences that could accrue from the appointment of an outsider to the CEO position who did not share its strong interest in the continuity of the company.

THE POINT

A board must be very careful when deriving a compensation package for a new CEO. The directors could, to their regret, find themselves facing unfortunate, unintended consequences. Their perception of the ideal choice of CEO may lead them into a new situation in which the best interests of shareholders from that point on requires a change in approach. Their best intentions to have the company continue as an ongoing entity may have to change to finding the exit strategy that maximizes the value received by shareholders for the company.

THE SUDDEN NEED FOR A NEW CEO

The situation in which the company finds itself will influence the process the board adopts in seeking a new CEO. There are instances in which time is of the essence, and the board must respond accordingly. For example, the CEO may have been killed in an accident or died suddenly from an illness. There may arise some scandal involving the company, or the CEO may have been accused of, or found guilty of, some indiscretion that triggered a clause in his or her contract that allows removal for cause. There could be some external event, such as the CEO leading an attempt at a leveraged buyout (LBO) of the firm. There are many such events that require the board to move with what the Navy terms *all deliberate speed*. All decision processes are expedited, and the task is to find and appoint a new CEO as rapidly as possible.

Each of these situations creates its individual dynamic. In the emergency situations, death or disability leaves no one to be blamed, although there is naturally some grieving for a respected friend. The event itself, though, usually creates no long-term fallout for the firm. Voluntary resignations cause employees and the public to ask why, wondering if the incumbent is aspiring to something or running from something. A complicating, accompanying issue is whether the departing CEO is likely to attempt to take other key people to a new employer. In the case of a CEO resignation, the board must act quickly to ascertain the answers to these questions and determine whether additional damage control might be necessary.

An involuntary termination is more complicated. The board must determine whether the management team generally understands the reasons for the termination and agrees with them or disagrees with the reasoning and remains loyal to the fired leader. Dealing with the consequences of the firing quickly, forcefully, and appropriately is essential; the board has to turn immediately to the issue of succession. Ideally, a contingency plan already would be in place. Many boards require the CEO to provide annually the name of the person or persons who could succeed him or her, at least on an interim basis. The suggestion or suggestions could be discussed with a key board member or committee chair or recorded in a sealed letter left with a legal counsel or the head of human resources. When the CEO has left a contingency plan, the board would carry it out unless it had some reason for not doing so.

In the absence of a contingency plan, the board must assess the situation and determine a plan of action. The two primary alternatives available to the board are to

- Appoint an interim CEO and proceed with a normal search process.
- Identify a preemptive candidate, either internally or externally, and make a permanent appointment. In general, the sooner the board installs a new CEO, the better, provided that the board does not rush to judgment.

As we mentioned previously, boards can rely on a number of their standing committees or a special committee to conduct the search and selection process for a new CEO. In the end, the full board must ratify the committee's work by endorsing the recommended candidate - as CEO. Identification of the best candidate(s) for CEO is often delegated to the nominating, executive, or HR committee because they are standing committees of the board as spelled out in the company's bylaws. In instances, though, when the stakes are considered high or when something must be done urgently, the board may appoint a special committee to carry out this work. This might come about when members of the standing committees are too busy with other duties to provide the time required to move rapidly.

A NORMAL PROCESS OF SUCCESSION PLANNING

Absent an emergency, the company can follow what might be termed a *normal* or *deliberative* process of succession planning and execution. The normal succession process begins perhaps as much as 2 years in advance of a planned retirement. The governance committee or a comparable committee of the board should work with the CEO to review the job description and the personal characteristics desired in a new CEO. Many of the considerations the board must take into account are discussed below.

Requisite Experience, Age, and Other Considerations

Naturally, a candidate for CEO would need to have the experience necessary to allow him or her to lead the company effectively. This translates into a certain level of maturity that comes with age, along with relevant functional and general management experience. Few candidates rise to the level of CEO of a major public company before the age of 40. On the other hand, few are appointed to CEO positions after the age of 55 because many companies now want their CEOs to retire between the ages of 62 and 65. Attaining a position as CEO is thus somewhat dependent on timing, since an opening must occur in the time frame during which an aspirant is eligible, and the candidate must be considered ready and available at that time. It is often the case that managers who would be excellent CEOs are effectively put out of the picture by the misfortune of the timing of the opening. The resulting selection of an individual who would be expected to hold the position for one to two decades, for practical purposes, closes the door on anyone "coming of age" during nearly all that time frame and certainly on those who are contemporaries of the appointee. The chances are indeed slim for qualified executives to rise to the office of CEO.

In determining the attributes of a potential CEO, committee members also would consider the board's perception of the needs of the company in the coming years. If the situation did not demand a drastic change in strategy, the board might seek a strong consensus builder who would work with the current management team to continue current successful strategies. If the board felt, on the other hand, that fundamental changes must be made, it would be more likely to seek a hard-charging change agent who would upset the status quo and move the company into new realms, including new products or services, increased international presence, or the sale of assets or businesses that were no longer considered to be strategic necessities.

Regardless of the need for change, prospective candidates for CEO should possess certain critical attributes if their term in office is to have a reasonable chance of success. The ideal candidate must

- Have had demonstrable, meaningful exposure to general management responsibilities
- Have exhibited a specific ability to deal with the key general management challenges that are currently facing the enterprise
- Have a strong functional understanding of the industry in which the enterprise operates
- Have a track record of unequivocal accomplishments in prior positions

Personal Attributes

The candidate also should possess a spectrum of personal attributes that extend beyond his or her specific enterprise-related skills. These include

- A personal value system of such strength that the candidate is immune to opportunistic actions that may operate to undermine the fundamental integrity of the enterprise
- A behavioral makeup ordinarily temperate in nature, although one that is capable of a high-energy force of personality at appropriate decision points
- A profound belief in the dignity of all people, regardless of their station in life, coupled with the ability to separate objectively superior performance from that which is unacceptable by the standards established for the enterprise
- A finely tuned ability to grasp the interests of the various constituencies of the enterprise and to blend them into a fabric of great strength and endurance in pursuit of the corporate mission and to the ultimate benefit of those whose assets are at risk

These characteristics may be summarized as describing four areas:

- Character and the emotional quotient (EQ)
- Technical competence in the industry and as a CEO
- Administrative skills
- Interpersonal skills

The Inventory of Internal Candidates

When the members of the designated board committee have clearly determined the attributes they are seeking in a new CEO, they should then determine if there are viable internal candidates. CEO candidates in large businesses as a rule will have acquired early in their careers the requisite experience to manage two or more functional departments successfully, such as marketing, finance, operations, or engineering. Success in these positions often leads to a general management position as head of a division, business unit, or profit center. These general manager positions test the executive's ability to lead a team of functional managers to achieve a balanced set of financial and marketing goals. The sequence of these positions typically involves moving from a smaller, more troubled unit to larger and more demanding situations.

The level of competition for the CEO position may be best illustrated by considering that in a company that operates 30 or more divisions or profit centers, only one of any "generation" of the division general managers will gain the CEO position. The board, which is charged with effectively representing the shareholders, must look to the business unit results carefully for clues as to the best executive to lead the entire company through its next leadership cycle.

On occasion, the committee may identify potential candidates who do not have the requisite experience to serve as CEO but have demonstrated high potential in their past performance. In such cases, the candidates should be assigned to positions that will provide them with the appropriate experience and the committee with an opportunity to observe their relative successes. Alternatively, the committee members sometimes may find that they do not have internal candidates in whom they are confident, and as a result, they may want to go outside the firm to hire into key jobs people who may have the potential of succeeding to the position of CEO. If the board committee finds only one high-potential internal candidate and that individual is satisfactory to the committee and the board, the board, then, must undertake the task to groom that person for the CEO position.

If there are multiple candidates, the process is necessarily more complicated. The one thing to be avoided is a public horse race. This creates a competitive environment that can be extremely divisive in management ranks and might undercut the eventual effectiveness of the winner. Essentially all the candidates must be given as much varied experience as possible, and the board must track their performance carefully. The replacement should be selected about one year prior to the retirement of the current CEO. If, at the end of this process, there is no acceptable inside candidate, then the board must conduct an outside search.

Competitors, suppliers, and customers will take note of the announcement of a new CEO and may react in unforeseen ways. A prudent search process should have uncovered any lingering doubts on the parts of these interested constituents with regard to the candidates. The unsuccessful inside candidates, many of whom may be contemporaries in age of the new CEO, likely will consider looking for employment elsewhere. The financial analysts who follow the company will be intensely interested in the new CEO and will scramble to understand the possible impact on their advisees (investors in the company). These interested parties most likely will want to interact with the new CEO immediately, perhaps more than with the lame duck still in place. It is thus advantageous to withhold the identity of the new CEO until the commencement of a transitional period in which the new and old CEOs overlap for the sake of a smooth transition.

WHEN THE SLATE IS UNIMPRESSIVE

As a change in the CEO approaches, it is very helpful if the board has adequate notice, providing time for the board to do this important work in a thorough and systematic way. No matter how careful the search process, inside or outside, it can become clear to the members of the standing or special committee leading the process or to the full board that the candidates identified are not the answer to the perceived needs of the company. This is the kind of situation that creates enormous stress on the board. There can be a great temptation to proceed in appointing the "least unattractive" candidate to get on with the process. The soon-to-be outgoing CEO may be impatient to get on with his or her postretirement life or already may be committed to a new assignment. It would be unfortunate if such circumstances led the board to move too rapidly. When necessary, the board should move to appoint the strongest insider to be the acting CEO, thus buying the time needed to come to a proper decision. In some cases, the acting CEO proves to be effective and, in the end, is chosen to lead the company.

PERFORMANCE EVALUATION OF THE NEW CEO

Once a CEO is in place, the board is responsible for evaluating his or her performance going forward. The process of performance evaluation should be used to influence the actions of the CEO to provide strong results for shareholders. Performance evaluation for the CEO has three prerequisites:

- The interests of the CEO and of the company must be aligned through compatible values and incentives.
- There must be mutually agreed-upon goals, standards, and time frames for the results.
- Accurate and timely measures of the key indicators of success must be shared with the board.

With these prerequisites in place, the board should assess the key issues noted below.

Strategy Implementation

On the premise that the board and the CEO have agreed on a strategy (we discuss the board's role in strategy formulation in Chapter 8), the board should conduct a continuous review of the efficacy of the strategy and the success with which it is being implemented. These reviews are part of the process by which the performance of the CEO is appraised and should lead to at least annual reviews that connect the CEO's compensation to the effective carrying out of the strategy. On occasion, differences of opinion arise between the board and the CEO as to the continuing effectiveness of the strategy and its implementation. While the differences of opinion may be wide and profound, they may not be sufficient to lead to removal of the CEO, given the upheaval and effort that necessarily accompanies the search for a new CEO.

One key attribute of the CEO that may not be tested until he or she is in the job for awhile is the CEO's capability to complete strategically important deals. Not all CEOs come to the job with experience in this area of acquisitions and divestitures. It is our experience that some CEOs seem to have an inherent knack for completing deals, whereas others propose, posture, even get to the negotiating table, but for one reason or another just cannot complete the deals. We believe that what enables some CEOs to complete dozens of deals over many years while others are stymied is the perception of the CEO's integrity or the reputation he or she may have developed as a straight shooter. The degree of satisfaction expressed by participants in previous deals no doubt has an influence on the possibility of consummating the current deal.

There is also, in our view, an element of ego involved. If a CEO has an unquenchable thirst to emerge as the clear victor in the negotiations, he or she will be unwilling or unable to make the kinds of concessions necessary in the normal give and take of reaching a deal. Such CEOs literally never get to complete a deal. This often happens with those described as "raiders," who propose but rarely, if ever, complete deals. Thus one of the key success factors for CEOs is the ability to negotiate any of a variety of deals with other entities, which may even include the ability to hire and retain outstanding members of the management team.

When the time approaches for the normal transition of the CEO position through the retirement process, the board may want to revisit the issue of strategy with those identified as candidates for the CEO position. The board may feel that a candidate's stance on strategic change is a pivotal issue that must be explored during the search process. The board should poll the candidates to determine whether they see a need for a change or adaptation of the company's strategy or whether they see "staying the course" as the best approach. The board has more clout to induce a change when the leadership is changing than it does when a long-term, incumbent CEO is in place. In some cases, the board may hasten the departure of the CEO through a scheme of early retirement in order to get on with a perceived need for strategic change. This approach recognizes that a CEO near the end of his or her tenure may not be inclined to pursue substantial change.

Benchmarking with Peers

The board and the CEO should continually compare the firm's financial performance with that of the Standard and Poor's (S&P) 500 Index, the Dow Jones Industrials Index, the Nasdaq Index, and a select group of peer companies chosen from the same industry or from others with similar cost, market, and/or competitive structures. The most important measures of corporate performance assessment are the interrelated goals of return on investment; growth in revenues, earnings, or market share; and adequacy of cash flow to fund growth. The efficacy of corporate goals and related performance is measured by comparisons with companies in the same or similar industries and, ultimately, with the wider array of investment opportunities across the spectrum of all industries.

Outside Assessments

The ever-present force that leads board members of public or private companies to engage in peer comparisons is the relentless appraisal of their company's performance by various outside agencies. Shareholders evaluate the performance of companies in terms of the profits earned, the dividends paid, the market price of the company's stock, and the public image of the company and its management. Customers continually appraise a business's performance in terms of the prices charged for its products, product quality and reliability, and the ability of the organization to meet delivery dates. Vendors demand timely payment of obligations. Government agencies maintain surveillance over such operational factors as market share, pricing policies and conformance to antitrust, environmental, and equal-employment opportunity regulations, among others.

Wall Street financial analysts and investors are interested primarily in the long-term earnings of the firm, and bankers evaluate companies in terms of debt repayments, various financial ratios, cash position, and general financial strength. Financial institutions, which are a significant factor in the market for corporate stocks, employ analysts to guide their investments. The market price of a company's shares is a major determinant of the firm's ability to raise capital by issuing public securities. Financial analysts thus exert considerable influence over the availability of equity funding for a firm. The assessment by bankers of the risk inherent in a firm's operations directly affects the interest rate the firm must pay for borrowed funds.

Performance Measures

What, then, are the principal attributes that professional evaluators prefer? Consider the most obvious measurable results (or expectations): profits, return on investment (return on equity), cash flow, growth, and finally, stability (predictability). The professionals assess the adequacy of the operating results of a business through a complex evaluation of the interrelationships of and trends in these attributes. The preferences among the performance criteria have changed in the past, with 5- to 10-year periods in which growth, return on investment, or stability was preferred. The measures of financial results gradually have become more sophisticated, with transitions from earnings to earnings per share to return on investment to cash flow to cash flow per share.

Typically, an initial level of assessment of a company and its management considers the earnings and the return on investment sustained over time compared with other firms in the same industry and with general industrial performance. It is possible, though, for a business to report consistently high levels of profitability and not be able to provide internally for its cash needs, particularly in fast-growth situations. Financial analysts and bankers therefore look beyond the levels of profitability reported to the cash the business would need to sustain its operations in the long term. If two businesses are each highly profitable relative to comparable companies in their industries and have ample cash flows to fund their operations, then professional analysts would prefer the company with the higher past or potential growth rate in sales, profits, and net worth. Finally, among companies achieving all the favorable attributes previously described, professional analysts prefer stability or predictability of results to volatility.

The Role of the CEO and the Board in Performance Assessment

Financial analysts guide investors in their choices of firms and in the timing of their investments. A need to forecast future profits is inherent in the process of capital formation because investment decisions are made based on the anticipation of future profits, not past performance. Analysts must depend on the CEO for assistance in the process of attempting to forecast future profit levels. CEOs regularly provide public projections of anticipated profits and potential problems. The accuracy of these public pronouncements builds a degree of credibility (good or bad) for the manager and the company with the investment community. The level of confidence in the manager and his or her company is a major determinant of the company's share price and its borrowing rate from banks.

It is reasonable that financial analysts should prefer a stable and improving earnings pattern, which suggests a high degree of management control. Indeed, in any industry, some companies consistently react to factors in their competitive markets and sustain higher earnings than their competitors with essentially similar facilities, labor, and raw materials costs. Beyond the figures, the analysts and bankers form opinions of their confidence in a firm's management, the potential available in its market segments, its degree of diversification, and other subjective attributes that are difficult to quantify.

The board invariably is led to consider this intricate pattern of external performance appraisal of the company, its strategy, and its operating results as it enters into selection of a new CEO and in the evaluation of the performance of a sitting CEO. Whether the board is satisfied with the current state of the company in all respects will influence its decision as to the type of CEO needed for the future.

CONCLUSION

Many students of corporate governance believe that selection of a CEO is the single most important action of a board of directors. As described in this chapter, the selection process is difficult and complex. Immediately upon selecting the new CEO, and perhaps concomitantly with the appointment, the board must consider carefully and reach agreement with the CEO as to how his or her performance will be appraised. They must jointly consider which specific goals for the company have to be clearly understood and agreed on, as well as the degree of subjectivity involved in the assessment process.

The performance appraisal process involves assessing the CEO's performance in executing the company's agreed-upon strategy, delivering strong financial results, especially the level of return on the shareholders' investment, and managing the state of the company with regard to its reputation, ethical standards, and morale of the workforce. The goals and objectives related to these areas of performance assessment are critically important because immediately upon selection of the CEO, the board must determine an appropriate level of compensation for the CEO, along with the various means (salary, bonuses, stock options, and so on) that will be used to deliver the compensation. These issues of compensation are discussed in Chapter 7.

REVIEW QUESTIONS

1. How should an outgoing CEO be involved in the selection of his or her successor?
2. What are the pros and cons of selecting an insider versus an outsider?
3. What risks accompany the decision to appoint an outsider as CEO?
4. What are the key steps in selecting a CEO?
5. How does a board assess the performance of a CEO?

CHAPTER 7

CEO Compensation

One of the more complicated tasks a board of directors must deal with involves determining the compensation of the chief executive officer (CEO) and senior managers. Management compensation must reward strong current performance and simultaneously provide incentives for similar future results. Additionally, the compensation should be structured to avoid paying premiums for average or poor performance. The task is not simple; the board wants to attract the right people, find the right alignment of their performance and shareholders' interests in both the short and long term, and use the most tax-efficient methods. Boards often worry much more about losing an obviously impressive CEO to another firm, with its attendant public scrutiny, than about the less threatening possibility of some outside pressure group questioning an expansive level of CEO compensation.

The task of developing compensation plans is complicated by the high public visibility of executive compensation in recent years. The media actively publicize CEO salaries, nationally and in local newspapers. Because the topic is so complicated, it is difficult to relate the dollar amount of compensation to performance in readily understood terms. Naturally, though, there is a dollar number, and the large ones look very large indeed, particularly to the average working person. Reporting the total compensation of CEOs makes for sensational journalism, usually at the expense of an informed debate. The predictable result has been that politicians have attempted to regulate CEO salaries. Because the tax laws were modified in 1993 to make the portion of salaries in excess of $1 million per year in public companies a non-tax-deductible expense, many companies have favored alternative forms of compensation to base salaries. This change has inadvertently triggered even larger payouts through more tax-efficient stock options. As these plans have received increasing publicity, the accounting standards board has looked for ways to disclose the cost of the issuance of stock options against current earnings, a task that is very complicated and for which a straightforward solution thus far has eluded it.

NORMS FOR CEO COMPENSATION

In order to calibrate our discussion in terms of prevailing levels of CEO compensation, we report some summary characteristics from a sample of more than 100 companies in a wide range of industries in Exhibits 7-1 and 7-2. These data were obtained from company proxy statements in a previously unpublished study. Proxy statements are issued prior to the annual meeting of shareholders to solicit the *proxies*, or votes, of the shareholders who cannot attend the meeting. The proxy statements are required to provide information on executive compensation, including realized and unrealized gains on stock options of the officers of the company. The data in Exhibits 7-3 and 7-4 came from the Dow Jones Industrials and Standard & Poor's (S&P) 500 samples described in Appendix 4-1.

Exhibit 7-1 provides a breakdown of average levels of total compensation between base salaries and bonuses contrasted with lower and higher levels of compensation. This exhibit shows that as the level of total CEO compensation increases, the base salary as a proportion of the total

Exhibit 7-1

Proportion of Total CEO Cash Compensation: Year 2000

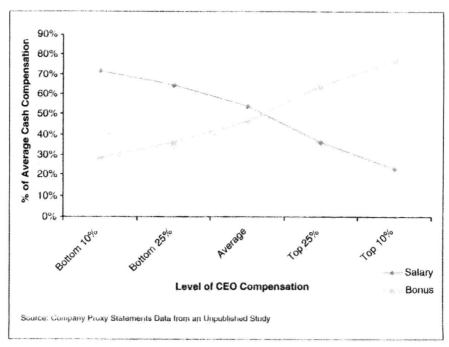

Source: Company Proxy Statements Data from an Unpublished Study

decreases and bonuses rise as a proportion of the total. Cash compensation refers to the current year and includes base salary and any annual bonuses. Long-term compensation includes long-term bonuses and gains from the appreciation in value of stock options and restricted stock.

Exhibit 7-2 shows that, in general, total compensation rises dramatically as the size of the organization increases. The same exhibit, however, also shows that CEO compensation declines as a percentage of company revenues as the firm becomes larger, demonstrating economies of scale. We could conclude logically from this chart that CEOs might inherently seek to enlarge their companies through acquisitions, for instance, in order to have a positive impact on their compensation.

To explain the prevailing levels of CEO compensation and the breakdown between cash compensation (base salary) and various types of long-term compensation, Exhibit 7-3 shows the highest, the average, and the lowest levels of CEO compensation by category in the group of 30 Dow companies.

Exhibit 7-2

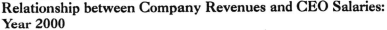

Relationship between Company Revenues and CEO Salaries: Year 2000

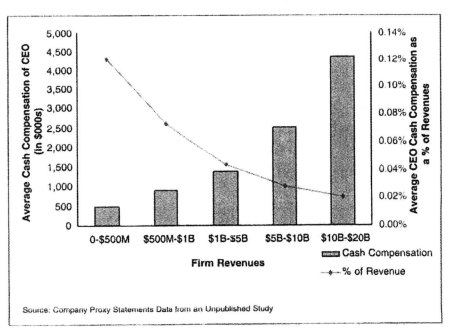

Exhibit 7-3

Cash and Incentive Compensation Levels for the 30 Dow
Company CEOs: Year 2000

	Cash Compensation	Long-Term Compensation	Total Annual Compensation
Maximum	$19,941,000	$108,131,000	$127,443,000
Average	$ 6,788,000	$ 20,363,000	$ 27,151,000
Minimum	$ 634,000	$ 0	$ 634,000

Exhibit 7-4 shows similar information for the sample of 25 companies from the S&P 500 list. The range of values within this sample is also large, and the differences between base salary and total compensation is likewise great, but the total compensation of the CEOs in the S&P 500 sample, on average, is approximately half that of the CEOs of the 30 Dow companies. These compensation levels most likely reflect the effect of the smaller sizes of the companies in the S&P 500 group, given the data of Exhibits 7-2 and 7-5.

Finally, Exhibit 7-5 shows how CEO total compensation rises dramatically as the size of the company and its revenues increase.

THE GOAL OF EXECUTIVE COMPENSATION

The goal of executive compensation is to find an equilibrium level that provides shareholders with the greatest return consistent with their risk tolerance, net of the cost of the compensation. The challenge facing the board is how to find and make the best deal for the shareholders. In arriving at the best amount of executive compensation, the board must first resolve a number of basic philosophical issues in forming the foundation for its compensation strategies. These include

- What constitutes good performance?
- Does management make a difference in performance?
- Does compensation make a difference in getting good management?
- How much, if any, of management's compensation should be "at risk?"

Each of these questions is addressed in turn below.

E x h i b i t   7 - 4

Cash and Incentive Compensation Levels for S&P 500 Sample
Company CEOs: Year 2000

	Cash Compensation	Long-Term Compensation	Total Annual Compensation
Maximum	$10,399,000	$67,888,000	$69,254,000
Average	$ 2,671,000	$ 7,680,000	$10,351,000
Minimum	$ 12,000	$ 0	$ 1,005,000

E x h i b i t   7 - 5

Total Average CEO Compensation in Relation to Company Size:
Year 2000

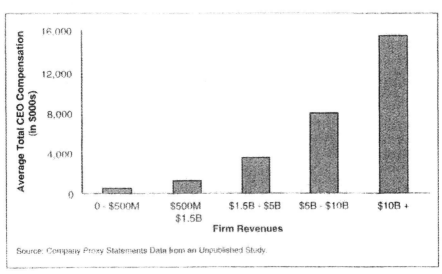

Source: Company Proxy Statements Data from an Unpublished Study.

WHAT CONSTITUTES GOOD PERFORMANCE?

A board wants to pay for good performance, but what is good performance? It is circumscribed by a company's current circumstances, its goals,
and the execution of its strategies. There is also an important time dimen-
sion. Goals should be both short and long term, so compensation plans
should include both short- and long-term components. The board must

search for a balance between the two perspectives. Sometimes, good short-term performance may be masking a deteriorating long-term outlook. Likewise, weak current performance may well be laying a strong foundation for the future. Generally, the board does not want to sacrifice the future for short-term gain. On the other hand, it has to recognize the need to achieve satisfactory current performance, particularly given the external fixation on quarterly results.

An objective way to quantify performance is to examine the achievement of financial goals. Using this approach, the board must find a way to deal with the importance of having and achieving strategic goals in the compensation plan. Generally, achievement of strategic goals provides the foundation for the achievement of long-term financial goals. Achieving strategic goals, therefore, ultimately should assist in achieving long-term financial goals. If there is a sound long-term component to the compensation package, there is no need to pay for achieving strategic goals in the short term. When the strategies are successful, the benefits ultimately will be there for both management and shareholders.

The company's circumstances and strategies will determine its financial goals. If it is a startup operation, it might not expect to have strong financial performance in the short term. If the firm has been successfully launched, it may be in a growth phase, with large investments required in operating expenses and capital to expand. Ultimately, the enterprise will achieve maturity, an era that should be marked by its greatest current profitability. The challenge then becomes one of renewal. If the company has begun to decline, it may need a turn-around strategy. The goals and compensation structures for these various phases differ. Vignette 7-1 describes a unique marriage of a strategy for change with a specially contrived compensation plan that produced dramatic results for General Dynamics.[1]

VIGNETTE 7-1

GENERAL DYNAMICS:
COMPENSATION AND STRATEGY

THE ISSUE

General Dynamics (GD) Corporation found itself in an untenable position, burdened with a plethora of mostly military products and services

Continued

Continued

at a time when the defense industry was experiencing large cutbacks in government procurement, which was leading to significant overcapacity in the industry. The issue was one of how the company could rapidly restructure itself to survive in this challenging environment.

THE SITUATION

By 1992, General Dynamics had built a proud history of conceptualizing, designing, and manufacturing a wide variety of advanced weapons and other systems for the armed forces of the United States. The company's products included military aircraft, nuclear submarines, tanks, space systems, missiles, and electronics systems. In 1991, General Dynamics was the second largest defense contractor, and revenues from defense-related activities were 82 percent of the company's total revenues. The board of directors hired William Anders, a former astronaut, away from General Electric as the heir-apparent CEO in September 1989 with the assurance that he would become CEO of General Dynamics on January 1, 1991. Anders thus had a little more than a year to study carefully the company's numerous activities with the objective of developing a viable strategy for the company going forward. Anders found a company seemingly in deep trouble.[2] The company's stock price had fallen from a high of $70 per share in February 1987 to only $25.25 at the end of 1990 (just when Anders was taking over). Additionally, the company reported a loss of slightly more than $800 million for 1990, and the company's senior and subordinated debt had been downgraded by rating agencies. Clearly, Anders had a difficult task before him.

Several events involving world affairs had aligned to reduce the likely demand for military equipment in the near term (in 1991) compared with historical levels. It seemed clear to Anders that GD needed to be scaled back in size and scope. He felt that the company had not been run efficiently and that a new emphasis would have to be placed on changing the company to one driven by shareholder interests. He felt that the company had to undergo a rapid transformation from a technology focus to a shareholder focus. Most of the top managers were changed or replaced, and a round of worker layoffs was completed. A blue-chip board of extremely competent directors oversaw

Continued

Continued

the operations of the company.[3] Anders then reported to the board that the company needed a large infusion of new managers and that he doubted that the company could attract the needed skills and experience in its current state.

THE BOARD ACTS TO CREATE THE INCENTIVE PLAN

In order to address this problem decisively, Anders received board approval for a sweeping incentive plan for a large group of managers and other key employees.[4] The incentives included a mix of salaries, bonuses, awards of restricted stock (stock awarded to an executive outright but with restrictions as to the time at which it can be sold), and awards of stock options. Anders' thinking was that in order to achieve the radical change in company culture that he perceived was necessary, the key employees would need strong financial incentives. One element of this plan involved issuing new stock options to replace older awards then "under water" and of no value to the holders. Anders' plan also included a stock investment plan (SIP), in which the company matched the investment contributions of more than 60,000 employees who participated, with an incentive to purchase company stock with the funds. By June 1991, 54 percent of the company's workforce was participating in the plan, and by June 1992, participants in the plan held 15 percent of the company's shares. Anders now had the structure in place that he felt necessary to make the massive changes needed to revive GD. He believed he would have all levels of management and most of the hourly workers thinking like shareholders (which they were) and willing to lead in changing the company rather than having to be forced to comply with actions dictated from above.

SIGNIFICANT CHANGES RESULTED

Changes followed rapidly as most employees embraced the need for a renewed company if GD were to survive tightening defense budgets and an industry suffering from excess capacity. The company proceeded with sequential rounds of layoffs, thinned out the management ranks, and began to sell off businesses that would be worth more to a purchaser than to GD. As these businesses were sold, the company

Continued

Continued

found itself with more cash than would be needed to fund the growth of the businesses that remained. Anders received the full attention of financial analysts when he announced that a diversification strategy would make no sense for the company and that the best use of the "excess cash" would be to distribute the cash to the shareholders through a share-repurchase plan or dividends. This announcement caused the stock price to continue to rise, as it had since announcement of the incentive plan. Financial analysts and investors could sense a strong, positive trend in the company's financial performance and were buying the stock in anticipation of further expected gains in shareholder value.

The turnaround of the company came with impressive speed. By the end of 1991 (Anders' first year), profitability had been restored, the company was holding $800 million in cash, and most of its long-term debt had been paid off. The company's employment had dropped almost 20 percent, through a combination of layoffs and the shedding of employees through the divestiture of several businesses. As a result of these improvements, largely mirroring the steady progress implemented by its dedicated and motivated work-force, the share price had risen to $53.75, a doubling of shareholder value during the year 1991.[5]

THE IMPRESSIVE RESULTS

The results brought about by this dramatic joining of a strategy of basic change and restructuring with an all-inclusive incentive plan aimed at increasing shareholder value proved more successful than anyone could have predicted. Between 1991 and 1993, GD sold seven divisions, for which it received $3 billion.[6] The divested units employed 44,000 employees at the time of their sale. The company shrank to one-third its former size, but the units retained were lean and profitable and had considerable competitive advantages in the defense products marketplace. This made the restructured General Dynamics Corporation a much more competitive enterprise, organized and led to compete in a slimmer, more demanding market for defense products. The corporate staff had dropped from 650 to about 200, with a plan to reduce further to 50 by the end of 1994.

Continued

Continued

This reduction was instrumental in lowering the overhead rate that had to be absorbed by the operating divisions.[7]

The company had raised almost $4 billion in cash by the end of 1993 through all its interrelated actions. This cash was used to retire almost all the company's debt, increase annual dividends to shareholders, repurchase more than 13 million shares with almost $1 billion, and return $50 per share to shareholders through three special distributions.[8] The effect of all these actions on the company's shareholder value was spectacular. The share price rose from $55 to $92 per share between January 1992 and December 1993 despite dividends totaling $3.25 per share and special distributions to shareholders of $50. The equivalent share price would have been more than $150 per share if the dividends and special distributions were taken into account. An impressive anecdote was that during this sharp upward trend in the company's share price, Warren Buffett of Berkshire Hathaway announced the purchase of more than 4 million shares (about 15 percent of the shares outstanding) for about $73 per share. He showed strong support for the management of GD when he announced that he gave the company his proxy to vote his shares as long as Anders remained CEO.[9] This was a much-revered endorsement of the company's strategy and ability to implement change by the foremost investor of the times.

THE PAYOFFS TO THE PLAYERS

Exhibit 7-6 shows the distribution of the increase in shareholder value among management, employees, and shareholders of GD during the period January 1991 through December 1993. Dollars are in millions; total gains include gain sharing, gains on restricted stock, and gains on stock options.[10]

Few shareholders would object to sharing of the results, given the dramatic turnaround in the company's fortunes. Here we see a very strong and highly competent board that recognized a need for sweeping change in the company and began the process by bringing in a very capable CEO from outside. The board gave the new CEO time to understand the company's problems and devise a strategy, approved a plan for a broad range of financial incentives available

Continued

Concluded

E x h i b i t   7 - 6

Distribution of the Increase in Shareholder Value among Management, Employees, and Shareholders, January 1991–December 1993

Participants	Total Gains	Percent of Total Gains
Anders (CEO)	$54	1.1 percent
25 other top executives	$258	5.3 percent
1300 other executives	$144	3.0 percent
48,000 SIP participants	$450	9.3 percent
Subtotal for GD employees	$906	18.7 percent
Other shareholders	$3958	81.3 percent
TOTAL	$4864	100.0 percent

to every employee in the company, and saw to the very effective implementation of the strategy. This is a powerful example of a board's use of an all-inclusive compensation plan to effect a complete reversal of a company's performance. One analyst who, early on, had been critical of GD's incentive plans said, "If we had spent less time criticizing Anders' pay package and more time increasing our investment in GD shares, we would have been a lot better off financially."[11]

THE POINT

Drastic situations call for bold, aggressive action. The board actively sought an experienced outsider to lead the company in making the required changes to its culture. The board and Anders were especially insightful in providing financial incentives for all levels in the organization. The entire workforce thus became change agents rather than resisters to change.

In addition to the maturity of the organization, the nature of the business is another important variable in the company's situation. For instance, if its industry is very cyclical, the company must be able to deal with the below-average, down years as well as the above-average, good years. The board must be careful in these situations to assess the firm's financial performance, especially relative to its peers, and reward management accordingly. Without the relative comparison, boards risk losing good management in bad times and overrewarding bad management in good times.

In summary, financial results must be the key indicator of performance. What are the metrics that indicate financial performance? There is no simple answer to this question. The goal of management should be for the company to earn a return on investment that reflects the risks inherent in and the cost of capital of the business, along with the goals of the shareholders. The board should establish a standard return-on-equity goal considering the average of all businesses, both current and historically, and the returns of peer companies. If the industry returns, as evidenced by peer companies, do not compare favorably with broader market returns, the board must grasp that it is in a below-average industry and adjust its strategies accordingly.

A company can use a variety of measures to improve and/or motivate change in its return on investment. These may include both absolute measures (such as sales dollars) or ratios and growth rates (such as the growth rate of sales). The approach of specifying quantifiable goals that are within management's control and linking rewards to their achievement is an extremely effective method of focusing management on desired results. Exhibit 7-7 lists a number of the key indicators frequently used for this purpose.

ISSUES IN MANAGEMENT COMPENSATION

Virtually all studies, as well as most intuitive observations, support a conclusion that management generally does make a difference in firm performance. Clearly, getting and keeping the right people is the foundation of success in every business. A number of factors should be considered in attracting and retaining qualified management.

While pay is only one of the factors in attracting and retaining talent, there is a competitive marketplace for labor, and it stands to reason that those who pay well will tend to do better in that marketplace than those who do not. The assumption is that shareholders will get more by paying more—if they get the right people. We saw the difference Anders made at General Dynamics in Vignette 7-1. One can only wonder if someone else would have done as well or better for a lower pay package. Accepting the principle that an organization reaps a return on its investment in human resources is important if one is to accept pay-for-performance packages. Consequently, boards of directors must recognize that this is an important area of gover-

Exhibit 7-7

Key Performance Indicators

Absolute Measures (in dollars)	Ratios and Growth Rates
Sales	Sales growth rate
Earnings before interest, taxes, depreciation, and amortization (EBITDA)	EBITDA as percent of sales
	Growth rate of EBITDA
Net operating profit after taxes (NOPAT)	NOPAT as percent of sales
	Growth rate of NOPAT
Net income (NI)	NI as percent of sales (Return on sales)
	Return on equity
	Return on capital
	Growth rate of NI
Earnings per share (EPS)	Growth rate of EPS
EBITDA per share	Growth rate of EBITDA per share
Cash flow per share	Growth rate of cash flow per share
Assets	Asset turns (sales/assets)
Capital	Capital turns (sales/capital)
Per share stock price	Growth rate in stock price
Market value of shares (market capitalization)	Growth rate in market value

nance. They also must resist the temptation to place too much emphasis on the issue of compensation at the expense of other significant matters.

Among the issues related to CEO compensation is the philosophical question of how much of management's compensation should be at risk, that is, based on performance, and how much compensation should be guaranteed, that is, without regard to performance. Many boards embrace the notion that plans improve as they motivate members of management to think and act more as if they were owners, which means having compensation at risk along with the owners' capital. Stock ownership is currently seen as the best way to bring this about.

BUILDING A COMPENSATION PLAN

The boards of most public companies approach the delicate issue of CEO compensation with caution. In order to avoid being perceived as out of line with the compensation schemes of similar or comparable companies, many boards make use of public data about CEO compensation (available from the proxy statements) or engage the services of consulting firms that specialize in compensation matters. Their goal is to ascertain and then establish *external parity* in CEO compensation. The use of consultants is intended to provide both expertise and objectivity that might enhance the board's credibility with shareholders and other constituencies.

Ironically, the use of such comparison processes has served to support the gradual rise in CEO compensation. In analyzing and tracking a set of comparable companies, one would notice that if any one of them raised the compensation of its CEO, the average of the pool would increase automatically. As other companies followed the rising trend, the increases would become more pronounced, and the steady upward trend would be reinforced. A board's intention to "stay in the pack" thus typically results in steadily rising compensation levels for its CEO.

Jack Welch, former CEO of General Electric (GE), employed a very effective form of peer comparisons. He insisted that the company only engage in attractive industries and that, further, GE's businesses should be number one or at least number two in the industries in which they competed. This series of definitions of suitable comparables rapidly led to GE being considered on a different scale relative to most other companies. We suggest that peer comparisons are merely the beginning of a process by which the board and its CEO lead a firm to excellence. Excellence does not result from being just anywhere in the pack.

THE COMPENSATION MIX

Exhibit 7-8 shows that the compensation systems for the CEOs of most public companies begin with a base salary, expected to provide a level of predictable income consistent with that of the CEOs of other comparable

E x h i b i t   7 - 8

Components of CEO Compensation

Current	Long Term
Base salary	Cash bonuses
Fringe benefits	Stock options
Perquisites	Stock grants
Cash bonuses	Stock ownership plans

companies. As we stated earlier, the problem for the board lies between not overpaying the CEO relative to other similar companies (which would lead to criticism by shareholders) and not underpaying the CEO (which might risk losing an outstanding executive to alternative employment). Once a base salary has been established, the board must determine the total value of the pay package at various levels of performance. The policy questions are how much should be at risk and how much guaranteed and what portion of the compensation should be short term and how much long term.

As we noted, a base salary is almost always the beginning of a compensation package. It is usually augmented by a short-term bonus arrangement and by a long-term compensation package. The components of the long-term package can include cash bonuses and any number of types of equity participation, all designed to provide incentives that will lead management to think and act like shareholders. These can include grants of restricted stock, grants of stock options, and/or required purchases of stock, perhaps funded by loans from the company to the executives, although this practice is increasingly frowned on because of the potential for substantial abuses. While the stock-based incentives may require a lengthy period before paying off for management (as we shall see), they often make possible levels of compensation that are remarkably attractive and clearly influence behavior. Stock-based compensation schemes bring both a long-term outlook and large compensation possibilities to the management team.

The Base Salary

The base salary is the starting point for the compensation package. The board has to decide to what degree it wants to compare itself to the external market in establishing a CEO's base salary. A policy many boards use is that if their company wants outstanding people to attain outstanding performance, it must offer compensation packages that provide the potential for high-end rewards. If the company only achieves average performance, it would want to pay only average compensation. The issue is often resolved by having average or slightly above-average base salaries, with at-risk compensation accruing when performance is superior. The worst case is to have it both ways—high base salaries without regard to performance and generous at-risk packages on top of that.

Fringe Benefits

The value of fringe benefits to the recipient typically can range from 30 to 50 percent of base salaries. Firms normally include standard employer

taxes, medical and life insurance premiums, the costs of holiday and vaca-
tion time, and retirement costs, among others. Fringe benefits typically
are more generous and complicated for higher-level executives, often
extravagantly so. In fact, fringe benefits can be an area of major abuse by
boards and CEOs, especially with regard to retirement packages.

Perquisites

The perquisites of a job also can be significant in some companies. Clubs
and expense accounts are justified as business expense reimbursements
for entertaining customers, or the executive's salary is "grossed up" to
cover these costs. Automobiles and airplanes are justified on the grounds
that they increase the efficiency of the executives. When the perquisites
are used properly, these are valid explanations. Unfortunately, they can be
another area of abuse because these are a valuable form of additional
compensation. Moreover, the recipient often pays little or no income taxes
on these benefits.

Bonuses for Short-Term Performance

The bases for short-term bonuses are usually some combination of individual performance (meeting personal objectives) and corporate performance. Senior executives other than the CEO often have some part of their
bonuses based on their business unit's performance.

The board normally has specific short-term goals and objectives for
the achievement of which it is willing to pay the CEO bonuses. These
goals and objectives might include bringing a new product to market in a
specified time, the successful acquisition of a competitor, completing the
closing of several obsolete manufacturing facilities, or identifying and
appointing a chief operating officer (COO), who also may be a potential
successor. Such short-term goals are usually quite specific, meaning that
their attainment can be measured unequivocally. The attainment of each
goal normally will accrue toward a rating of the executive's performance
leading to a bonus as a percentage of the potential payout. All of these
amounts of bonus compensation have to be within the boundaries of base
salary and total compensation considered appropriate for the CEO.

Bonuses for Long-Term Performance

In its discussions with the CEO about the company's strategy, the board
may conclude with the CEO that the achievement of certain goals and
objectives of a long-term nature are of paramount importance to the future

of the firm. These long-term aspirations may include the timely completion of a much-needed new product development program currently in research and development, which brings along with it the likelihood that many of the company's current products would be made obsolete. There may be a long-term objective to cripple a competitor through a program of price reductions that the competitor is thought unable to meet while remaining profitable. There may be a perceived need to put into place a worldwide sales and distribution network to ensure the long-term viability of the company in increasingly global markets.

Long-term objectives of this sort necessarily may be costly to the firm in the short term. In order to ensure that the CEO concentrates on these long-term objectives and is not penalized financially in the process, the board often puts into place long-term incentive awards for their achievement, over and above the existing short-term objectives and incentives. Given that we all act in our own perceived best interests as well as that of our employers, the patterns of these short- and long-term incentive payouts likely will determine how the CEO approaches their attainment. The ideal situation presents the possibility of mutual success on all fronts, with the incentive payments intended to assist the CEO in assessing the mutual attainability of all the objectives. The board must carefully consider the possible ramifications if the CEO should achieve all the short- and long-term goals simultaneously, thus earning the award of the total bonus package. This unlikely and often unexpected event can lead to embarrassingly large total pay for the CEO. In the case of General Dynamics, the large bonuses appeared warranted. In other cases, such simultaneous peaking in several aspects of incentive plans has provided unwarranted and embarrassing payouts.

Stock Options

Stock options have been available and have been used as facets of management incentive plans for many years. Stock options are rights to purchase a specified number of shares of the firm's stock at a stipulated price during some forward time period. Most options are classified as *nonqualifying*, meaning that they do not qualify for capital gains treatment in regard to taxes. Gains will be taxed as ordinary income at the time the option is exercised. The awarding of the total number of shares is often staggered over time, with the total number awarded vesting gradually, year by year. *Vesting* is the technical term for the moment at which the stock options actually become the property of the holder. For example, a CEO may be awarded options to purchase 1 million shares at a so-called strike price of $10 per share. The options, however, may *vest*, meaning that ownership becomes final, at a rate of 100,000 shares each year for 10 years.

At any time after the options vest, the CEO will be free to buy the shares from the company at the stipulated price. This purchase is not an open-market transaction. The CEO is then free to hold them or sell them and pocket the difference between the strike price (purchase price) and the current market price. The gain on such a transaction is subject to federal and state ordinary income taxes in the year in which the transaction takes place, provided the options are exercised. If, on the other hand, the options are *qualified* (versus *nonqualifying*), taxes on the gains on the options are deferred until they are sold, and any profits will be taxed as capital gains. The capital gains treatment is one of the attractions of qualified options. There are very tight restrictions on the offering of qualified options, and thus they are limited in use.

Other definitional terms related to stock options include so-called underwater options, those for which the strike price of the options is more than the current market share price, thus rendering the options valueless. Conversely, options are considered *in the money* when the current market price of the shares is greater than the option price. Stock options that are vested and in the money can be *exercised* (cashed in) at any time up to their expiration date. As a general rule, the market frowns on resetting the exercise price of underwater options because the net effect is to reward management for failure, absent some traumatic external event. Boards may, with shareholder approval, reset the exercise price of hopelessly worthless options in order to provide an incentive for executives going forward. This might happen after a collapse of the company or might be needed to attract a quality CEO to a poor situation.

Other Nuances of Stock Options

There is an implicit understanding that a CEO with confidence in his or her firm's future, and thus the prospects for its share price to increase, would want to hold rather than sell any shares effectively owned. The exercise of vested options combined with their sale would send a negative signal to shareholders, investment analysts, and the public at large regarding the firm's likely future. The CEO thus would be more likely to hold the options until they expire, which might be after, say, 10 years. There would be no logical motive for exercising stock options that are vested and underwater because they would present a loss to the holder of the options. Finally, there would be no reasonable motive for holding options past their expiration date, so there would be no negative perception of the CEO's exercising the options and selling the shares at that time.

The increase in recent years of the inclusion of stock options in the mix of usual and customary forms of incentive compensation has been encouraged by several events exogenous to the boards of public companies. First, the change in the tax policy and law described earlier has rendered large salaries (greater than $1 million per year) unpalatable to prudent boards of directors. Second, there has been an increasing call from advocates of shareholder interests for both members of the board and CEOs to have a financial stake in the future of the firm's share price through share ownership. Third, investment advisory firms assist public companies through initial public offerings (IPOs) of their shares and afterwards in maintaining a strong market for the company's outstanding shares by advising their investment clients on the strengths and weaknesses of companies. In positive advisories relative to the prospects for the future movements of share prices, they often cite the stock option plans in place as positive evidence of the alignment of the interests of the board and management with those of all the shareholders.

Stock Grants

Some companies prefer to include stock grants in CEO compensation in lieu of stock options. The disadvantages of stock grants are that the grants are taxable when granted, and they are more expensive per share to the company than options. On the other hand, they do provide some downside risk to the recipients, assuming the recipients hold, rather than sell, the shares. Grants are treated as cash compensation for tax purposes.

Stock Purchase Plans

Warren Buffett has an unfavorable opinion of options because they provide no downside risk to management. He prefers firms to make stock grants or to make it possible for managers to purchase shares in the company, often with loans. In such cases, the company loans the executive the funds required to purchase a stipulated number of shares of the company's stock. The loans are subsequently "paid off" by the executive by means of bonuses earned for superior performance. These purchases are more tax-efficient than stock grants and can create even stronger incentives for the managers.

EMPLOYMENT CONTRACTS, INCLUDING NONCOMPETE AGREEMENTS AND SEVERANCE ARRANGEMENTS

Boards and their CEOs enter into employment contracts for a variety of reasons. CEOs may seek to preserve some independence and, as a result, would want specificity as to the term of employment, the level of compensation, and the other supplemental perquisites. Boards may seek to protect the firm's competitive position, creating employment contracts that usually take the oblique approach of forbidding the CEO to work for competitors or other similar businesses during the period of the contract and for a given time after leaving the firm rather than binding the CEO to serve the employing firm. This is a common feature of almost all employment contracts, such as those of professional athletes, actors, school principals, and scientists. Because involuntary servitude is illegal in the United States, employment contracts do not require a CEO to work for the given company. Rather, they limit or stipulate the alternative employments in which the CEO may engage, thus enhancing the attractiveness of the CEO's continuing to serve the company.

We should note that unlike most contracts, employment agreements of CEOs are more binding on the company than on the CEO. Because the agreement cannot require the CEO to serve the company any longer than he or she wishes, the board normally attempts to limit the alternative employment possibilities available to the CEO. In the end, however, the board and the company are liable for all the conditions to which they have agreed, whereas the CEO has more latitude in his or her options. Thus the company cannot compel the CEO to continue, but the CEO can hold the company to all its agreed-on conditions, except for circumstances falling under the definition of *cause*. Most CEO employment contracts include a clause stipulating the situations under which the CEO is considered to be in breach of contract. Such terms as a rule relate to character, dishonorable acts, evidence of dishonesty, or other acts that are detrimental to the reputation of the company. The CEO can be removed for the violation of these terms, but otherwise, the board and the company are required to fulfill the terms of the agreement, often including handsome severance payments, if they decide to remove the CEO for reasons other than for cause.

GOLDEN, EVEN PLATINUM, PARACHUTES

The term *golden parachute* has come to have a very negative connotation in the context of CEO compensation. The phrase brings to mind a vision of a CEO who may be retiring, may have effected a merger with another firm and is moving on, or who may be underperforming, necessitating his or her removal from the position. Regardless of the reason for the CEO to be moving on, all too often the financial arrangements attendant to the act of leaving the position provide the departing executive with a handsome, often expansive set of rewards. These types of generous parting arrangements began some years ago with seemingly large packages but not necessarily at obscene levels.

Recently, however, such arrangements have reached a level that is unacceptable to many. CEOs whose unsatisfactory performance called for their dismissal have been perversely rewarded with payments of $1 or $2 million per year for life, with provisions that if their spouses outlive them, the spouses will get half the amount for the rest of their lives. This tendency toward expansive payments is even more apparent in the event of mergers of public companies. In one instance, the terms of the merger between two companies called for the CEO who was leaving to receive $5 million per year for life, along with the generous extension of the benefit to his wife. In some cases involving the merger of two firms, the package is so rich that both CEOs prefer to leave rather than stay and work. In one well-publicized case, as shareholder indignation mounted and a shareholder vote on the merger approached, the agreed-on amount was reduced by about half out of fear that the deal would not be approved by shareholders. Such cases lead to the need for upgrading the descriptive adjective of the parachute from *golden* to *platinum*.

Similar situations occur when a CEO considered to be performing poorly needs to be removed in order for the company to move forward. The terms of the CEO's employment agreement may include a provision for a rolling 5-year term, for instance, with an additional year added each year to keep the horizon of employment at 5 years. In such a situation, the board's determination of cause or its straightforward determination that the CEO needs to be replaced for any reason may lead to a difference of opinion about the CEO's performance or behavior. The board's perception of the circumstances obviously will be quite different from that of the CEO. Given the general reluctance of boards to call attention publicly to the company's problems, if the CEO is reluctant to leave or is inclined to fight any attempt to remove him or her, it is not unusual for the board to contrive some exit strategy for the CEO that involves a special retirement package, full payment for the remaining years of the CEO's contract, or even an additional negotiated financial settlement. It can be extremely expensive to dispose of a CEO, leading to the understanding that the board must be very careful in choosing one.

EVENTS THAT NORMALLY TRIGGER OUTSTANDING OPTIONS

The length of the lives of options awarded is subject to certain events that can trigger the vesting of all options, regardless of their originally intended lives. For instance, most stock options, regardless of their stipulated schedule of vesting, vest immediately on the occurrence of a change in control of the company. Any point in time at which some new set of shareholders holds 50 percent plus one share of the total outstanding shares of the company is defined as a change in control (from those previously in control to the new controlling group). If an exchange of shares among any parties leads to a new set of shareholders being in control of the company, a *change of control* is said to have taken place. Concomitant with the change of control, all outstanding stock options vest immediately, allowing their holders to cash the options and sell or hold their shares as they see fit.

CONCLUSIONS

In the general zero-sum game between the board, representing the shareholders, and the CEO, representing himself or herself, there is a continuing debate as to how much compensation is too much. Instances in which CEOs have been enriched to the extent of even hundreds of millions of dollars remind us that the best-designed systems for CEO compensation are devised by humans and are thus capable of producing unintended consequences. Regardless of the absolute level of the CEO's total compensation over some time period, the board, shareholders, and the world at large will look at this compensation in terms of the market value of the company's shares created during the relevant time period, as measured by the increase of the market capitalization of the firm. If the market capitalization of the firm had risen by a total of $20 billion during the time a CEO received $100 million, most shareholders would consider the CEO compensation fair, given that it represented one-half of one percent of the increase in market capitalization created. Only the shareholders themselves can answer the question as to the fairness of the CEO's compensation—and then only in the context of the gains (or losses) that accrued to the shareholders during the relevant time period.

As noted earlier, there are numerous components of a CEO's compensation. Items of direct payment or award must be reported in the firm's proxy statements. Other elements may not be obvious to investors. Board members must be watchful over all components of compensation as they execute their duties to represent the best interests of the shareholders. Board members also must carefully balance these interests with their perceptions of the need to offer market-driven rewards to competent corporate officers.

We will discuss the relationship between the board and the CEO further in Chapter 8.

REVIEW QUESTIONS

1. How does a board determine the proper level and mix of compensation for a CEO?
2. How does the board assess the performance of the CEO?
3. What are the advantages and disadvantages of the various types of compensation?
4. What is the purpose of stock options and other stock-based forms of compensation?
5. Why do boards employ severance agreements, sometimes referred to as *parachutes*, in phasing out a CEO?

CHAPTER 8

The Board–Management Relationship

The board of directors chooses the chief executive officer (CEO) and delegates to him or her the responsibility for running the company. Thus begins a hopefully productive, albeit complex, relationship. The board's role in this relationship is first to understand and approve of the CEO's strategies and plans and then to monitor the execution of those plans and to periodically evaluate the results. Finally, the board must decide whether, when, and how it should intervene. How the board executes its role is critical to the success of the relationship and, ultimately, of the business.

There is a fine line between the responsibilities of the board and those of the CEO, and it is usually disastrous for the board to become enmeshed in the details of running the business. Most members of the board are, at best, vested with a part-time interest in the company. While they are charged with "looking out for the interests of the shareholders," most have other full-time positions that limit the time they can devote to their oversight function. With a myriad of activities going on in the company every day, it is impossible for members of the board to have an ongoing, first-hand view of operations. They must rely on the CEO (management) to keep them updated on successes, opportunities, and problems.

The board may meet for a day or two, six or eight times a year. As mentioned in Chapter 5, a short time before the meetings, the directors usually receive a package of materials related to the upcoming meeting. The package of materials will include results of recent operations, forecasts of likely future performance, some mention of strategic issues, and perhaps some information about proposals for which management needs the approval of the board. The quality of this material and of management's briefings at the meetings is the foundation of the board's understanding of the situation. If board members are not comfortable with what they are hearing, they can pursue the matter in other ways, such as by conducting studies independent of the CEO. The end result is that the board depends on management in the normal course of business for candid and timely information about the company.

A board that crosses the line by interfering or micromanaging can undermine the effectiveness of the CEO and will find it difficult to hold the CEO accountable for poor results it may have had a part in bringing about. On the other hand, a board that is too detached from what is happening or too passive in carrying out its responsibilities may, in fact, be abdicating its role in the governance of the organization. Board members must strive to find the right balance between these two extremes, staying proactive in carrying out their responsibilities as directors without interfering.

In finding this balance, it is of primary importance that the members of the board remain independent of the CEO. Independence requires board members to refrain from providing legal or consulting services to the CEO or the company because board members cannot objectively hire and appraise the performance of a CEO to whom they are beholden. Similarly, board members should not let personal friendships with the CEO interfere with carrying out their responsibilities. Independence of board members from a CEO does not require an adversarial relationship; to the contrary, the parties must establish and develop effective ways of communicating and working together in a collaborative partnership built on mutual respect. Both parties must remember that, ultimately, the CEO is accountable to the board. A good CEO understands this and makes it easy for the board to execute its responsibilities.

To execute its responsibilities well, the board must have a workable governance model. Such a model should address issues central to establishing and maintaining an effective process for making and administering corporate policy. A governance model should include routine approaches to the following:

- Choosing or clarifying the business or businesses in which the corporation will operate
- Hiring the right people in terms of both their abilities and their values
- Aligning the interests of the board and management with those of the shareholders
- Developing mutually agreeable goals, policies, and standards of performance for the CEO
- Evaluating plans to achieve agreed-upon goals
- Remaining knowledgeable about the firm's activities and performance and evaluating the results
- Reacting appropriately to the results by holding management accountable and rewarding or intervening as necessary

Boards of directors creating and following this or a similar governance model should be well on their way to establishing productive partnerships with their CEOs. Board members are advised to recall the paramount importance of hiring an effective CEO for the firm. The right person for the situation will strive to solve problems that might exist and seek to improve upon established methods. The wrong person, however, is likely to create new problems for the firm and the board. Vignette 8-1 describes in some detail a major corporate restructuring over a 5-year period and the resulting positive outcomes reflected in the company's financial statements.

VIGNETTE 8-1

A SUCCESSFUL STRATEGIC CORPORATE RESTRUCTURING

THE ISSUE

A major consumer goods company, PepsiCo, needed to complete a significant restructuring in order to continue to grow profitably in a more narrowly focused competitive environment. In such situations, management must recognize the need or opportunity at hand and develop a workable solution. As part of this process, senior management must present the problem and its recommendations to the board. The board must come to understand the problem or opportunity and advise management on and consent to its recommendations before a new course of action may be taken.

THE SITUATION

PepsiCo enjoyed a strong position in its industry, with a focus on both convenience foods and beverages, after emerging from a 3-year restructuring effort. The company maintained dominant market positions in three key product areas: salty snacks (number one worldwide), beverages (number two worldwide), and branded juices (number one worldwide). Further, PepsiCo led the world in brand recognition with 15 brands that generated more than $500 million in revenues per year each, including 11 brands that generated more than $1 billion each in revenues. The marketing of this impressive portfolio of products was augmented worldwide by a powerful distribution network.

Continued

Continued

The major restructuring of this company began in 1996 when management recognized the lack of strategic fit between its restaurant businesses and its other businesses. Management recommended the spin-off of Pizza Hut, Taco Bell, Kentucky Fried Chicken, PepsiCo Food Systems, and several other noncore U.S. restaurant businesses into Tricon Global Restaurants, which the board approved. In 1998, PepsiCo completed the acquisitions of Tropicana Food Products and The Smith's Snackfoods Company (TSSC) in Australia. In addition, acquisitions and investments in unconsolidated affiliates, various bottlers, and other international salty snack food businesses brought the aggregate cost of acquisitions to $4.5 billion in cash in 1998. The company also completed a spin-off of bottling operations through an initial public offering (IPO) and completed a major acquisition of Quaker Oats.

THE RESULTS OF THE ACTIONS OF THE BOARD AND THE CEO

The strategic moves to restructure the company through acquisitions and spin-offs led to a dramatic improvement in the company's financial results over the next 5 years. Results for the years 1996 and 2001 are shown in Exhibit 8-1.[1]

E x h i b i t   8 - 1

PepsiCo's Transformation

1996	Measures	2001 (Estimated)
$31 billion	Revenues	$27 billion
12 percent	Operating profit margin	16 percent
$1.22	Earnings per share (EPS)	$1.66
$1.4 billion	Operating cash flow	$2.5 billion
15 percent	Return on invested capital	26 percent

On May 2, 2001, PepsiCo announced that Steven S. Reinemund was being appointed chairman of the board and CEO and Indra Nooyi was being appointed president. Between 1998 and 2001, five new

Continued

Concluded

directors were appointed to the board; three were CEOs of other companies, one was president of a large subsidiary of one of the largest
companies in the United States, and the other was the president of
PepsiCo.

New strategic initiatives included focusing on convenience in
beverages and snack foods, completing the integration of Quaker
Oats, leveraging existing broad distribution channels, and maintaining a balanced brand portfolio in the targeted market segments. The products were balanced as to times of the day of
demand, consumer age groups, and consumer need states (healthy
versus indulgence).

THE POINT

As a result of these strategic initiatives, the board and management
of PepsiCo achieved a major restructuring of the company during a
period of transition to a new CEO. These results speak well for the
environment in which the board and the CEO could work together
to reposition the company in a major way. The restructuring essentially involved pruning away less effective businesses in terms of
growth potential and returns on capital and leaving a smaller but
richer mix of businesses for the future.

HOW THE BOARD SHOULD FUNCTION

Given that the board has an effective person serving as CEO, that an
arm's-length relationship exists between the board and the CEO, and
that there is a workable governance model, the board can focus on its
ongoing tasks. Most of these tasks may be grouped into three primary
activities:

- Reviewing and influencing decisions in an advise-and-consent role
- Reviewing and understanding the firm's results
- Determining when and how to intervene in management's
  affairs

Among the board's most important duties are its responsibility for
actively participating with the CEO in the development of the company's
strategy and the formulation of detailed plans for the strategy's successful implementation. As a practical matter, the CEO prepares a list of the

strategic options available to the company, explores the advantages and disadvantages of each option with the board, and recommends one or more to the board. A board must determine whether to support management's recommendations. The CEO must consult the board on such matters because execution of the strategy may require actions that have to be approved by the board and perhaps by the shareholders. For instance, if the strategy involves capital expenses or leases for plant and equipment or other facilities, the board would need to approve the capital expenditures. If the strategy involves repurchasing the company's shares or instituting a stock option plan, it may be necessary to gain approval of the shareholders through a formal vote, which would follow board approval.

The decisions related to the board's posture toward a proposed strategy are easier made when there is an orderly planning process in which the board can participate. The planning process provides the means by which the board sets expectations for the company's future performance, which, in turn, become the basis for making strategic choices and evaluating the performance of the CEO.

Of special concern to conscientious board members is the spectrum of advising the CEO and consenting to his or her plans on the one hand and acquiescing to a CEO's desires on the other. In determining its approach to this critical interaction, the board must address its role as both partner with and employer of the CEO. The board should avoid providing so much advice and assistance that the CEO could claim that he or she was simply following the board's lead in making critical decisions. If the board is successful in imposing its will regarding strategy or staffing on the CEO, it likely will find itself conflicted when the company's operations proceed poorly and someone must be called to account for the problems. This situation is most likely to occur if the CEO is weak or easily influenced by others.

On the other hand, the members of the board are chosen because they bring relevant and valuable industry or general business experience to the board and thus have much to offer the CEO in the form of guidance and providing a sounding board. Members of the board often couch their questions or comments in language that reminds the CEO that they want to express their feelings on an issue but that the CEO should take the questions or comments as advice to be considered rather than direction intended to encroach on the CEO's prerogatives. Vignette 8-2 presents a situation in which a board's decisive actions likely saved a company from ruin.

V I G N E T T E   8 - 2

A TEXTBOOK APPROACH TO HANDLING A CRISIS

THE ISSUE

When a board is faced with a crisis, often unanticipated, the way in which it immediately responds may determine whether the company survives.

THE SITUATION

Some years ago it was made public that a major Wall Street securities firm had engaged in the illegal manipulation of securities and faced indictment by the Justice Department. No financial services firm had ever survived a federal indictment, and the share price of the firm's stock began to plummet on release of the news.

THE BOARD'S ACTION

The board, largely made up of outsiders, moved swiftly to address the problems and quickly announced the resignation of the top officers of the firm and the temporary appointment of an acting chairman and CEO. The board immediately announced that it would cooperate fully with investigators and that it would, through its new CEO, institute a rigorous compliance program without delay. The acting CEO announced to the company's employees and to Congress that those activities believed to be over, on, or near the line of acceptability would not be tolerated and that all employees responsible for or involved in the illegal activity would be terminated. To emphasize his commitment to the employees and to resolve the scandal, the new CEO gave out his home phone number to employees so that they could call if they had problems or questions.

THE RESULTS

We suspect that the swift action of the board to cooperate fully with regulators, terminate all implicated employees responsible for or involved in the violations, and restore confidence through a new management team and rigorous internal safeguards saved the firm. An indictment was avoided, and investors rallied with new confidence.

Continued

Concluded

The swift actions of the board illustrate the way that boards are intended to act, but too often they lack the courage, knowledge, or independence to do so.

THE POINT

Crises test the independence and the action orientation of board members both individually and collectively. The survival of the company and the best interests of the shareholders are often at stake. Board members must be willing to take action swiftly, when necessary, to uphold their duty to shareholders. Board service, as we are coming to recognize more clearly, requires a principled action orientation on the part of board members.

STRATEGY FORMULATION VERSUS IMPLEMENTATION

The board must recognize the crucial importance of each of two aspects of corporate strategy. First, the strategic planning process begins with decisions regarding the firm's strategic goals and objectives, followed by the formulation of strategies for their attainment. Second, plans must be devised for implementing the strategies and managing the myriad of detailed actions that are required to execute the strategies effectively. The board cannot be content to endorse automatically the strategy devised by the CEO and senior management. The directors must ensure that operational plans are in place to carry out the strategic intent effectively. After a strategy has been adopted and the journey has begun, the board should systematically monitor the progress of execution of the strategy. When the board and the CEO share a mutual understanding of the strategic goals of the company and the indicators of success to be tracked, this process is monitored and evaluated more easily. Because strategic goals eventually must translate into financial success, financial measures and progress toward goals also need to be monitored.

Every strategic plan is based on some critical assumptions, particularly about the firm's market(s), competitors, and other environmental variables. These assumptions also should be tracked to assess their relevance and validity. Furthermore, there needs to be a continual scanning of the environment to identify any new forces that may have an impact on the strategy. Drastic variation in the assumptions underlying strategic plans and objectives and/or related new forces may necessitate their revision, particularly when the variation was unforseeable and beyond the control or influence of management. Typically, this timely feedback is not accomplished easily. Considerable thought must be given to designing practical, systematic approaches to these tasks, and the board should insist on discipline in regular reporting of the findings by management.

THE BOARD, THE CEO, AND THE SEARCH FOR A SUSTAINABLE COMPETITIVE ADVANTAGE

In many ways the strategic planning process in the business world is analogous to the search for the "ultimate weapon" that has characterized military initiatives throughout history. In seeking "sustainable competitive advantages," commanders have hoped to acquire access to a weapon so unique that it would tip the battle in their favor. Unfortunately, this hope has, for the most part, been futile. Consider the small number of ultimate weapons we can recall and the relatively short time during which they afforded the fortunate a competitive advantage. From the spear, bow and arrow, crossbow, longbow, gunpowder, and firearms to machine guns, artillery, and nuclear weapons, the competitive advantage lasted only until opponents internalized the advantages of each weapon and copied them. Even with all the science and technology involved with nuclear weapons, the competitive advantage was only sustainable for at most 3 years.

Consider, on the other hand, the success of the Greek phalanx, the Roman legion, Genghis Khan's cavalry, modern military logistics, and the ever-present use of alliances to rein in those who appear too powerful. It is apparent that, for the most part, history has belonged to the *organizers and implementers* and only for fleeting periods to those with some undefendable ultimate weapon. So it is with business. Unique strategies are few and seldom can be perpetuated for very long. Even patents expire at the end of some specified time interval.

Boards must recognize that, as a result, in our system of free enterprise and competition with unprecedented capabilities for communication, ideas do not remain proprietary very long. Competitors become aware of the strategies of others from suppliers, customers, industry connections, former employees, and especially from the CEOs' statements in the annual reports of most public companies. Success in the business environment surely depends on the derivation of effective strategies but at least equally depends on superior ability to execute the strategies. Firms with superior strategies and the ability to execute them successfully are the big winners in the free enterprise system. This dual theme of strategy formulation and concomitant superior execution is closely related to what is sometimes referred to as the execution of a *sustainable competitive advantage.*

Thus the board must recognize the importance of strategy that creates the dual needs for the company to manage change effectively and to move decisively in implementation decisions. In fact, success of the entire process of strategic planning and execution depends on the ability of the board and the CEO to lead change and execute decisions swiftly and decisively. We learned from the master of understanding and explaining human nature, Niccolò Machiavelli, that these traits are essential for the "prince" who wishes to defend and expand his realm (read business). Machiavelli wrote, "There is nothing more difficult to execute, nor more dubious of success, nor more dangerous to administer than to introduce a new order of things,"[2] thus warning of the difficulties of implementing change.

THE EVER-CHANGING NATURE OF STRATEGY

Regardless of how it comes about, the board must ensure that the strategies essential to business success are in place and that proper incentives exist to guarantee their successful implementation. This involvement in strategy formulation takes place in the relative chaos created by the persistent, ongoing restructuring of American industry. Over the last three decades and continuing today, the basic strategies of American industry have evolved continually and have adjusted in response to competitive and financial pressures that have created a popular view of a particular approach to strategy.

The First Movement: Diversification and Decentralization

The decades of the seventies and eighties were identified with a sustained period during which large corporations tended to diversify into different businesses. This was done to placate financial analysts' preferences for risk aversion, which were, in turn, brought on by concepts from *portfolio theory*. This theory was one of risk management, promoting the concept that a diversified company was at less risk from market downturns than a single, focused business because numerous industries were unlikely to experience problems simultaneously. As a result, most of the Fortune 1000 largest U. S. companies became diversified and decentralized, and their boards were in a position of "advising and consenting" to these arrangements.

It was natural that these diversified companies embraced a decentralized form of operations for planning and control. Typically, the breadth of the businesses within a corporation precluded anyone from completely understanding all the operations. This led to a natural division of labor wherein the corporate staff was responsible primarily for deciding on and financing the portfolio of businesses to be included in the company holdings. The various division managers were responsible for all aspects of their respective operations, including the product, marketing, and pricing strategies appropriate for their focused businesses.

Pressure to Focus

After operating in this mode for many years, American businesses saw the late 1980s usher in the beginning of a period of new trends in industrial organization. At that time, financial analysts began to profess that they found the diversified businesses difficult to understand. They feared that the numerous business units provided opportunities for companies to mask their risks or troubles in certain profit centers with the successes of another subset of more prosperous business units. These concerns emerged gradually, accelerated in the nineties, and have become major impediments to most diversified, decentralized corporations in the twenty-first century. The impediments come in the form of reduced valuations of the share prices of diversified companies.

In today's corporate world, financial analysts and institutional investors characteristically afford more focused and pure-play (read narrow-product-category) companies the opportunity to achieve much higher stock price multiples than more diversified companies. Furthermore, corporations that paid large sums for acquisitions during the expansive 1990s found optimistic forecasts and expected synergies failed to materialize in the harsh economic climate of the early 2000s. As a result, CEOs and boards of directors of many public companies have been led to unwind much of the diversification previously cherished. This has led, in recent years, to a continuous stream of divestitures of operating units, as companies lessened the diversification (and debt) within their portfolios at the behest of the financial community. These divestitures often have resulted in improved operating results and accompanying higher returns on shareholder investment and naturally have led to more favorable share price-to-earnings multiples for many firms.

The New Economy

The explosion in the 1990s of the "new economy," centered on high-technology, telecommunications, computer, and Internet-related businesses, upset the strategic status quo of the "old economy." The careful equilibrium that had existed in the financial markets and in the consumer and industrial markets for a century was pushed aside by a new breed of "technocrats" who marshaled formidable technological advances in electronics to create whole new industries. Their success, in turn, first attracted the attention of venture capitalists and then large numbers of mainstream investors who saw a means for participating in a new economy perceived to possess almost unlimited upside potential.

This development changed the strategic perceptions of risk and return for the board and CEO of virtually every major U.S. corporation. Boards of directors and their CEOs have had to decide whether their businesses were threatened by the new technologies as well as whether their companies should attempt to capitalize on the new developments in their normal competitive environments. The century of stability and predictability of competitive pressures, relative market shares, and labor and material costs had spawned generations of risk-averse managers. Numerous authors had commented on the predilection of managers to substitute planning for risk. They observed that multiyear contracts with labor unions and suppliers were examples of attempts by managers to remove major risks from pricing decisions.

The new economy offered the prospects of almost unlimited returns on investment at the cost of a level of risk and uncertainty unknown for generations. The strategies of the old economy were shaken and subjected to scrutiny as never before. Would the company be left behind? Should the company make major investments in the new economy, and if so, how? The world of the boards and the CEOs of many old economy companies had permanently changed overnight.

Current Strategic Issues in the Mainstream of U.S. Businesses

Recognizing these important trends in new technology and the still-surviving range of corporate portfolio diversity in U.S. corporations today, we note the key strategic issues related to management of a multidivisional organization. The board and the CEO must ensure a proper strategic interface between a parent corporation and its operating divisions, with a strong emphasis on the analytical and financial relationships. The board and the CEO must recognize corporate strategies as primarily revolving around determining the appropriateness of including various divisions (and potential acquisitions) in the corporate portfolio of businesses. There is also a need for corporate strategies to encompass the allocation of resources among the businesses of the portfolio.

Divisional strategies, or those of focused businesses, on the other hand, require extensive understanding of competitors and realistic product, marketing, and pricing strategies based on the division's role in its competitive environment and the corporate portfolio. In this context, the board and CEO must place particular emphasis on operating improvements as a critical, continuing competitive factor.

The board and the CEO must mutually focus on growth, consistent with our philosophy that in a free enterprise competitive environment there is no substitute for the energizing phenomenon of growth. It is our belief that all strategic issues can be dealt with more effectively in a growth environment than in a stagnant one. And so our basic premise, for all businesses in all industries, is that the strategic planning process begins with managers devising strategies for growth, followed by addressing the accompanying issues their firms face.

RESTRUCTURING VIA ACQUISITIONS AND DIVESTITURES

The board's role in the direct management of a company's affairs takes on a more critical flavor when acquisitions or divestitures are being considered. A company's bylaws often lift the board's oversight responsibilities to a higher level when there is a move to sell a portion of the company's assets or to make major asset acquisitions through a proposed merger or by acquiring another company. While there is a general tendency on the part of the board to endorse actions recommended by the CEO, proposed mergers or acquisitions often lead to the excercising of substantial caution because the board may want to rethink or reevaluate previously adopted strategic plans.

Boards may rationally consider, in abstract terms, an acquisition that will double the size of the company or a divestiture that will remove the original product line on which the company was built. It is quite stressful, however, when the previously approved strategic initiative leads to an actual proposal for major change. Some boards are strong advocates of strategic change and lead the way for such bold moves. Other boards, though, become very reluctant participants in projects involving broad changes. These boards sometimes lose very effective CEOs who recognize the need for fundamental change and leave when the board refuses to endorse the new direction for the company. In the final analysis, boards have the responsibility to consider *all* options in carrying out their duties to shareholders.

KNOWING WHAT THE RESULTS ARE: THE OVERSIGHT RESPONSIBILITY

The board must, in the end, maintain an effective oversight of the CEO, the company, and its assets from the standpoint of shareholders. This means asserting itself when it must, challenging the CEO when trouble is apparent or suspected, supporting the CEO in difficult situations when it believes that support is warranted, and even altering the make-up of the board through the nomination and election process if there is a perceived need for the highest level of change. It is far better for the board to readily assume this incontrovertible responsibility than to acquiesce to a forceful CEO and learn later that the company has made a serious mistake.

The board always must be informed as to industry and general business trends; the most recent strategic initiatives of suppliers, competitors, and customers; and the strengths and weaknesses of its own organization. The board ensures this through an established process of receiving and reviewing data, with appropriate analysis provided by management, including periodic competitive analyses, industry analyses, and benchmarking studies. The board must be especially wary in the area of the firm's capital structure, its debt and equity structure, and its general long-term financial outlook and results. Examination of these important financial issues should follow from results and projections provided by management. In particular, board members should monitor compliance with lending agreements (covenants) and the firm's bond rating. These responsibilities were covered in detail in Chapter 3 and Appendix 3-1 on audit committees.

WHEN AND HOW SHOULD THE BOARD INTERVENE?

If the board does not fully support the strategy or its implementation by the CEO, or if it is faced with an untenable crisis situation, then the board should either persuade the CEO to reformulate his or her plans and actions or find a successor who is more in consonance with the board's vision of the proper strategy for the company going forward. One of the key requirements of the board's appropriately making such a determination is that the board must know what is actually happening and what the results of the CEO's decisions are. Only by having such information can the board evaluate the performance of the CEO and know when to intervene.

Based on Past Events

From a historical perspective, the board should intervene when the firm's results are not satisfactory and board members believe that the CEO neither understands the situation nor has a plan for dealing with it. Similarly, if there is a plan in place, the board should intervene when it lacks confidence in the CEO's ability to execute the plan.

Based on Views of the Future

Attempting to look forward, the board and the CEO may disagree at times as to the most desirable strategy for the company. Superior products may be available from competitors. A disruptive technology may be looming. Foreign competitors may be gaining market share with equivalent products at much lower prices based on lower costs. In fact, one general manager of a large business unit of a major corporation was removed because his unit had small, single-digit losses in market share for 3 consecutive years. This action was taken despite all the other 20 or so performance measures of his division being rated as strong to outstanding. It was felt that most other performance measures could be managed in good fashion in an environment in which the business unit was giving up market share. In short, if the board and the CEO do not agree on the strategy, there must be a change. The change can involve resolving the differences between the board and the CEO as to strategy or replacing the CEO with a successor who can relate to the board's position. As we said earlier, the board almost always wins in a showdown with the CEO.

Loss of Confidence in the CEO

Boards can lose confidence in a CEO either because board members do not feel that the strategy is appropriate for the firm at the time or because they do not have confidence that the CEO and his or her team have been implementing (or will be able to implement) the strategy successfully. The CEO may be convinced that a new product will win the market; the board may have doubts. The CEO may feel strongly that an international strategy is essential; the board may not be convinced that the company is pressed to become an international enterprise. The board may be convinced of the desirability of a recommended strategy, but it may feel that the CEO and the management team are not capable of carrying it out. Or the results are inarguably poor, and the CEO is not addressing the situation appropriately. An aggressive acquisition strategy, for instance, may be felt to be appropriate, but if the CEO and the company have failed to integrate several recent acquisitions effectively, the board may be reluctant to agree with such a strategy. In such cases, the board may seek to remove the CEO and look for stronger leadership to carry out the perceived superior strategy.

In order to act with confidence, the board must keep itself informed about all aspects of the company's operations. If board members doubt the CEO's candor or honesty or his or her ability to understand the situation, they must take the necessary steps to inform themselves. The shareholders deserve nothing less, and board members have committed themselves to responsibly carrying out this duty.

SUMMARY

This complex relationship between the board and the CEO requires genuine independence—but with a mutual commitment to work toward the achievement of common goals in the interests of shareholders. It is very difficult for the board to force its strategic preferences on the CEO for many reasons. Such a move by the board would leave the CEO with an unassailable alibi in the event of future troubles. When board members feel an imperative to alter the course of strategy espoused by the CEO, intervention by the board is more likely to take the form of replacing the CEO. The board cannot properly exercise its oversight responsibility unless it has faith in the CEO and his or her strategies.

We now move on to the role of the board in determining corporate organizations and capital structures in Chapter 9.

REVIEW QUESTIONS

1. What elements would characterize an effective working relationship between a board and the CEO?
2. What is the role of the board in formulating a corporation's strategy?
3. What are the odds of a corporation's developing a sustainable competitive advantage?
4. How has the concept of business strategies evolved over time?
5. What are the dominant strategic issues in U.S. business today?

CHAPTER 9

Corporate and Capital Structures

One of the first decisions the founders of a business must make is the legal form the organization will take. As the business grows, its founders or board members may need to modify the initial form to reflect new and changing circumstances. They similarly must decide on the capital structure, determining how the business will be financed initially. The capital structure usually will be some mix of equity capital and debt. The more risky the business venture is thought to be, the more equity the lenders of the debt financing will want to see in the capital structure. The initial decision regarding the capital structure will be revisited constantly during the life of the organization, although subsequent financing decisions always must relate to prior financial commitments.

The owners or shareholders generally must approve any changes in the initial corporate structure. Substantial changes in the capital structure, such as the creation of new classes of stock, the issuance of new shares, the sale of substantial assets, or even the sale of the company, are also subject to shareholder approval. The board of directors, however, generally can approve the issuance of debt on its own authority. Any restrictions on the board's authority to manage these aspects of the business should be spelled out in the bylaws.

In this chapter we discuss the important points that stockholders and particularly directors need to consider in making thoughtful corporate- and capital-structure decisions. There are two basic guiding principles in making structure decisions:

- The structure should reflect the inherent nature of the business.
- The strategy of the business should drive its structure.

CORPORATE STRUCTURE

The size and complexity of a business and its underlying strategy determine to a large degree the appropriate form of business structure. The nature of the business, its degree of capital intensity, and the nature of its assets and operations, along with the risks they create, determine the appropriate or requisite capital structure for the business.

Organization Forms

Numerous forms of organization exist in today's marketplace. Distinguishing characteristics of each form make it more or less suitable under specific circumstances. The most often-used alternatives include

- *Proprietorships.* Generally, single owners are fully engaged in operating the business. The owner is the business, in that the enterprise has no economic value apart from the owner's efforts and capabilities. Examples of proprietorships are small service businesses or professional businesses.
- *Partnerships.* Generally, there are multiple owners, some of whom, but not necessarily all, are engaged in managing the business. While many small businesses are partnerships, there are also some large partnerships in real estate ventures, oil drilling, and the like.
  - *General versus limited partners.* In large partnerships, there are often general partners and limited partners. One difference in the role of the partners is that the general partner often has full authority to manage all affairs of the business. Another difference is that the general partner often has unlimited liability, whereas the liability of the limited partners is the capital they have invested or are committed to invest under specified conditions. The details of the authority and responsibility related to the various classes of partners in a particular business will be spelled out in the partnership agreement. The general partner may be a corporation, in which case the stockholders of the corporation will have taken on a limited liability.
  - *Limited-liability partnerships (LLPs).* In recent years, most states have created a limited-liability form of partnership that provides liability protection while maintaining tax advantages. This form of partnership is used primarily by professional organizations, such as lawyers and accountants.
- *C Corporations.* The C Corporation is the standard form of corporate organization.

- *S Corporations.* The S Corporation has many of the characteristics of the C Corporation, except that its income is taxable as a partnership. It is a creation of the Internal Revenue Service and is subject to its limitations in terms of the number of owners. An S Corporation cannot have more than 75 shareholders. Further, these shareholders must be individual citizens or residents of the United States, estates, or certain qualifying trusts. Corporations and partnerships cannot be stockholders. The S Corporation cannot have more than one class of stock. Voting rights can vary among stockholders, however, as long as other rights are identical.
- *Limited-liability corporations (LLCs).* This form of a corporation is taxed as a partnership as well. There are very few differences between S Corporations, LLCs, and LLPs. An LLC has *members*, an LLP has *partners*, and an S Corporation has *stockholders.* All three organizational forms serve to allow profits to flow through to the partners or stockholders without the double taxation that characterizes C Corporations.
- *Public corporations.* Public corporations meet ownership criteria defined by the Securities and Exchange Commission (SEC). Such public corporations are required to report financial results to the SEC on a regular basis. For a company to be deemed a private company and thus be exempted from reporting to the SEC, the company must have (1) fewer than 300 shareholders or (2) less than $10 million of assets and less than 500 shareholders. The ownership of public corporations can be subdivided by the exchanges on which they are traded, including the Nasdaq Exchange, the New York Stock Exchange, the American Stock Exchange, and so-called over-the-counter (OTC) trading. Each of these exchanges has its own rules and regulations for qualification.

Determining the Most Appropriate Organization Form

A degree of judgment is involved in selecting the appropriate organization form. There are at least five variables that should be considered as major determinants of the most appropriate form of organization for any business. They are

- The size and complexity of the business
- The number of owners
- The life span of the business
- Tax considerations
- Liability considerations

Generally speaking, smaller, simpler businesses are more apt to be proprietorships or partnerships. The primary advantages of these forms of organization are simplicity in record keeping and forms of taxation. These advantages of the simpler form of organization are also the two disadvantages of the corporate form. Obtaining a state charter forms a corporation; in reality, it is fairly simple and inexpensive to form a corporation, so a desire for simplicity alone is not a compelling reason to avoid the corporate form.

Tax considerations are more compelling, however. The owners of a C Corporation are subject to double taxation, first paying corporate income taxes and then paying full personal income taxes as well on any corporate dividends paid out to shareholders. If the owner is a taxable entity (as opposed to tax-exempt retirement or charitable funds), the combined tax rate on corporate profits and dividends can approach 64 percent, depending on a shareholder's personal tax bracket, as shown in Exhibit 9-1. Small corporations traditionally have a somewhat lower corporate tax rate, and the owners may be in a lower personal tax bracket, so the tax burden on a small business owner might not be as great as that of shareholders of large corporations. The details of these differences change from time to time as the tax code changes. Exhibit 9-1 shows the effective tax rate that results from the phenomenon of double taxation.

Many people think that double taxation should be eliminated by making dividends tax free to the shareholders. As we will see shortly when we discuss capital structures, taxation is a major factor in capital structure decisions and typically leads to a bias toward more tax-efficient debt over equity.

An additional consideration is whether the owners work in the business and whether their ownership is in proportion to their relative salaries. When the owners work in the business, they can, within limits, avoid the double taxation by taking excess funds out as salaries or bonuses.

Exhibit 9-1

The Effect of Double Taxation

Corporate pretax income	$100
Corporate tax rate	40 percent
Corporate after-tax income	$60
Assuming that all after-tax income is distributed as a dividend and the individual tax rate is 40 percent, individual after-tax income	$36
Total effective tax rate	64 percent

By *excess funds*, we mean cash in the business beyond the normal needs of the company in the foreseeable future. As a business gets larger, particularly in terms of the number of owners, the advantages of the corporate form of organization quickly come into play so that corporations become the preferred form for businesses of any substantial size. Any tax considerations are outweighed by the advantages of limited liability, unlimited life, and the ease with which ownership is divided and transferred.

Public versus Private Ownership

When we speak of public companies, we are referring to companies whose shares are widely owned and publicly traded. There are public debt markets, but these are used primarily by larger companies, whereas smaller companies rely largely on banks for their debt needs. These generalities prevail because of need and convenience. Small and medium-sized companies are free to use public debt markets if they choose, and large companies certainly use banks, when convenient, for part or all of their debt needs.

When we refer to public companies, we are also referring to companies that are required to report financial and other data regularly to the SEC. As noted earlier, a company does not have to file with the SEC if there are (1) less than 300 shareholders or (2) less than $10 million in assets and fewer than 500 shareholders. Companies with fewer shareholders are free to handle their investor relations and reporting as more or less a matter of personal or company preference. Some will provide formal annual reports, whereas others will communicate more informally or perhaps not at all.

Why Do Companies Go Public?

In the not too distant past, the most prevalent reason companies went public through initial public offerings (IPOs) was to raise capital. The growth of the venture capital and private equity markets, as well as the tax efficiency of debt, has brought about the current environment in which going public is probably more of an exit strategy for the venture capital investors than a necessary means for the company to raise capital. This is certainly true of smaller companies.

There are, however, a few larger companies that have grown profitably and chose to go public to fund a strategy of rapid growth that required capital in quantities beyond that available at attractive rates in private equity markets. Companies with a strategy to grow by acquisition may go public to create a currency (shares) with which to make acquisitions. This works well when they can buy target companies at a lower multiple of stock price to earnings than that for which their stock is selling. Probably the most common motive for going public is to gain liquidity for the previous investors in the company.

When a business has been successful, the question always arises as to how best to capitalize on the success. When it is an owner-managed business, the owner can find ways to withdraw substantial sums from the business, thereby creating wealth outside the business. However, when there are other investors, particularly venture capitalists or private equity investors, this avenue is not as readily available. The choices of the investors/owners are generally to have the company buy them out, sell the business to another company, or go public. Often, when these alternatives are compared, the highest price for the shareholders is attained by the public offering.

There is, unfortunately, another motive often at play that best can be described as self-interest on the part of both investment bankers seeking a fee and the owners of the company. These parties traditionally seek a short-term profit on the transaction to go public, and are not always trying to build a business for long-term profitability. A classic example of this phenomenon was the dot-com bubble that burst in the spring of 2000. The role of the investment bankers and management was to convince the public that these companies had a great future and to sell shares of the companies to the willing public.

This is not a new phenomenon. One of the most famous examples of such behavior was the South Sea bubble in 1720. The South Sea Company was chartered in England in 1711 and granted a monopoly of British trade with South America and the islands of the Pacific Ocean. During the next several years, the monopoly rewarded investors handsomely. With the company's stock appreciating rapidly, the task of persuading new investors was easy. Between January and July of 1720, the stock grew eight times in value, attracting all manner of speculators and inspiring no end of imitators. By November, however, nearly nine-tenths of the value of the stock of the company had vanished, disgracing the directors of the company (who proved to have collaborated in assorted shenanigans with the company's accounts), ruining thousands of investors, and wreaking havoc on the finances of the entire British Empire.[1] To many, this sounds quite familiar when reflecting on the market activities of the early 2000s.

When Should Companies Go Public?

Many people see going public as a mark of success, something to strive for. The reality is that running a public company has all the challenges of running a private company and then some. In addition to the costs of regulatory compliance, there is the need to maintain good investor relations to support the stock price. Investor relations bring in the need for sponsoring brokerage firms and their analysts, who assist in creating interest in the stock. Financial analysts who follow public companies tend to have a very short-term perspective, with an undue emphasis on quarterly earnings.

There is also the problem of the structure of the market for the shares of public companies. For a number of reasons, *small cap* (small capitalization) stocks often find it difficult to get a fair valuation, given the system of analysts and investment advisers. The large institutional investors normally steer away from small caps because there are not enough shares outstanding to permit them to make a meaningful minimum investment without moving the market or acquiring too great a percentage of the company. They also fear a lack of liquidity if and when they might want to sell their shares. From the perspective of brokerage firms, there is not enough potential commission volume in small cap transactions to warrant a great deal of attention.

Because of these difficulties, going public should be undertaken only when there are solid business reasons and when the company is large enough to create a meaningful market for its shares. The major business reasons are access to capital, stockholder liquidity, and a currency to execute an acquisition strategy. The question of being large enough is a matter of judgment, but a market capitalization today of $100 million is a realistic minimum size, although many public companies are smaller.

When outside investment is an attractive alternative, companies in a startup or early growth stage generally find venture capital or private equity partners a better alternative than going public. These investors tend to be more sophisticated in understanding the company's strategy and evaluating its performance and are comfortable taking a longer-term view. These investors, however, expect a very high return for their risk, which at some point in the company's growth cycle makes going public a less expensive source of the required additional capital.

CAPITAL STRUCTURE

The details of the capital structure of a business describe the financing of the organization. Traditionally, *capital structure* refers to the relative amounts of debt and equity on a firm's balance sheet. The need for capital is driven by the nature, size, and growth rate of the business. Some businesses are more capital-intensive than others. Service businesses may generate as much as $10 of sales for each $1 of capital invested. A major process manufacturing operation such as a utility, chemical plant, or oil refinery might generate as little as 50 cents of sales for each $1 of investment. Exhibit 9-2 shows the varying levels of investment intensity across a number of sectors of the Standard and Poor's (S&P) 500 set of companies.

While larger companies require more capital than smaller companies in the same business, it is a change in size that creates the need for more or less capital at any point in time. After the size has stabilized (growth has slowed), new funds usually are not required. A basic maxim is that the nature of the business's assets dictates the type of investment capital that is appropriate. Illiquid, long-term assets, such as specialized plant and equipment, need to be funded by permanent capital, either long-term debt or equity. The more risky the business in terms of the unpredictability of earnings, the more equity is needed. One of the principal mistakes that companies make is to overleverage (take on too much debt). In such over-leveraged situations, if the financial results (net income and cash flow) fall short by as little as 20 or 30 percent or require only a year or so longer than planned to develop, the overleveraged company can find itself in default on its debt and have all of its equity wiped out. Exhibit 9-3 depicts how the nature of the assets influences the appropriate capital structure.

Trading assets minus trading liabilities equals trading capital required. Short-term bank lines of credit can provide seasonal trading capital that is self-liquidating at least once a year. Fixed assets are ideal for long-term debt financing, in that the debt can be serviced by the cash flow from earnings and tax advantage of depreciation of the assets. While the practical limits on the amount of debt are established by the amount of cash flow available to service (pay interest on) the debt, we typically would expect to find new assets carrying fairly high levels of debt, perhaps as much as 75 or 80 percent of the book value, with the amount of debt declining gradually as the

Exhibit 9-2

Investment Intensity across Sectors of the S&P 500: Year 2001

Sector	Investment Intensity*
Communications	176%
Utilities	149%
Transportation	146%
Energy	141%
Basic Materials	97%
Consumer Staples	67%
Health Care	56%
Capital Goods	53%
Technology	53%
Consumer Goods	46%
Financials	44%

* Investment Intensity is measured by
Depreciable Assets divided by Revenues

Source: Standard and Poor's Research Database, 2002.

E x h i b i t   9 - 3

Asset Types and Capital Sources

Assets	Capital Source
Seasonal trading assets—accounts receivable, inventory, and prepaid expenses	Trading liabilities

	Trade credit
	  Accrued expenses
	  Seasonal bank line
	  of credit

Permanent trading assets	Trading liabilities Revolving bank line of credit Equity
Fixed assets—land, building, and equipment	Long-term debt Equity

assets age and their book values decline. A conservative rule would be that all assets other than fixed assets are financed with equity, although there may be exceptions to this, depending on the nature of the asset.

One of the key decisions a board must make is the amount of leverage that the firm will assume. Leverage is a two-edged sword. When the interest rate on the debt is lower than the return on capital of the business, the difference accrues to equity and leverages up the return on equity. The reverse, however, is also true.

This mix of debt and equity determines two very important things:

- The allocation of risk, income, and control
- The cost of capital

Each of these outcomes is examined below.

Allocation of Risk, Income, and Control

If the capital structure of a business is entirely equity, the owners own all of the income, have all the control, and take all the risk associated with the business. The owners of a company taking on debt or issuing shares to the public or to private equity investors want to shift as much risk to the company's lenders or new equity holders as possible, giving up as little of the income and control as they can negotiate.

For a strong company, the best debt gives up little control (it is unsecured but has tight covenants indicative of the strength of the company without being onerous to the company) and carries a low interest rate, reflecting the low risk. As the risk increases, a lender will want more control (collateral and more restrictive covenants) and a higher interest rate (more income). The most risky debt is subordinated to senior debt and carries high rates (often called *high-yield* or *junk bonds*) and may even have equity features (such as conversion rights or warrants to purchase common stock).

Leasing is another form of debt. Because the leasor retains ownership of the asset, the leasor automatically has collateral. While the legal form of ownership is different, the economics are essentially the same, except that sometimes the rent is cheaper than the interest and debt repayment, particularly for companies that are strapped for cash. Of course, the leasing company does not own the leased asset at the end of its payment horizon.

Equity as a source of capital may involve the relinquishing of various degrees of control. Different classes of equity exist that give varying rights, such as preference to dividends, voting, or repayment in liquidation (usually called *preferred stock*). Preferred stock can provide funds that give up less income than issuing straight equity shares (less dilution) without the risks related to having to service a debt obligation.

Lenders will charge a corporate client a market-based interest rate that reflects the perceived risk in the business. They will minimize their investment risk by limiting the amount they will lend related to collateral values and by their required coverage of debt service ratios. They will exercise control through the loan agreement and covenants that are triggered by breaches of the minimum required ratios. The remedies to breached covenants available to the lenders will lie along a continuum from simply conferring with management to review financial plans to restricting certain actions by the company to actually calling in the loan.

More complex capital structures will have layers of debt—from senior debt secured by the firm's assets, to unsecured debt, to subordinated debt—with each level carrying a progressively higher interest rate. The interest rates will reflect the total amount of leverage, so the incremental cost of high-interest, subordinated debt will approximate that of the cost of equity, as shown in the example in Exhibit 9-4.

The exercise of Exhibit 9-4 raises the question of what is a correct, or optimal, amount of debt for a company. The answer depends, of course, on the nature of the business. Banks with very liquid assets (investments and short-term loans) typically will have debt in excess of 90 percent of their total capital. Manufacturing firms probably are considered conservatively financed, with about 35 percent of their total capital in debt, corresponding to an AA bond rating. Exhibit 9-5 shows that, in general, the interest rate rises as the debt-to-capital ratio rises, reflecting the increased risk of the debt.

As Exhibit 9-5 indicates, interest rates vary directly with the perceived risk of the organization, as assigned by the rating agencies, such as Standard & Poor's or Dun & Bradstreet. The directors of a company should

E x h i b i t   9 - 4

An Example of Interest Rates on Incremental Debt

	Company A with 50 Percent Debt	Company B with 80 Percent Debt
Total book capital	$1000	$1000
Debt	$ 500	$ 800
Book equity	$ 500	$200
Interest rate	7 percent	12 percent
Annual interest cost	$35	$96
Incremental interest paid by Company B		$61
Incremental debt for Company B		$300
Interest rate on incremental debt for Company B		20 percent

E x h i b i t   9 - 5

Corporate Bonds: Debt to Capital Ratios and Interest Rates of Various S&P Ratings: Year 2001

S&P Bond Rating	Debt / Capital Ratio	Effective Yield*
Treasury Bonds	N/A	4.97%
AAA	30.9%	6.05%
AA	36.8%	6.10%
A	41.5%	6.63%
BBB	47.9%	7.42%
BB	56.6%	8.19%
B	64.6%	10.50%

* Effective Yields for Five-Year Corporate Bonds as of May 22, 2001.

Source: Standard and Poor's Global Fixed Income Research.

be aware of this relationship and seek out that point at which the benefit of the increased leverage just outweighs the increase in interest rate.

Off-Balance-Sheet Financing

No discussion of capital structure would be complete today without mentioning off-the-balance sheet financing. In its simplest form, it involves operating leases whose terms permit them not to be shown as a liability. This is an accounting technicality and has no economic impact. In more sophisticated efforts, it involves financial instruments and investments that can be accounted for by the equity method. There are situations where off-the-balance sheet obligations make good economic sense. Unfortunately, those who have wanted to cover up their actions or who have not wanted to disclose the full amount and nature of their debt leverage have abused them. Often, the complexity of off-balance-sheet vehicles makes it very difficult for an outsider to understand a company's true financial picture and sometimes for insiders as well, it appears.

There should not be a blanket condemnation of the practice of off-balance-sheet financing, but directors need to ensure the sound rationale of using such vehicles and that they are fully disclosed in company statements.

The Cost of Capital

The concept of the cost of capital is imbedded in this discussion of capital structure; it is a concept of which boards must be ever mindful. Debt clearly has a cost—the interest rate paid less the tax savings. Equity also has a cost, although not so obvious. The cost of equity is the return that the owners desire on their invested funds. This return is a figure based on investors' comparison of a given investment with their other opportunities. The cost of capital of a business can be estimated by computing the weighted average of the costs of debt and equity. Exhibit 9-6 provides an example using a 40 percent debt, 60 percent equity structure.

The return on capital before interest but after taxes should be compared with the cost of capital. If the company is earning more than its cost of capital (that is, its return on capital exceeds its cost of capital), it is cre-

E x h i b i t   9 - 6

An Example of Determining the Weighted-Average Cost of Capital

Type of Capital	Percentage of Total Capital	Cost	Weighted Cost
Debt	40 percent	4.2 percent*	1.68 percent
Equity	60 percent	14 percent	8.4 percent
TOTAL	100 percent		10.08 percent

*7 percent interest rate less 40 percent taxes.

ating shareholder value. If the company is earning less, it is destroying shareholder value. The return on investment earned is one of the primary tools used in valuing businesses, in making capital investment decisions, and as the basis for determining the level of incentive compensation of executives. The underlying assumption is that encouraging the earning of positive returns for shareholders, after all costs and including capital costs, is the basic intent of incentive systems.

THE EVOLUTION OF THE ORGANIZATION AND THE FINANCIAL STRUCTURE

As companies grow and circumstances change, it is often necessary to restructure the business. We have already described how many businesses start as proprietorships or partnerships and progress on to become corporations. The corporate organizational structures also evolve along with the gradual development of the requisite financial structures to support the more sophisticated corporate structure. One of the most common changes as a business grows is to create subsidiary corporations or operating divisions, a process referred to as *decentralization*. This approach is usually chosen when distinctly different operations develop or are acquired, such as the development of a completely different business or establishing a location in another state. Subsidiaries, in turn, can be wholly or partially owned, for example, through a joint venture.

The Results Expected of Premium Companies

The most important measures of corporate performance assessment are the interrelated goals of return on investment; growth in revenues, earnings, and/or market share; and adequacy of cash flow to fund growth. The efficacy of corporate goals and performance is measured by comparisons with companies in the same industry and, ultimately, with the wider array of investment opportunities across the spectrum of all industries.

The natural development of most public corporations during the last 30 years or so has resulted in some degree of diversified, decentralized operations. The diversified, decentralized form of corporate organization is still the dominant mode of operation of most large public U.S. companies, although the investment community has pressured companies in recent years to become less diversified by rewarding focused companies with higher multiples of stock prices to earnings.

The Constraints on Performance

Each industry has its inherent pattern of investment intensity, gross profit margins, degree of labor intensity, rate of new product development and introduction, prevailing rate of research and development expenses, and degree of market elasticity. Each operating unit (division or subsidiary company) of a diversified company has a characteristic set of feasible financial results based on the industry competitive structure it faces. The performance of the divisions on these variables leads to a set of boundaries that define reasonable corporate expectations with regard to return on investment, growth, and cash flow.

It is difficult to achieve high returns on investment in industries that are highly investment-intensive. It is also difficult to grow significantly faster than the industry's market growth rate. Finally, it is almost impossible to grow faster than the market if the product or service is a commodity. Any attempt to capture market share by reducing prices in this situation will lower the prices and margins of all the competitors because competitors will as a rule meet the lower prices to protect their market shares. It is also axiomatic that fast-growing businesses require injections of cash to grow capacity and to provide the necessary working capital to fund their growth.

It is apparent that many focused businesses would have difficulties achieving high returns on investment, high relative growth rates, and self-sustaining cash flow simultaneously. If the business were to grow rapidly over a long time frame, it would need continuous injections of cash. If it were required to maintain some level of debt to total capital, it would invariably and continually reach points in time at which its debt would encounter limits imposed by lenders, and it would have to issue additional equity to continue to grow. This process would relentlessly dilute the ownership of the company and would be counterproductive from an investor standpoint.

Some businesses with market leadership through new product innovation or through patents are able to earn sufficient profit margins and the resulting cash flow to support almost any market growth rate. Such situations are very rare, however, and are found most often in so-called high-tech, research-oriented businesses. Finally, investment-intensive businesses producing commodity products or any business facing price pressures from strong foreign competition will find it difficult to earn attractive returns on investment in the long run.

The Advantages of a Portfolio of Businesses

These challenges, however, are offset in each situation by concomitant advantages to a company with a portfolio of businesses. Despite their needs for cash, fast-growing businesses provide their corporate parents with the growth for which financial analysts long. Businesses with market leadership provide their parent companies with high profit margins. And investment-intensive businesses, despite thin margins and low returns on investment, often provide steady, high levels of cash flow, resulting largely from high levels of depreciation. As a result, many companies resist pressures from financial analysts for more focus and prefer to operate through a portfolio of business units that brings the proper mix of desirable results to the corporate totals.

This advantageous combination of performance measures does not necessarily represent synergy among the businesses of the portfolio. Many companies seek synergies between operating divisions, such as supposedly advantageous supplier-customer relationships created through vertical integration. The advantage would seem to be the capturing of supplier margins, which would tend to increase the company's profits. In reality, the disadvantages inherent in attempting to achieve synergy often considerably outweigh the advantages because of the internal squabbles that naturally arise over fair transfer prices, reasonable inventory levels, and acceptable delivery dates.

The Relationships among Business Units

Many well-run companies have come to realize the power of the free enterprise system in resolving these situations. The divisions are left to do business with one another at their discretion, based on arm's-length relationships, without corporate edicts with regard to transfer prices or product schedule dates. Division managements are left to fill their procurement needs on the open market, with a caveat that they should "buy internally," all other things being equal. Supplier divisions must compete by meeting market standards as to prices and delivery. The general notion throughout this book is that synergies are advantageous when the free enterprise system is left to work, and the most effective rules are those provided by competition.

THE CORPORATE CHALLENGE TO MANAGE THE MIX OF BUSINESSES

In a diversified, decentralized company, the corporate challenge is to provide an effective set of consistent results over the long term from a given mix of businesses, each of which has some inherent pattern of achievable results. The divisions are charged with producing outstanding results compared with similar companies, their own past performance, and that of other well-run companies. In such a corporation, the results of the total enterprise depend on the sum of the results of the operating units.

It follows that the only way the corporate office can make significant changes in the firm's results for the important performance measures of return on investment, growth, and cash flow is to make changes in the portfolio of businesses. That is, it can choose to acquire new, more desirable businesses and/or it can choose to divest less attractive businesses. In the end, its long-term results will be determined by the mix of businesses and their potential for contributing to the crucial performance measures. Corporations that perform superbly will find ready access to equity markets, will enjoy lower interest rates than competitors, and will be able to use strong stock prices to acquire additional businesses. The overriding objective of contemporary corporate management is to enhance shareholder value, and this will be the ultimate objective of the boards of both public and private companies.

Analogous reasoning holds in the more focused business. Management can make substantial changes in the performance outcomes by adding or acquiring new, attractive product lines and/or by selling or closing less attractive lines, categories, or even facilities. For both the decentralized corporation and the focused company, "fixing" the results of the constituent businesses or product lines is always an option—but a less immediate and often less certain one than restructuring.

Corporate-Level Strategies for Restructuring

In a diversified, decentralized corporate setting, strategy at the corporate level may be narrowed to a set of choices that are not mutually exclusive. First among these, a corporation may choose to continue operations as an ongoing enterprise with the business units currently in its portfolio. This more or less commits the corporation to the pattern of results reasonably available from the current business units. If the business units compete in attractive industries and are well managed, this may be a viable and desired strategy. This commits the growth of the company to the limits imposed by the natural growth rates available to the several business units. Closing businesses is a similar option, where typically the assets of the business are sold, but not the trademarks, contracts, or liabilities.

Sell One or More Businesses

A corporation instead may choose to sell one or more of its current business units. This could result from a perception that these business units lack long-term prospects consistent with the company's objectives. It could follow from environmental or other regulatory requirements that require extensive capital investments for continued operations in one or more business units. The company may not have the cash for such investments or may not wish to commit the investment at this time. Divesting (selling) the unit would bring in cash that could be used in what would be considered more advantageous ways. It also may improve performance relative to the company's specific goals.

Spin Off One or More Businesses

A corporation also may choose to spin off one or more of its current business units. Spin-offs offer certain advantages to a company and to its shareholders as compared with the sale of operating divisions, especially related to taxes. Spin-offs occur when management feels that greater shareholder value can be achieved by separating operations. In such a case, the shares in the newly separated business are distributed pro rata to the holders of the parent company's shares. Because this transaction is considered a substitution of one item of a stipulated value for another item of similar value, the transaction is deemed to create no gain for either party and is thus a tax-free exchange. (A number of restrictions apply, however, in order for the event to be considered tax-free.) Spin-offs are increasingly popular as a result. This process allows the individual shareholders to decide whether to sell or hold the new stock, thus controlling the occurrence of a taxable event. Whether the mechanism employed is a sale or a spin-off, the result is the same—a leaner, more focused corporation.

Sell the Entire Business

Occasionally, a company may find itself in a strategic and/or operational situation from which it cannot readily extricate itself. An aggressive competitor may have neutralized a competitive advantage formerly enjoyed by the company. The firm may face prohibitive labor or material costs that are uncontrollable. It may find itself "in play" as a result of an unsolicited offer for its shares. The company may find that its focused market segment is vanishing as a result of shifting consumer trends or substitute products. For these and other reasons, the corporation may conclude that shareholder interests are best served by going out of business. The company would thus sell out to another company, and its shareholders would receive cash or stock in the acquiring company in return for their shares.

Acquire Additional Businesses

Alternatively, a company may choose to use cash accumulations, debt, or use equity to purchase into strategic acquisitions. Management may feel that the company should proceed in a different direction and that certain focused acquisitions may enhance the competitive position of one or more of its business units. This choice precludes simply reinvesting all available cash into existing operations. These acquisitions, if thought out carefully, can improve the company's performance with regard to return on investment, growth, and/or cash flow.

Repurchase Its Own Shares

Finally, a company may choose to use its cash accumulations to buy back its own shares. In the past decade, share repurchases have become a widely used strategic tool for U.S. corporations, as shown in Exhibit 9-7. This has become an increasingly popular strategic option in recent years as many companies, faced with holding levels of cash beyond their reasonable operating needs and believing their stock to be underpriced, reason that buying their own shares constitutes the best use of these funds from the shareholders' point of view. The cash accumulates as a result of an imbalance among the company's growth rate, its needs for cash, and its ability to generate cash.

After debt is paid down to optimal levels, the cash in excess of internal needs normally earns less in interest income than the prevailing return on investment from operations and thus results in a lower overall average return on investment for the corporation. This follows from the practice

E x h i b i t   9 - 7

Share Repurchase Totals for U.S.-Based Securities.

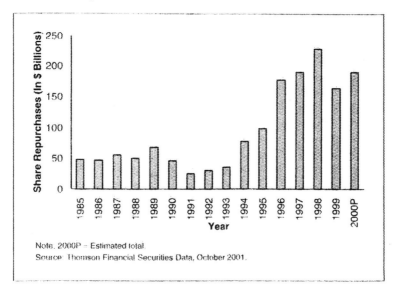

Note. 2000P = Estimated total.
Source: Thomson Financial Securities Data, October 2001.

that public companies normally invest excess cash in risk-free government bonds because management is not expert at investments and companies are not normally formed for the purpose of investing in other companies. We note that the repurchase of shares is effectively a tax-free dividend, increasing the remaining shareholders' investment with no tax penalty. We digress here to discuss the strong current sentiments for companies to repurchase their shares when the conditions warrant.

Why Repurchase Shares?

Not too many years ago, the repurchase of its shares by a company was frowned on. This left many companies with excess cash and only limited options for dealing with the situation. They could increase dividend payouts, but this would lead to a cohort of unhappy shareholders who would be subjected to taxation of the dividends as ordinary income. As a result, many companies looked to diversification through acquisitions as the next best alternative for dealing with the excess cash. This, in turn, led to the formation of numerous unwieldy, unmanageable conglomerates. The current, more favorable disposition of the investment community and government regulators toward share repurchases has provided a valuable tool to boards of directors seeking to maximize shareholder value. Thus many highly regarded companies regularly buy back their own stock as a matter of policy. In the first quarter of 1999 alone, five companies, including such corporate powerhouses as Time Warner, Citicorp, and Morgan Stanley Dean Witter, each announced share repurchases of more than $1 billion.[2]

There are four key reasons for a company to repurchase shares. These reasons are to transfer excess funds to shareholders, to increase the proportion of debt in the company's capital structure, to signal management's confidence in the company's stock to the financial markets, and to mount a corporate takeover defense.

Return Excess Funds to Shareholders

Companies strive to achieve the consistent returns desired by their investors. To do so, a company might turn down new business opportunities that are expected to generate lower than desired returns. Shareholders would be better off if the company simply returned the excess cash to them and allowed them to reinvest their capital in a different investment that would provide the desired returns. This situation drives companies with a strong balance sheet, solid cash flow, and a lack of compelling new investment opportunities to undertake share-repurchase programs.

Certainly, though, there are other ways to return excess cash to shareholders than through share repurchases. In fact, year after year companies distribute billions of dollars to investors through regular and special dividend distributions. Therefore, why should a company choose to repurchase shares instead of paying out dividends? Because in the United States shareholders pay less taxes on gains from share repurchases than they do on dividend distributions. Given the tax benefit shareholders receive from share repurchases, one might expect companies to always choose to distribute cash in the form of repurchases instead of dividends. This is not the case, however. Most companies undergoing stock-repurchase programs continue their dividend payments.[3]

Investors often choose to buy the stock of a particular company because of the expected regular income that the company pays out in dividends. If a company were to halt its dividend payments, those investors would be upset about the loss of dividend income. Most companies therefore continue to pay their regular dividend and opt to use repurchases for larger, one-time cash distributions. If a company has an unusually large amount of cash, it may not choose to increase dividend payments because it does not want to set a precedent for higher future dividends.[4]

Increase the Proportion of Debt in the Capital Structure

When companies decide to increase the proportion of debt in their capital structures, they often use share repurchases to make the change, a process called *decapitalization*.[5] This follows from the example presented earlier, in which increasing the proportion of debt to equity in the capital structure lowered the firm's cost of capital. While this illustration might suggest that taking on more and more debt would relentlessly decrease the firm's cost of capital, this is not the case. A company's equity becomes more costly as the company takes on more debt. The cost of equity increases slowly for initial increases in debt and then much more quickly as the company takes on excessive levels of debt. It is precisely this phenomenon that creates an optimal mix of debt and equity for a company.[6]

Signal Management's Confidence in the Company's Stock

Stock repurchases also may be used to signal confidence in the future of the company. For example, stock prices plummeted on Black Monday, October 19, 1987, and the next day many companies announced large share repurchases. Citicorp was the first to announce a share-repurchase plan of $250 million, but many other companies followed quickly. In fact, within 2 days of the crash, firms announced a total of $6.2 billion in share repurchases as management and boards attempted to regain market confidence.[7] To underscore the shareholders' and management's commitment to the company's future, senior management and directors usually hold onto their stock when companies offer to repurchase their stock at a premium.[8]

Deter a Takeover Attempt

A company may choose to use share repurchases to deter a takeover attempt. Share repurchases protect a company from a hostile takeover in three ways.[9] First, the repurchase may persuade shareholders not to tender their shares in a takeover. Second, the share repurchase alters voting rights within a firm, making it more difficult to acquire the firm. Third, a repurchase removes the shareholders with the lowest threshold price, thereby making it more expensive to buy the remaining shares.

Methods for Share Repurchase

There are three principal ways to repurchase stock.[10] The most common is for the firm to announce that it plans to buy its stock in the open market. Alternatively, a company can buy back a stated number of shares at a fixed price, which is typically set at about 20 percent above the current market level. Shareholders can choose whether or not to accept this offer. Finally, a company can undertake a share repurchase via direct negotiation with one or more major shareholders. The most notorious examples of these negotiations are greenmail transactions that occur when the target of a takeover attempts to buy off the hostile bidder by repurchasing any shares that it has acquired.

Market Reaction to Share Repurchases

When a share repurchase is announced, the market tends to react positively, and the share price rises, as would be expected. By reducing the number of shares outstanding through a share repurchase, the company lowers the denominator in the earnings-per-share (EPS) calculation, thereby increasing EPS (see Exhibit 9-8 for an example). Because the performance of the company has not changed materially with the share repurchase, it is reasonable to expect the market to apply the existing price-earnings (P/E) multiple to the EPS. Because the postrepurchase EPS is higher, the stock price should rise accordingly. The fundamentals of the company have not changed, so the total market value (share price times the number of shares outstanding) should remain the same.

Exhibit 9·-8

The Impact of Share Repurchases on Share Price

Before Stock Repurchase	
Net income ($)	500,000,000
Shares outstanding	300,000,000
Earnings per share ($)	1.67
Price-earnings (P/E) ratio	20×
Share price ($)	*33.33*
Market value ($)	10,000,000,000
After Stock Repurchase (Assume Company Bought 50 Million Shares)	
Net income ($)	500,000,000
Shares outstanding	250,000,000
Earnings per share ($)	2.00
Price-earnings (P/E) ratio	20×
Implied share price ($)	*40.00*
Increase in share price	20 percent
Market value ($)	10,000,000,000

Restructuring to Improve Shareholder Value

If a company's businesses are well positioned, compete in attractive industries, and are well managed, corporate management must accept the results they produce. If it is believed that the unit could be managed better, then a management change is in order. In the final analysis, corporate performance is determined largely by the aggregate performance potential of the firm's several business units. This is, of course, predicated on the premise that corporate overhead is in line with that of other well-run companies. No degree of divisional excellence in performance can overcome the negative effects of a bloated, out-of-control level of corporate overhead expenses and/or punitive interest charges brought on by excessive levels of corporate debt.

SUMMARY

In summary, the strategic problems or opportunities for the board and the chief executive officer (CEO) can be encapsulated in the following questions:

- In what businesses should the firm compete?
- Should the company be restructured through acquisitions and/or divestitures?
- How should the company's ongoing operations be financed?
- Is the level of corporate expenses consistent with that of other well-run companies?

The board and the CEO thus face a set of unique problems and opportunities. The more diversified the corporation, the more difficult it is for directors and corporate executives to understand the detailed problems and opportunities faced by its operating divisions. There is a fundamental axiom for directors: problems are always accompanied by opportunities. Most of us would consider the divestiture of several divisions of a large company to be drastic, to the point of being unthinkable. However, we should recall Vignette 7-1 that reported the significant gains in shareholder value that resulted for General Dynamics Corporation from divesting numerous businesses, leading to a more focused corporation.

Thus effective corporate strategies frequently involve thinking the unthinkable. The greatest unknowns in strategy formulation, and in decision making in general, are the likely actions or reactions of competitors and the firm's own ability to execute. Any restructuring moves a company makes will be carried out in an atmosphere of intense competitor reaction and a risky internal morale climate. The preferences of investors and influential analysts for focus and corporate clarity, however, have led many firms to restructure their businesses, unlocking extensive value for their shareholders.

We now move on to discuss in Chapter 10 the numerous external events with which a board has to contend and the pitfalls boards must avoid.

REVIEW QUESTIONS

1. What are the advantages and disadvantages of the various forms of business organization?
2. Why is the corporate form the dominant one?
3. What factors determine the best choice between a business being private or public?
4. Why is a business's capital structure so important to its success?
5. What are the results expectations for companies striving to be considered premium companies?
6. What strategies are available to boards and CEOs to restructure their companies?

CHAPTER 10

Dealing with External Pressures

A public company operates in a fishbowl, under vast scrutiny and exposed to a wide range of external pressures. The board of a public company, therefore, must learn to function effectively in such an environment on a continuous basis. The company normally can trace some of the pressures to its own actions or inaction, but to a large extent, they are attributable to forces beyond the company's control and often must be addressed without delay. Many pressures are time-consuming, some are embarrassing, others are infuriating, and on the whole, the board would prefer not to have to deal with them. They are disquieting to board members who would much prefer to move along in relative obscurity. External pressures may challenge not only the board's patience but also its resolve, making the position of a director of a public company something for those who are not faint-hearted.

Consider the wide range of uncontrollable, external events that routinely complicate the work of boards of directors. For example, recent years have seen a rise in the number of organizations engaged in shareholder activism and in the intensity of their attempts to interfere with the normal processes of board oversight. Other examples include the offers that may appear at any time for the company to merge with one suitor or to sell out to another, occasionally in the form of a hostile takeover bid rather than a friendly solicitation. These gambits have increased in frequency and in size as the financial community has provided the capability to finance larger and larger deals. When the overtures are friendly in nature, the board has the luxury of dealing with them in a thoughtful, deliberative way. In other circumstances, offers may have a very short fuse and must be dealt with in a less than relaxed, more adversarial fashion.

External pressures can come to bear in certain situations in the form of shareholder dissatisfaction. One such circumstance involves board entrenchment, which results when the board appoints and reappoints members from a close group that gradually, over time, gains control of the board, often in alliance with the chief executive officer (CEO). Likewise, the pressure of dissatisfaction can come when directors have multiple board memberships. Over the past few years, there has been an escalation in the fees paid to directors of public companies and a parallel rise in the number of boards on which certain directors serve. Individual investors, investment analysts, major institutional shareholders, and governmental regulatory bodies all point out the implied risk of casual involvement on the part of overcommitted directors to the important affairs of multiple companies.

Pressures also may arise when it is necessary to determine who will survive the natural reductions that attend the amalgamation of companies through mergers. When two companies merge, or when one company acquires another, there is usually a reduction in the number of directors as the two boards are consolidated. This process of reduction or consolidation is vital in determining who will control the new company. Each of these situations brings scrutiny to the workings of the board(s) with regard to details that the directors would prefer to keep private because they are subject to the spotlight of public interest, examination, and possibly criticism. While such scrutiny may be undesired by the directors, it is frequently a constructive force in bringing about better governance processes and decisions.

As we have described previously, the board sometimes has to deal with aggressive investors (either individuals or groups) who purchase a significant portion of the company's shares in an attempt to begin a process leading to a hostile takeover. In certain instances, for the right price, the hostile investor group may be persuaded to sell its significant level of shares back to the company for a handsome premium over the price at which the shares were purchased originally. This process was given the name *greenmail* as its occurrence became more frequent.

Dissident shareholders have a means through the process of the proxy statements (usually annually) to suggest basic changes to the company's policies or even to influence the process by which directors are nominated and elected. Such conflicts are termed *proxy fights* and involve much rancor on both sides of the quarrel. In the end, such fights are resolved by the highly sought-after votes of shareholders.

The board also must contend with class-action lawsuits, which may be brought by shareholders, customers (with regard to product safety), suppliers (over procurement agreements), governmental regulatory agencies (over compliance with laws and regulations), or even activist groups (on behalf of the environment or seeking the removal or replacement of a board perceived to be weak).

Finally, there are unpredictable and limitless sets of crises that may arise at any time without warning. The board must be at the ready to deal with any and all of these perturbations that may appear. In general, crises requiring board response can be divided into three broad categories:

- Shareholder actions directed at the board
- Hostile takeovers
- Regulatory actions

SHAREHOLDER ACTIVISM

At the beginning of the last century, in an admittedly gentler time, many people accepted the status quo with regard to most public institutions. In recent years, though, there has been a growing tendency for activists of one sort or another to seek change. As a proven example, agitation by activists brought about extensive changes in the area of ensuring a safe supply of food and drugs for the U.S. population. These activists were successful in pointing out the prevalence of unhealthy conditions in the preparation of food and drugs and in the basic ingredients from which they were produced. These unsavory conditions were seen to result from the unbridled greed of capitalists, often monopolists, who, in the pursuit of higher profits, resorted to unseemly practices and procedures. Through numerous changes in both state and federal laws, and through the establishment of the Food and Drug Administration, the activists succeeded in establishing suitable standards for these important aspects of our lives. They also succeeded in setting in place regulatory bodies to ensure compliance by companies engaged in the affected industries and in levying civil and criminal legal penalties on those who attempted to thwart the standards.

Issues around Labor Relations

In the area of labor relations, activists exposed less than sterling practices on the part of companies in the areas of child labor, minimum wage practices, minimum safety and health standards in work environments, and a reasonable length of the work week. These abuses were so apparent that they eventually led to legal protection for most workers with regard to these basic workplace characteristics.

The existence of trade unions and their rights to represent workers were prescribed through laws, as were standards for a healthy and safe workplace, a reasonable length of the work week (through laws requiring the payment of overtime for work beyond 40 hours in a week), and a federally mandated minimum wage. While the unions were instrumental in fighting the early battles for these basic rights, the continued need for unions has been diminished because the laws and regulations that have been established apply to nonunion as well as union situations. As more and more of these conflicts, originally espoused by unions in very difficult situations, have become legal and regulatory entitlements, the perceived need for unions has declined. Thus the total percentage of eligible workers belonging to unions has been declining steadily for the last 50 years or so.

Issues around Full Disclosure

In a similar way, activists representing shareholders and other pressure groups have increasingly come to question the activities of boards and the companies they oversee in areas related to shareholder fraud, legally required disclosure of appropriate facts and figures, conflicts of interest on the part of directors, and the carrying out of the other duties of directors. For instance, over the past decade, as the use of stock options has grown as a form of incentive payment for CEOs, other executives, and board members, regulations have been put in place that provide shareholders much more accurate information about the present and possible future value of stock options awarded to directors and executives. One of the basic tenets of American capitalism, with the shares of thousands of companies listed on the major stock exchanges, is that all investors and potential investors (the public) should have access to the same information regarding all aspects of the operations of these companies.

Thus it has been made illegal to engage in *insider trading*, where one or a few people have and use so-called inside knowledge of pending events not known to the public at large. The entire body of legal requirements and regulations has been put into place gradually over many decades in response to the sequential appearance of newly perceived threats to free markets. It is a sort of thrust and parry in fencing terms, in which each new threat to full disclosure is met by a countermeasure intended to restore the availability of full information to all members of the public.

The latest developments involving ENRON and other companies with regard to the use of apparently legal partnerships to both shield profits from taxes and remove significant debts from the balance sheets of listed companies surely will lead to further tightening of the legal requirements and regulations on such disclosures. Unfortunately, the boards, CEOs, and senior managers of companies who perpetrate such acts in the first instance often cannot be prosecuted criminally or held personally liable because the laws and regulations invariably follow the occurrence of severely adverse consequences. In the case of widespread public disclosure of especially reprehensible acts and unfortunate outcomes for numerous people, the Congress, and the major government agencies may lead shareholder activists in the push for reforms.

Proxy Fights

When there are strong differences between a board and a company's shareholders as to the strategy being followed, the financial results of the firm, the long-term outlook, or a proposed merger or acquisition, the stage is set for a proxy fight. The fight occurs when the board sends out its proxy statement for which it seeks shareholder approval of a variety of intended actions. Disenchanted shareholders may institute a public fight against the board's proposals. These fights take the form of mailings to shareholders, advertisements in widely read newspapers, or even the initiation of lawsuits. The board has an advantage in such situations because it can use company funds to promote its preferred course of action.

The process of a proxy fight was thoroughly illustrated by the hard-fought proxy battle between the Hewlett Packard Corporation and some dissident shareholders over its proposed acquisition of Compaq Corporation in 2002. Almost every aspect of proxy fights played out in this prolonged, classic struggle which pitted the board and its CEO against a disaffected director who represented a major group of shareholders. In the end, after an acrimonious public squabble, the shareholders voted to support the board's and the CEO's proposed acquisition of Compaq, a decision that actually went into the courts and was upheld.

Class-Action Lawsuits

The use of lawsuits brought against companies has increased dramatically in recent years, consistent with the growth of litigiousness in society. Class-action lawsuits have been brought into the courts on behalf of environmental activists, groups of individuals who feel they have been denied fundamental rights by companies and large numbers of people who claim to have been hurt as a result of negligence on the part of manufacturers who have delivered allegedly unsafe products. The possibility of such lawsuits reminds boards of directors that all of their actions are subject to scrutiny by all parties interested in their operations.

EXTERNAL EVENTS AND BOARD MEMBERSHIP

As we described earlier, poor performance by the board and the company can lead to outside pressures to reform the governance of the company, creating a pivotal point in time for the board and the CEO. If the reaction to the criticism is open and responsive, such pressures can lead to effective reform. If the reaction, however, is defensive, the board and the CEO may retrench by replacing any board members who leave or retire with additional close friends who will assist in perpetuating the status quo. The term *retrenchment* has come to signify such courses of action. It usually leads to a continuing spiral of poor decisions and poor company performance that only can be corrected by the process of a hostile takeover, as described earlier.

Other instances when external events affect board membership include situations in which an acquisition of a company that is similar in size to the acquiring company takes place or two companies of similar sizes or market values merge. In these cases, given that the optimal size of a company's board is usually thought to be from 12 to 15 members, and given that each company has a board of the proper size, the new board of the surviving company will need only about half the current directors. Many of the decisions as to which directors will be retained follow from the perceptions of their relative experience and expertise. It is also understandable that the CEO of the surviving entity will want a majority of directors on whom he or she can depend for support in building the new company and carrying out the agreed-upon strategy. It is logical that directors' and CEOs' views of potential mergers or acquisitions would be tempered by their perceptions of their likely positions in the hierarchy of directors that would result if the merger or acquisition were to occur. The actual structure of the new board (the number and identity of directors from each company) is usually stipulated in the merger or acquisition documents.

FRIENDLY MERGERS VERSUS HOSTILE TAKEOVERS

Opportunities for companies to consider the advantages and disadvantages of friendly mergers, acquisitions, and/or divestitures arise often in the normal context of conducting business. In many industries, U.S. companies have found themselves in a fragmented competitive situation in which no firm has the economies of scale inherent in the industry structure of larger foreign competitors. The recognition of such situations has led the boards and CEOs of numerous companies to simultaneously arrive at the conclusion that the consolidation of two or more smaller firms would provide the missing economies of scale. Commencing discussions about friendly consolidations can take place over lunch, on the golf course, or at an industry conference.

When both parties are already thinking along the same lines regarding the desirability of a merger, agreements often can be reached very quickly, lessening the trauma to the employees, lenders, suppliers, customers, and shareholders of both companies. The announcements of such friendly mergers often include most details regarding the financial terms on which the merger will be completed, along with the degree of synergy expected in the consolidation. The word *synergy* in this context should be interpreted to mean primarily the number of employees who will no longer be needed, whose release will provide a concurrent reduction in operating costs, which, in turn, will allow the surviving company to pay a premium for the shares of the acquired company. Such friendly mergers also minimize the legal and investment banking fees associated with such transactions. Vignette 10-1 describes the delicate balancing act a board must conduct between shareholder and stakeholder interests in handling a hostile takeover bid.

VIGNETTE 10-1

BALANCING CEO, BOARD, AND SHAREHOLDER INTERESTS AFTER A HOSTILE TAKEOVER BID

THE ISSUE

CEOs and members of boards of directors naturally become comfortable in their positions of power and authority. As directors, they have the duty to represent and act in the best interests of the shareholders; however, many find that regardless of what is best for the company's stockholders, it would be difficult to support a lucrative hostile takeover bid that ultimately might leave the CEO without a job.

THE SITUATION

A regional energy company was approached recently by a competitor with an offer to purchase all its outstanding shares for cash in the amount of $63 per share. Two weeks later, the target company rejected this bid and announced that it would make its own unsolicited proposal to acquire another competitor for $9 billion. This unsolicited bid was rejected one month later, and the company chose to walk away from the proposed deal. Fifteen days after the energy company withdrew its offer to purchase the third party, its competitor

Continued

Continued

seized on the opportunity to take its original bid directly to the company's shareholders. The competitor released a letter indicating an offer of $68 cash per share and citing numerous benefits to a combination. The offer represented a 31 percent premium over the average closing share price of the target company's common stock for the preceding 20 trading days and a premium to the all-time high stock price.

THE BOARD'S ACTIONS

The target company's management responded immediately that the company was "not for sale and was not interested in any merger transaction in which another company would acquire control." The board then made this decision official by unanimously rejecting the offer and adding, "The decision not to pursue this proposal is final." The company further indicated that the offer did not fully reflect its expected earnings potential.

The competitor did not give up, however, and instead met with industry analysts and actively courted the target company's institutional investors. In response, the target company's board strongly recommended that shareholders oppose the takeover attempt by not tendering shares to this competitor. The board then authorized a $400 million buyback of shares and increased its change in control benefits or "golden parachutes," approving new severance packages for the CEO and other senior executives totaling in the tens of millions of dollars. Other tactics the board employed in its defense included

- Appealing to and agitating local politicians
- Dangling prospects of a "white knight" rescuer
- Purchasing full-page newspaper ads in communities served by its competitor to warn them darkly about the competitor's "disturbing environmental record"
- Defending against lawsuits brought by the competitor

THE RESULTS

None of these actions convinced the unwanted bidder to go away. Instead, the competitor announced that it had received pledges for

Continued

Concluded

60 percent of the outstanding common stock and that it would extend its cash offer for 2 months. The competitor then dramatically increased the pressure by raising its hostile bid to $74 per share and clearing room in its boardroom and executive suites for current target company board members. The target company board promptly rejected this sweetened proposal but a few weeks later decided to put the firm on the auction block by disclosing talks with other potential bidders. The company sent the competitor a proposed confidentiality agreement and invited it into the auction process.

Unfortunately, this proved to be a difficult time to be on the block. Interest rates and oil price increases, along with a mild winter, fueled a slide in the hostile bidder's stock, which fell by 43 percent as the industry index slid 28 percent during the same period. As a result, the competitor officially withdrew its $74 per share hostile bid, ultimately lowering its final bid for the company. With industry stocks beaten down, the preliminary bids from other suitors never materialized, and the company was left with little choice but to accept this reduced bid.

THE POINT

Thus, after approximately 7 months and $15 million in legal fees, the company accepted a merger offer from the competitor valued at $6 billion in cash, or $70 per share for the company's common equity. Asked why the company did not simply accept the $74 per share cash offer 4 months earlier, the CEO said that the board decided to "check what was out there and get the best price." Obviously, there is some pain in relinquishing control to a rival. A public company, however, can only delay a reasoned consideration of a lucrative hostile bid for so long before stockholders become actively involved and demand a vote.

Hostile transactions come about when an aggressor company attempts to take over another company without the consent of its board. The suitor may have acquired on the open market the percentage of the company's shares at which a public disclosure is legally required. The company then must state whether it has acquired the shares strictly as an investment or whether it intends to seek to acquire a majority of the shares of the target company, effectively taking it over. If a hostile takeover is the intention, the target company may employ a variety of defensive measures, some of which were mentioned earlier. The laws vary from state to state, but the act of a potential acquirer making a firm offer to buy the shares of a company at some premium price over the current market price of the shares also may precipitate the conduct of an auction. The end result of the auction is to achieve the best possible exit price for the shareholders. In these cases, the board is no longer able to deflect the hostile offer and simply must try to use the leverage of the auction to get the best possible transaction price.

In hostile takeover situations, as a consequence of the bitterness that results from the combative process, most of the management, including the CEO, and most of the board usually will be displaced. This brings to mind one of the advantages of hostile takeovers from a governance perspective. Many companies have been found to have weak boards, CEOs, and management teams, which is readily apparent to informed industry analysts, potential investors, and current shareholders. In many cases, it is virtually impossible to displace the underperforming board and CEO because the board has come under the control of the CEO through the gradual appointment of a majority of the board who are cronies of the CEO.

Hostile takeovers are, in fact, one of the few mechanisms by which an inept board and its misguided governance can be removed. If the performance is poor enough and the share price drops low enough, it will be in the best traditions of our competitive system for a stronger, better-managed company to take over the firm via the mechanism of a hostile takeover. This process invariably leads to a premium being paid for the shares over the current market price, providing a more favorable exit for unfortunate or fortunate shareholders, depending on their point of view. In the case of a stock transaction, the shareholders may have an option to convert their shares into shares of the acquiring firm, providing for a possible future upside to their investment and avoiding the tax consequences of a sale of the shares for cash.

In the final analysis, hostile takeovers can be advantageous or deleterious, depending on one's point of view. They also provide the ultimate safety valve for the shareholders of poorly managed, underperforming companies. They are the final arbiters of the effectiveness with which the board and the CEO of a company perform. In the case of a superbly governed and managed company with strong, consistent financial results, the market will value the company at a level that will inhibit all suitors except those willing to pay the highest possible price. Even then, the existing shareholders will have the right, through their votes, to accept or reject any offer. The operative rule is for the company to produce and compete effectively or perish. This is one of the principal strengths of our capitalist system of competition.

Poison Pills

As we described earlier, attempted hostile takeovers began to accelerate in number in the 1970s. Some of the most venerable companies in the United States were targets of these aggressive takeover attempts. As one would expect in our highly competitive capitalist system, the boards of many companies were unwilling to acquiesce to unwelcome overtures but were groping for an effective means of at least being able to control the process of assessing options for the best long-term interests of their shareholders. Otherwise, the aggressive suitor could make an unsolicited offer for the shares at some premium to the current share price but significantly less than the intrinsic value of the company and win a vote of the shareholders eager for a fast gain on their shares.

The legal community came to the rescue by devising the highly effective "poison pill." This stratagem works through a company's capital structure to thwart hostile takeovers. The board and the shareholders adopt a plan providing that, when an unwanted agency acquires a given percentage of the company's shares, there is an automatic triggering of the release of a very large number of stock options for each of the prior shareholders at a very low price, say, one penny. This process would dilute the value of the holdings of the unwanted suitor so effectively that such a poison pill has never been triggered. This countermeasure has effectively removed the possibility of a hostile takeover when adopted by a company.

We could ask why most companies do not have such a defense mechanism. Some companies simply do not want to deter the possibility of an auction, especially when the board or the shareholders are unhappy with the performance of the CEO and the company. The boards of some companies may have sought the approval of shareholders for such a plan, only to have it rejected by unhappy shareholders. Finally, some boards may think that their companies are immune to such takeovers because of their size or their strong performance and related strong share price. It is difficult to enact such countermeasures after a bid for the company has been received because of the need to secure shareholder approval, unless it is a part of the proxy materials prepared in anticipation of the annual meeting of shareholders. It has thus become commonplace for boards to put poison pills into their capital structures well before there are any takeover attempts.

White Knights

In the event that an effective poison pill is not in effect, a company may find itself totally defenseless against an unwanted takeover attempt. If the company's shares are felt to be underpriced, there is little to prevent a suitor from making a tender offer for the shares at a price the shareholders may be reluctant to turn down. The board may feel that the aggressor has ulterior motives, such as a breakup and selloff of the company's assets, which would make some other alternative best for the company. The board may then proceed to seek out other possible acquirers for the company, perhaps a firm that has approached the company previously or one that the board feels would be a better strategic fit. Underlying this strategy would be a strong desire to achieve the best possible price for the shareholders of the company, which would be more likely to result from an auction.

While the board, in the end, would have to accept the best offer, the board still might have the final say on the future direction of the company if the final offers are close or differ in important ways. For instance, two offers might appear to have similar prices for the company's shares, but an all-cash offer might be preferred to a stock offer or a mix of cash and stock. Similarly, multiple offers requiring risky financing would be judged on the strength of the financing and the perceived ultimate value to shareholders. The firm invited into the contest by the target company has come to be called a "white knight." Companies approached in this way have an edge in the bidding process and in the ultimate decision because the board of the target company has a great deal of control over the give and take of closing out the deal. While the board may not be able to prevent the company from being taken over, it may, in the end, thwart the intentions of the company that originated the hostile takeover attempt.

Greenmail

As we have noted, over the past two decades a new form of corporate predator has become well known to the investing public. These aggressive investors may be individuals or corporate entities. Their modus operandi is for the aggressor to begin to buy shares in a target company. After some time period, if the total accumulation of shares acquired reaches some stipulated percentage of the total shares outstanding, the aggressor company must file a form with the Securities and Exchange Commission (SEC) announcing the firm's intentions regarding the target company. The intention may be to hold the shares as an investment without any intent to interfere in the management of the company. However, the intention may be to continue to acquire other shares and seek control of the company.

Alternatively, the intention may be to hold the shares, seek a position on the board, and otherwise attempt to influence the governance of the target company. The target may be chosen for its general and prolonged poor performance, for a perceived weak board and/or CEO, or for a disparity between the actual value of the firm or its assets and the prevailing market value of the company. The aggressor (whether an individual or a company) essentially sees opportunities to gain in market value by removing the board and/or the CEO, whether the acquirer keeps the governance structure in place or not. These instigators of mischief came to be called *raiders* in the press and in the general business vernacular.

Raiders present a slightly different approach from the attempt at a hostile takeover. They may or may not seriously want to take over and run the target company. On some occasions, the board and the CEO of the target company, in order to be rid of the potential threat the aggressor may pose, will negotiate to repurchase the shares held by the raider for some premium above their acquisition cost. The raider thus walks away with a rather fast and sometimes handsome premium on its investment. These transactions came to be called *greenmail*, the term emanating from the similarity of the process to *blackmail*, a rather well-understood term. The difference is that greenmail is not illegal, as long as all security laws and regulations are scrupulously observed.

While this process is not universally admired, it is in the spirit of the competitive free enterprise system of capitalism under which we live. The free market in the shares of public companies, together with the rules about any agency acquiring certain levels of shareholdings, makes this form of pressure quite legal. This gambit is not without its risk for the raider, though. The board of the target simply may ignore the raider group, leaving it to the fate of all minority shareholders, or it might institute some procedure in its capital structure that would effectively dilute the ownership of the raider, thus inflicting upon the raider significant financial losses.

REGULATORY AGENCIES

In addition to the pressure brought by shareholders and hostile acquirers, boards experience the scrutiny of regulatory agencies. The primary agencies overseeing public companies are the federal Securities and Exchange Commission and the related state corporation commissions. They are interested in timely, accurate, and complete disclosure of information designed to maintain orderly and fair markets. When fraud is detected, the justice system comes into play with criminal proceedings. As with all businesses, the Internal Revenue Service, the Federal Trade Commission

(FTC), and other similar governmental agencies require compliance with regulations and standards. Perhaps the most active among the agencies in recent years has been the Environmental Protection Agency (EPA). A significant number of commissions oversee specific industries, such as the Federal Reserve Bank and the Comptroller of the Currency, which regulate banks, and the Federal Communications Commission, which has seen its purview expand with the explosion of wireless communications and data-exchange media. Transportation and utilities are also examples of industries that have been closely regulated.

SUMMARY

In addition to the ongoing task of overseeing the complex operations of the company, we have seen in this chapter that numerous external and uncontrollable forces greatly complicate the agendas of boards of public companies. Responses to external events are often more important to the survival of the company than the routine operations. Thus directors must have a practical capability to deal effectively when these unpredictable perturbations. Individuals who are uncomfortable when dealing with the unexpected may find themselves unsuited for board service.

We next discuss in Chapter 11 the ways in which directors may find themselves in trouble.

REVIEW QUESTIONS

1. What are the most prevalent external pressures that boards face?
2. What is the important role proxy fights play in the corporate governance process?
3. What special duties and responsibilities for directors accompany hostile takeover offers?
4. What is the role of poison pills, white knights, and greenmail in the process of dealing with hostile takeover attempts?
5. What is the responsibility of the board in the climate of increasing scrutiny from governmental regulatory agencies?

CHAPTER 11

How Directors Get into Trouble

A review of the popular press reveals that corporate directors occasionally get into trouble. What do we mean by trouble? There are numerous answers to this question, with some occurring more frequently than others. Notable forms of trouble occur when the corporation does not produce acceptable results, perhaps placing it in fiscal jeopardy, or violates the civil or criminal law and is sued or prosecuted for its actions. Directors can get into trouble because of individual actions, and they also can get into trouble as a group, which means that directors want to be careful about those with whom they associate. They also can get in as much trouble, individually and collectively, from the things they did not do that they should have done as from having done things they should not have done.

What makes being a director even more perilous is that often it is not what one has or has not done as much as how things have worked out that determines how a situation is evaluated. This implies that a single course of action may be deemed right at one juncture and wrong at another, depending on the accompanying circumstances. Frequently, as the nature of the business and the relevant issues evolve over time, the requisite knowledge and experience for board service change, and once-competent directors can become relatively less so. As a result of these many factors, performing effectively as a director can be a difficult, demanding, and somewhat risky task. It is easy to get into trouble, particularly in today's litigious society. We will break the discussion of these challenges into four parts:

- Avoiding a bad situation
- Potential individual problems
- Potential collective problems
- Directors' exposure to litigation and prosecution

In closing this chapter, we will suggest proactive measures board members may take to stay out of trouble.

AVOIDING A BAD SITUATION

Avoiding a potentially troublesome situation is a most important aim for boards because problems can be avoided in the first place more easily than they can be solved after they are apparent.

Understanding Motivations for Board Service

The first and most prevalent reason that directors get into trouble is that they allow themselves to be drawn into wrong situations. There are a variety of motives for joining a board. They include friendships, potential economic gain, networking, learning and exposure, and for many, enhanced prestige. None of these motives is negative, but it is important that the motives of the aspirant director are compatible with the existing corporate situation. People who are attractive board candidates generally have full calendars and must set priorities for the use of their time. They should consider carefully whether membership on the board of a particular organization fulfills their objectives as well as or better than service on another board or some other use of their time.

Due Diligence: Understanding the Situation

An important rule for recruited board candidates is to know well those with whom they will be associating, recognizing the potential to be judged by the company they keep. If a board candidate does not share common values and objectives with the other directors, it is unlikely that he or she could have a positive relationship with the board. If those in control at the company are not forthright and trustworthy, the potential for trouble is great. There is a basic asymmetry in access to information between management and directors, with the board dependent on the chief executive officer (CEO) for full, accurate, and timely information. There is often a similar information gap between controlling directors and less involved directors. In the end, new directors will, of necessity, need to count on those with the relevant information for full and honest disclosure of the issues about which a director needs to know. New directors cannot assume honesty on behalf of the other members of the board simply because they have no knowledge of dishonesty. It is important that board candidates know the current board members and their reputations well enough to know the degree to which they can be trusted. In effect, the person being considered to be a director must come to a positive conclusion regarding the honesty and integrity of those already on the board rather than simply relying on the absence of a negative impression.

Along with integrity, the other members of the board also must demonstrate unquestioned competence. The candidate for the board must have absolute confidence in the judgment and experience of each director. If an aspirant director does not respect the competence of the directors and is not confident that they are capable of fulfilling their responsibilities, he or she should decline the opportunity to join the board.

Understanding the Responsibilities and Duties of a Director

A second part of the due diligence process for board candidates is to understand clearly why they, as individuals, are being invited to join a board. They should determine what the board's expectations of them are as directors and whether these expectations are consistent with their objectives, available time, and competencies. It is essential that board candidates have confidence in their abilities to deliver on the board's expectations, or they may end up in a situation where they are unable to be effective or possibly where they can be effective only at great personal sacrifice.

In addition to the specific demands of the current situation, board candidates also need to understand the legal obligations regarding their duties as directors, as well as the attendant limitations. These limitations include restrictions on directors' ability to buy and sell stock in the company and their freedom to reveal information they become aware of as insiders. Failure on the part of a new director to understand these legal requirements can lead to serious consequences.

Understanding Individual Limitations

Once a board candidate understands the situation of the firm, the organization's expectations in terms of contributions, and the time required to commit to the effort, the candidate must make an honest assessment of whether the proposed board service fits with his or her personal expectations and limitations. The candidate should take stock of his or her strengths and weaknesses, as well as the demands on his or her time, as part of this assessment. In the end, the responsibility for understanding the requirements of the director appointment lie with the candidate and should be taken seriously.

POTENTIAL INDIVIDUAL PROBLEMS

A director always should act with integrity. This means not only honest behavior but also ethical behavior. Blatantly dishonest behavior, such as stealing and outright lying, is universally frowned upon. Much unethical behavior, however, is excused with a "business is business" attitude. Common behaviors in this latter category include the abuse of power in a situation to drive a hard bargain and the attitude of *caveat emptor*, or "buyer beware," when products do not live up to perceived or agreed-upon standards.

It is not always easy to determine when and where one crosses the line from behavior appropriate for a good, tough businessperson to that of an unethical opportunist and eventually to that of a dishonest scoundrel. There are conventional norms to guide us in judging behavior, but often the degree of acceptability depends on one's point of observation and personal values. Some people, though, drift into unethical behavior because of arrogance, selfishness, or greed. These individuals either lack the introspection to understand their personal weaknesses, or they have not yet developed a strong enough set of values to deplore unsavory acts. This type of person does not make a good director because being a director means, at its core, representing others. A director has a fiduciary obligation to act in the best interests of the shareholders of the firm.

It is essential that a director grasp the seriousness of this fiduciary obligation and act accordingly. There is a wonderful dictum, "Let me be true for there are those who trust me." A director is in a position of trust and must place his or her obligations above personal interests. This means that it is essential to avoid conflicts of interest that force the director to make a painful or costly choice. If such a conflict exists, real or perceived, a director first should disclose it to all concerned and second should not participate in any deliberations or decisions that relate to the conflicted position. A director can get into trouble when the conflict is not disclosed and the director does not excuse himself or herself from the discussions and/or decision. A good maxim for a director is, "When in doubt, always fully disclose."

Conflicts can be either situational, such as when a director is on the board of a competing company, or temporary, transaction-driven events, such as the sale of property to or other dealings with a close friend or relative. Sometimes directors are selected specifically because they represent some particular interest, frequently that of a major shareholder or shareholder group. The problem for such a director is that under the law, every director represents all the shareholders as a group. Conflict may arise if the director repeatedly has a narrow agenda reflecting the interests of the sponsoring shareholders, such as trying to gain control of the company by buying up shares or by making a hostile takeover offer.

A second broad area of concern to the individual director is staying properly informed about the affairs of the business. As mentioned previously, the relevant legal requirement for a director is the duty of care, which was described in Chapter 2. In practical terms, the duty of care requires directors to take care to understand the business and the major issues that it faces. Equally important, it encompasses a director's knowing the capabilities of the CEO and the key senior managers and judging their competence in dealing with the prevailing issues and running the business. Executing this duty does not come through passivity, where the director simply relies on what management chooses to tell him or her. Rather, the director must proactively engage in the work of the board and in particular confirm that the company has a strong management team in place, especially an effective CEO. The individual director must then be sure that the CEO provides, on an ongoing basis, a thorough assessment of the company's competitive and financial situations. The director must be certain that he or she understands what is being said to the board and must press for answers when the information is difficult to understand or is incomplete or inaccurate. Ignorance is not an excuse for a director's failing to intervene in a situation involving inappropriate dealings.

Based on the director's individual assessment of the veracity of the information being provided, he or she must work with the CEO to establish mutually satisfactory goals that address the important issues before the board. The individual director must then systematically track performance against these corporate goals to his or her individual satisfaction. It is not enough to be a loyal member of the board. A director is not effective unless, as an individual, he or she is willing to challenge unsavory acts as they come to the attention of the board. When company performance falls short of meeting the specified goals, the director must work hard to understand why the shortfall in performance occurred and what response might be appropriate.

On the other hand, an active director can get into trouble or cause trouble by interfering with management's prerogatives. The process of the director proactively understanding the business, participating in the setting of goals, and monitoring progress must respect the very thin line between the roles of the board and management. Directors should be careful not to cross this line into attempting to micromanage the company.

One of the most important challenges for a director is an interpersonal one—developing a productive relationship with the CEO and key managers. How does one maintain a collaborative and open problem-solving relationship while at the same time preserving the independence necessary to judge the results? This task becomes even more difficult when the director and the CEO are or have become friends. One of the great temptations for the individual director is to rationalize poor performance because of loyalty to or concern for the manager.

While individual directors can get into trouble, typically due to conflicts of interest, it is more often how the board functions as a whole that determines the long-term potential for problems.

POTENTIAL COLLECTIVE BOARD PROBLEMS

There are many ways in which a board, collectively, can get into trouble. General causes of these disturbances include

- Conspiring in or tolerating legal violations
- Poor results that bring about the wrath of shareholders
- Lack of board leadership
- Internal political or personality conflict problems
- Ineffective board organization and processes
- Securities violations

Each of these topics is addressed below in turn.

Conspiring In or Tolerating Legal Violations

It should go without saying that all boards should avoid any violation of laws. The most culpable act of boards is to intentionally conspire to defraud investors or other stakeholders, but unintentional violations due to ignorance or lax oversight can be nearly equally troublesome. As many directors have found to their discomfort, severe problems can come from the act of tolerating legal violations within the organization. Ethical behavior is a product of cultural norms and internal controls, both of which begin in the boardroom. Directors must establish policies and maintain behaviors that set the ethical climate, and they must be ever vigilant in protecting that climate.

Poor Results That Bring on the Wrath of Shareholders

Board troubles often begin with someone's voicing a complaint. To counter complaints about financial performance, a board's best defense is to deliver strong, positive results. When this is done within the law, shareholders often ignore as irrelevant virtually every other board defect. The goal of the board must be to conduct itself so as to make the right decisions that, in turn, deliver favorable results, done in a manner consistent with a firm's values and in pursuit of its stated mission. An important issue for board members, then, becomes one of how to make good decisions. As we have noted previously, the board is responsible for a select series of important decisions regarding the firm's strategy and management. Each of these decisions must be managed well to avoid conflict and trouble.

A foundational decision for the board is selecting the business or businesses in which the firm will engage, preferably ones with great potential. Warren Buffett, CEO of Berkshire Hathaway and recognized investment expert, has said, "When a management with a reputation for brilliance tackles a business with a reputation for poor fundamental economics, it is the reputation of the business that stays intact."[1] Thus a board must understand the potential of each of its businesses and be very involved in and knowledgeable about all acquisition and divestiture decisions, as well as substantial capital allocations.

The second key decision of the board is the hiring of a competent and honest CEO to run the business, one with whom the board can establish an effective working relationship. The future results of the firm depend on the effectiveness of this decision. Even with unrivaled diligence and sound decision making, however, some shareholders may raise objections to the organization's chosen path. Board members should be prepared for dissonance at every turn.

When a firm is in a good business with a competent and ethical CEO, the actions or inactions of a board may cause poor results. There are a number of causes of poor results, and they are described below.

Lack of Leadership

A board is a group of human beings and, as such, is subject to all the dynamics found in any group. If the group lacks effective leadership, it is apt to make mistakes when confronted with difficult decisions. In the corporate setting, the greatest potential problem for the group that is the board arises when the leadership of the group comes from the CEO. If the leader of the group is also the key individual whose performance must be evaluated continually, obvious difficulties may arise. A large majority of publicly held companies currently have a combined CEO/chairman of the board structure, in which one executive holds both positions. This organization may appear to work well until the board has to evaluate the performance of the CEO or his or her recommendations on a crucial issue. The antidote to the situation in which the joint CEO/chairman position creates a dilemma is to separate the jobs of CEO and chairman of the board. If the two jobs are combined, the board should have a lead director or chairman of a committee of outside directors. This individual would manage the affairs of the board when it is dealing with the CEO.

Ideally, an effective board is a self-managed group in which, as colleagues, all collaborate and individual leadership rotates in an informal way depending on the issue and each director's expertise and interests. As in most situations, the ideal is not always attained. The board, to work as a group, must then rely on one or a few seasoned, experienced individuals whom the other board members respect and trust to keep it focused on its responsibilities. The danger, of course, is that the leadership will emerge as strong-willed individuals who strive to gain power and control rather than help the group to function more effectively.

Political or Personality Conflicts

When a board lacks effective group leadership, political or personality conflicts can develop that may prove very disruptive for the entire group. Such a conflict may be as simple as two members disliking each other or having severe conflicts of style or as complicated as the presence of competing cliques with very different agendas. Frequently, there is some dissident individual who is out of step with the group as a whole. This individual may have a different agenda than other members or simply a controlling personality that creates conflicts in a group setting. Strong group leadership is required to handle these kinds of problems and keep the board functioning effectively.

Typically, such political and personality problems are the result of flawed nominating processes. The wrong people become members of the board for the wrong reasons. This possibility emphasizes the need for an effective nominating or governance committee to manage the membership, structure, and performance of the board.

As noted previously, a significant element of the governance process should be a regular peer review of individual and collective board effectiveness. The best boards include some up-front training in how a group functions in general and how a board should function in particular. A board should reach a consensus regularly (or reconfirm previous agreements) on how the group is to operate and evaluate its individual and collective effectiveness. At least annually, the chairman of the nominating or governance committee should follow a formal process of interviewing or surveying the members of the board about individual and collective performance and report the results back to the entire board. If this process identifies problems, the board may be reluctant to confront the unpleasant realities. Board leadership should remain committed to improvement and recognize that one test of an effective group is its ability to deal openly with its problems.

When the behavior of a particular individual is disrupting the board, the ideal result is informal peer pressure from the other directors that confronts the problem and achieves a behavioral change on the part of the individual. If this kind of reconciliation is not obtained, the best alternative is for the individual to leave the board. A classic example of this problem was the situation that developed between Ross Perot and General Motors (GM). Perot had sold Electronic Data Services (EDS) to General Motors with the understanding that it would take over GM's management information systems. In addition, Perot was guaranteed membership on the board of GM while he continued to run EDS. This arrangement soon produced a very disgruntled Ross Perot and an equally disgruntled GM. While much of Perot's criticism appeared justified by GM's performance history, his approach to attempting to change the situation did not work. A strong resistance to change set in on both sides of the situation, and the two parties separated, with Perot leaving the GM board. GM had very little leverage with Perot because, as part of the deal in which GM purchased EDS, he had the right to remain on the board, regardless of his opposition to the other directors.

Ineffective Board Organization and Processes

If a company is in a good business, has an effective CEO, and has assembled strong directors who function as an effective group, the board must make sure that it organizes itself and its processes to produce effective results. Furthermore, regardless of whether strong results are achieved or not, the board should possess a record that demonstrates that it fulfilled all its legal duties. The board's organization and processes are very important in this regard.

Every board should have an effective committee structure through which much of the detailed work of the board is accomplished. The committees then bring actions or recommendations to the whole board, with the evidence of good advice and effective staff work. This kind of work within the board leads to a rule of reason that is more apt to produce good results than one that may be driven by good intent or even passion. If these appropriate structures and processes are in place, the board may still face problems. Too often boards concentrate on the trivial, usually because it is easy and gives the impression of activity. They tend to live in the past, reviewing, rehashing, and redoing. To be sure, one must understand how the company came to be in its current situation because there are lessons to be learned from the past. The principal focus of the board, however, must be on shaping the future and resolving substantive issues and policies. To accomplish this, boards require good information, as well as the knowledge and experience to interpret it correctly. Information about the future, though, is not easily attained.

When a board has clearly established a focus on the future and appropriate strategies for going forward, it is still left with having to hold management accountable for execution of the strategy. This is another area where boards get into trouble. Responsibility and thus accountability may not be clear. Or if they are clear, managers may not be held accountable for results, meaning that the board is not reacting aggressively to rectify poor performance. The board must understand the causes of any problems in performance and ensure that action is taken to correct them. Boards, in general, probably react fairly aggressively in crises. It is gradual deterioration in performance that they may fail to address. Vignette 11-1 describes the disastrous results that may ensue when a board is out of touch with corporate activities.

VIGNETTE 11-1

WHEN A BOARD IS OUT OF TOUCH WITH CORPORATE ACTIVITIES

THE ISSUE

A primary duty of a board is to keep itself fully informed about the affairs of the company.

THE SITUATION

An Internet startup business launched its initial public offering (IPO) with much fanfare at $23 per share, closing the day at $55 per share. Yet, within just 9 months, nearly half the company's 600 employees had been laid off, the stock had plummeted to just $2 per share, the chairman and founder had been ousted, and bankruptcy appeared imminent. The story of this company is a saga of gross mismanagement, abuse of corporate funds, an erratic CEO, and a lack of oversight by the board of directors.

This company had a high-powered and prestigious board that somehow missed the following critical warning signs:

- *Questionable expenses.* Expenses included $69.6 million for advertising; $800,000 for a corporate jet, plus $250,000 per year for pilots; $5 million for land for a company headquarters, later appraised at $2 million; $750,000 to sponsor a prominent yacht race; and $4.5 million to Yahoo! for ads that brought in less than $100,000 in revenue.

Continued

Continued

- *Struggles to meet expenses.* Unable to meet its growing payroll, the company began to delay payments to its suppliers.
- *Founder and chairman acting in self-interest.* As investors infused cash to keep the company going, the chairman sold shares out. For example, while one investor put in $15 million, the company chairman sold a portion of his stock holdings, collecting $5.7 million while the board remained quiet.
- *Founder's troubled history.* The first company he founded had ended in bankruptcy. In the current venture, he had little of his own cash at risk and no technology experience.

BOARD ACTIONS SIGNAL A BRIGHTER FUTURE?

The board finally took action in a vote to fire the chairman (accepting his resignation a month later). One board member was named chairman, and the chief operating officer (COO) was promoted to CEO. After resigning, the former chairman rapidly liquidated his stake in the company, selling a total of 7.5 million shares and gaining over $35 million in 5 months.

Unfortunately, a crisis situation was required to compel this board to take action—and then only after long delay. From a governance perspective, however, the following actions were implemented rapidly:

- An experienced board with 10 directors and an independent chairman was put in place.
- The board became very involved in designing a strategic restructuring plan to focus on narrower product lines.
- A special turnaround committee was created to explore strategic opportunities available to the company, including financing alternatives to increase the available cash.

THE RESULTS

Unfortunately, these efforts were a little too late, because the company eventually went into bankruptcy. We are left to wonder to what degree the company was the victim of the "irrational exuberance" of the dot-com era or a board of directors that seriously neglected its oversight responsibilities.

Continued

Concluded

THE POINT

A powerful, prestigious board is no guarantee of success. The directors simply may not devote the time to understand what is going on in the business and execute their duties effectively. This situation allows a CEO to go his or her own way to the benefit or detriment of the shareholders.

The final area of organization and processes that gets boards in trouble is that of so-called benefits, the small or large perquisites that directors are apt to find personally convenient or attractive. These "perks" may include trips on the company plane, first-class travel and accommodations, or participation in celebrity sporting events. Except in the most egregious cases, the cost of these may not be material to the business, but the signal they send is loud and clear—and very destructive of a high-performance culture. While there is a tendency to emulate other companies with regard to such perks, boards must keep in mind the negative impressions such uses of the shareholders' funds may invoke.

LEGAL CONCERNS AND INDEMNIFICATION

Quite simply, in our increasingly litigious society, almost anyone or any group of individuals can sue anyone else or any organization for almost any real or imaginary slight. Individuals or organizations can sue to put in place restraining orders, recover damages, or force another person or organization to cease some activity. Groups of individuals who do not even know one another can file class-action suits in the pursuit of some common goal. These individuals may sue as employees of a corporation, or they may sue collectively as members of a labor union. Similarly, customers may sue individually or collectively to recover damages they perceive to be the responsibility of the corporation.

We have seen a rash of suits against corporations and boards on behalf of shareholders who seek to overturn some board action, force some desired action, or prevent some undesired direction the company may take. Suppliers of raw materials, purchased parts, or capital equipment may sue the company over delivery dates or payments supposedly due or for other damages incurred. Governments and governmental agencies may sue a firm in order to enforce some disputed regulation or to require the company to cease taking some undesired action.

Lawsuits can be initiated by individuals or by entities, such as churches, trade associations, fraternities, or garden clubs. They can be class-action suits that seek some remedy by a group of individuals or entities with some mutual dispute with the company. The various types of suits are almost limitless and are as varied as are the state codes under which they may be brought.

One of the principal objectives of the Securities and Exchange Commission (SEC) is to ensure that all interested parties have access to the same information base regarding public corporations—that there is no opportunity for advantageous insider trading. As a result, regulations place a great deal of emphasis on full disclosure of all pertinent facts to the public at the same time. Directors get into trouble when full disclosure does not take place or when they trade in their company's securities in violation of SEC regulations and securities laws. The responsibility for understanding the limitations of insider-trading legislation lies with the directors, and awareness of legislative and regulatory requirements should be part of director orientation and ongoing director education programs.

As we stated earlier, directors can be sued for almost anything by a variety of seemingly aggrieved parties. Directors can only be prosecuted, however, for real violations of criminal law. Most companies indemnify (protect) their directors and officers from personal liability that might be incurred in the process of carrying out their duties as directors. This indemnification is acquired through the purchase of directors' and officers' indemnification (DOI) insurance. There is a very simple rule that governs the applicability of the indemnification to a given situation. Legal actions of the board and/or directors acting on behalf of the corporation are covered; illegal acts of the board and/or directors are not indemnified. Thus a director who participates in an illegal act by the board is personally liable to the fullest extent of his or her personal assets for any damages deemed to have been inflicted on others.

HOW DIRECTORS STAY OUT OF TROUBLE

An obvious step toward staying out of trouble for a board is to avoid the pitfalls that commonly lead to poor board performance. At the least, a board that comprises strong, effective members and which is well organized to carry out its duties should effectively represent its shareholders. Several publications report from time to time on their impressions of the best and worst boards among the public companies in the United States that are listed on major stock exchanges. It is difficult for any outside observer to know the intricacies of any board's actions and relative effectiveness. We assert that the vast majority of boards could be termed "adequate." That is, they are neither spectacularly good nor bad. They are doing the jobs they are chartered to do in a professional manner. The financial and other results of these companies could be described as "in the pack," or on a par with those of most other firms in their industries or among other public companies in general.

On the other hand, certain companies stand apart from the larger group either because they consistently, over long periods of time, produce spectacular results or because they are consistently among the very worst performers. The financial analysts who delve into the details of company performance are constantly seeking to understand the underpinnings of either success or failure. They may decide that a company has a failed strategy or an unsustainable strategy. They may conclude that foreign competition or labor problems or new, disruptive technologies have set the company at a disadvantage. They have increasingly, in recent years, looked at the details of the board's membership, organization, independence of directors and the reported results of the company to determine if part or most of the company's financial results (strong or weak) are attributable to board activities or inactivity.

THE ATTRIBUTES OF A GOOD BOARD

This scrutiny has led a number of major publications to report on their assessments of the best and worst boards among U.S. companies. The information reported here is drawn from articles in *Business Week* dated November 26, 1996 and January 24, 2000. The criteria used for identifying the boards that were highlighted were reported in the articles and are included below.

Independence of Directors

The reporters preparing the articles carefully examined all interrelationships among each board's members. Obvious friends and cronies of the CEO were considered a liability to the company's image to outsiders or the public at large. Crucial panels, such as the audit committee, were expected to contain no inside directors as members. Additionally, among the most egregious faults of board membership were so-called cross-directorships. *Cross-directorships* were defined as situations in which, for instance, the CEO of Company B was a member of the board of Company A and the CEO of Company A was a member of the board of Company B. The relative independence of such directors was suspect because each director might tend to support the other's proposals in a quid pro quo arrangement.

The following criteria were used to judge the relative independence of directors. Boards that did not meet these criteria were considered less than satisfactory in independence. A board was judged on its having the following:

- No more than two inside directors
- No inside directors on its audit, nominating, or compensation committees
- No outside members who directly or indirectly drew consulting, legal, or other fees from the company
- No interlocking directorships

Furthermore, extra points were awarded for meeting regularly with the CEO.

Quality of Directors, Individually and Collectively

Those preparing the ratings of the boards attempted to ascertain the extent to which the board's meetings included real, open debate. An attempt also was made to determine whether directors were sufficiently familiar with the company's managers and conditions in the field. This assessment included an attempt to understand whether the board was taking steps to be informed, or whether its members were totally dependent on the CEO for relevant information.

The articles used the following descriptors to judge the overall quality of each board:

- Fully employed directors should sit on no more than three corporate boards, and retired directors should sit on no more than six.
- The board should include at least one outsider with experience in the company's core business.
- There should be at least one outsider on the audit committee with a financial or accounting background.
- Extra points were awarded if the board included at least one CEO of a company of similar size or stature.
- Directors should attend 75 percent or more of the board's meetings.
- The board should have no more than 15 directors.

Accountability

Those assessing the effectiveness of boards reasoned that because directors are intended to represent the shareholders of their company, the directors should hold serious financial stakes in their companies.

Directors also were expected to challenge underperforming CEOs. These circumstances were felt to be crucial in sustaining independence of thought and action by the directors.

The following criteria and requirements were deemed important with regard to directors having proper accountability to shareholders:

- All directors should own a minimum of $100,000 in stock.
- Extra points were earned for not offering pension benefits to directors.
- Extra points were earned for having elections of directors every year.
- Boards should meet at least four times per year.
- Audit committees should meet at least three times per year.
- Points were lost for boards that failed to evaluate their own performance.

THE BOTTOM LINE ON POORLY FUNCTIONING BOARDS

The following excerpts summarize the unsavory attributes of boards considered poor. They included directors who were

- *Underinvested.* The articles included a list of individual directors (by name) of major U.S. companies who owned zero or insignificant amounts of their companies' shares.
- *Stretched too thin.* The articles listed 7 directors, each of whom served on from 9 to 13 boards. The major companies on whose boards they served also were listed for each director. The obvious question was whether directors could serve on from 9 to 13 boards, attend the requisite meetings, stay informed, and most important, understand any of the businesses they were presumed to be directing.
- *Absent too often.* The articles highlighted 10 directors whose average attendance records at board meetings ranged from 25 to 45 percent. Poor attendance was considered a problem, given the important opportunity that board service provides for representing shareholders.

THE BEST BOARDS

For the 5-year period from 1995 to 1999, General Electric, Johnson & Johnson, Campbell Soup, Intel, and IBM were among the companies consistently designated as having the "best boards." This could be interpreted as indicating that these companies and others fully met the stringent criteria described earlier as strongly related to effective board performance. Conversely, companies designated as having the "worst boards" could be assumed to have fallen short with regard to some or all of the criteria outlined earlier.

The underlying objective of the *BusinessWeek* study and of other similar studies was to identify companies that may outperform (or underperform) similar companies with superior (or inferior) organizations and operational processes of their boards of directors. The question remains, however, how direct or strong the link may be between company performance and the perceived quality of the board of directors. We report here the results of a review of the financial performance of the two groups of 25 companies designated as having the best and worst boards of directors by *BusinessWeek* in late 1996 over the 5 years following the reporting of the designation.

As shown in Exhibit 11-1, the performance of each company during the 5-year period was categorized as one of the following:

- Tracking the average results of companies in the Standard and Poor's (S&P) 500 Index within plus or minus 10 percent of the cumulative returns to shareholders
- Underperforming or outperforming the preceding metric
- Ceasing to exist due to insolvency or having been acquired by another firm

The results are interesting, although they scarcely could be considered conclusive regarding the relationship between apparent board effectiveness and company performance.

During the period examined (May 1997–May 2002), a company on

E x h i b i t   1 1 - 1

Performance of the 25 Best and 25 Worst Boards:
May 1997–May 2002

	Underperformed the S&P 500	Performed with the S&P 500 (±10% Cumulative Return)	Outperformed the S&P 500	No Longer Exist
Worst boards	12	1	4	8
Best boards	6	4	12	3

Note: Companies are from lists in *BusinessWeek*, November 26, 1996. Stock performance was measured from May 20, 1997 to May 20, 2002 from public sources.

the "worst boards" list was twice as likely to have underperformed the S&P 500 Index than a company on the "best boards" list and almost three times as likely to have ceased operating as an independent company. Conversely, a company on the "best boards" list was three times more likely to have outperformed the S&P 500 Index than a company on the "worst boards" list, with "best boards" list companies either meeting or beating the index almost two-thirds of the time, as compared with 20 percent of the time for the set of "worst boards" companies. To repeat, these results are subject to the frailties of the small sample sizes, the lack of adjustment to the financial returns for the varying market and industry trends and other risks faced by the companies, and the unavailability of specific information about the fates of the companies that no longer exist as independent companies. No degree of elegance of board organization or processes could lift a company to achieve outstanding financial returns if it faced a technological revolution or innovative substitute products. In a similar way, we have no way of knowing how the shareholders fared when a company merged with or was acquired by another firm during this period, which could have happened to companies on either list. The results do show, however, support for the general notion that superior board processes scarcely retard the creation of shareholder value, a very conservative conclusion.

Some companies identified in the 1996 survey of the best and worst corporate boards appeared again in the same category in the 2000 survey, which reinforces the notion that the effectiveness of boards does not change precipitately and that, further, boards as a rule do not get into trouble or become strong overnight. Rather, boards evolve over time to adopt a set of patterns of operation that are very resistant to change. We conclude, therefore, that the status quo of a board situation is very difficult to alter in a short time frame. Time will tell as to whether the criteria used in the surveys to identify strong, independent, high-quality boards continue to relate positively, on average, to strong financial performance.

SUMMARY

It should be apparent at this point in our discussion that the functioning of a company's board of directors is influenced by an indescribable amalgamation of the skills, experiences, and particular motivations of the individual directors at any point in time in the life of the company. The effectiveness of the board as a whole is circumscribed by the board's ability to organize itself and rise to the challenging occasions that surely confront every business. A board must commit to educating its members and regularly evaluating its performance to remain effective. Moreover, a board must be vigilant in keeping apprised of the firm's performance and the initiatives of the CEO. Such watchfulness in itself is no guarantee against shareholder or stakeholder agitation, but it is a sound step toward reducing the likelihood of being drawn into such conflicts.

While this work was written to address primarily the governance of public U.S. firms, we broaden our discussion in Chapter 12, where we discuss the similarities and differences of for-profit and not-for-profit board service.

REVIEW QUESTIONS

1. What are the primary ways in which individual directors get into trouble?
2. What are the principal risks facing a board of directors as a group?
3. What is the role of leadership in the proper functioning of a board?
4. What are the primary ways in which a board or a director may face litigation?
5. How do directors stay out of trouble?

CHAPTER 12

Not-for-Profit Organizations: The Differences

Our form of society is commonly described with approbation as *pluralistic,* and it is commonly added that pluralism is essential to a democracy. Among other implications, the term signifies that such a society contains a wide variety of institutions: business concerns, welfare agencies, museums, churches, trade unions, colleges and universities, hospitals, foundations, rod-and-gun clubs, and many others. Some are profit-seeking; others are not. Many of the duties and problems of governance are common to both for-profit and not-for-profit organizations, whereas others are characteristic of or peculiar to one or the other.[1]

Thus far in this book we have been addressing the governance of corporate organizations, particularly publicly owned U.S. business concerns. Because there are more than a million not-for-profit organizations (1,627,000 in 1998[2]) and many of our readers are serving or will serve on not-for-profit boards, it is important to discuss how the governance of not-for-profit organizations differs from that of for-profit companies.

THE MEANING OF THE TERM *NOT FOR PROFIT*

The terms *nonprofit* and *not for profit* generally are intended to describe an organization whose purpose is to serve the public rather than to earn a profit for its shareholders. While *nonprofit* is used widely and is actually the preferred term in academic circles, we find *not for profit* (NFP) preferable precisely because it implies purposeful nonprofitability. There are many for-profit organizations that inadvertently have nonprofit results and many nonprofit organizations with the purpose of serving as a venue for socializing rather than serving the public. As a result, we have chosen to use the not-for-profit nomenclature here.

Not-for-profit organizations (NFPs) generally are very purpose-driven. They are organized to serve some group, usually composed of individuals but sometimes other organizations. Many people see this emphasis on purpose as the basic difference between not-for-profit and for-profit organizations, but the distinction is more complex.

The conventional response to the question, "What is the purpose of a business?" is "To make a profit." As the objective of the investors, this reply is generally true. As Peter Drucker, the management guru of the twentieth century reminds us, however, the purpose of a business is to create and satisfy a customer. Profit is the reward for doing that well. When thought about in this way, both NFPs and for-profits are purpose-driven organizations.

A legal perspective provides a second meaning of the term *not for profit*; such organizations are tax-exempt if they comply with Internal Revenue Service regulations. If they provide a benefit deemed to be in the public interest, they may qualify for tax-exempt status, meaning that they do not have to pay income taxes. In addition, those that have a charitable purpose also may receive contributions that are tax-deductible to the contributor.

NFPs are exempt from taxes, but they are not exempt from basic economic principles. All organizations must find a revenue stream that will cover their expenses and thus balance their budgets. This revenue is frequently from client fees, which are quite similar to the revenues of a for-profit business. If NFPs do not charge fees, they must generate funds from grants or contributions. While the accountants might call this *unearned* income on the financial statement, generating contributions or securing grants takes a great deal of planning, effort, and skill. These activities essentially represent a basic marketing challenge. An NFP competes for contributions and grants just as for-profits must compete for customers. Equally important, an NFP, similarly to for-profits, must manage its operations to achieve a positive, or at least nonnegative, bottom line.

THE ROLE OF NFPs

Economists and business people often divide our productive society into three sectors—the public government sector, the for-profit commercial sector, and the private not-for-profit service sector. The not-for-profit sector plays an important role because the other two sectors in a capitalistic system cannot meet all social needs. Commercial enterprises with their emphasis on profits are not motivated to do so, and governments are not organized to deliver services effectively and efficiently, as they have demonstrated repeatedly. The NFPs gather resources, both financial and human, and focus them at the grass-roots level on meeting human needs. The result is a social and political stability that contributes to a healthy economy and a sound democracy. Indeed, there is rich irony in the reinforcing of our for-profit economic system by the NFPs and their restraining influence on public-sector welfare expenditures.

The NFP sector represents a substantial portion of our gross domestic product (GDP). According to *The New Nonprofit Almanac and Desk Reference, 2002*, the NFP sector has $785 billion in expenditures, not an insignificant number when compared with the GDP.

TAX-EXEMPT ORGANIZATIONS

The Internal Revenue Service Code defines tax-exempt organizations under Section 501(c). The definitions include 501(c)(3) organizations, which are operated for philanthropic purposes and contributions to which are tax-deductible. In addition to these groups that are widely recognized as not for profit, there is a wide range of associations and service organizations that have 501(c)(4) and (6) exemptions from income taxes. Contributions to these organizations, though, are not tax-deductible. They include social clubs, fraternal organizations, professional groups, labor unions, chambers of commerce, industry associations, and civic leagues, among others.

The major categories of organizations and their distribution of revenues in 1997 are shown in Exhibit 12-1.

E x h i b i t   12 - 1

Revenues of NFPs: 1997

Category	Percent
Health services	49.0
Education and research	18.0
Religious organizations	11.5
Social and legal services	11.5
Foundations	5.0
Civic, social, and fraternal organizations	2.7
Arts and culture	2.3
	100.0

Source: Urban Institute, The New Nonprofit Almanac and Desk Reference (San Francisco: Jossey-Bass, 2002), p. xxxiii.]

Tax-exempt organizations may be required to pay taxes on unrelated business income (UBI) when the source of the income is not directly related to its philanthropic purpose. Moreover, the fact that a tax-exempt entity owns some or all of a taxable enterprise does not exempt the taxable subsidiary from taxation; the taxable enterprise is still subject to normal taxation, both federal and state. In such instances, it is often the wisest course for the NFP to convert such ownership to cash or its equivalent and make alternative investments, thereby rendering future income received tax-exempt. An excellent example of such board action is that undertaken by the Public Welfare Foundation in Washington, DC. This foundation's sole asset was a chain of daily retail newspapers, all taxable corporations, that were paying roughly $4 million per year in after-tax dividends to the foundation. Following the sale of these newspapers to the New York Times Company for cash, the foundation's tax-exempt annual income grew to over $20 million because the sale proceeds were invested more efficiently.

GOVERNANCE DIFFERENCES

The governance differences between for-profits and not-for-profits can be classified into two broad categories: the legal form of the organization and governance practices.

The Legal Form

NFPs typically take one of four general forms: corporations, foundations, trusts, or associations.

Corporations

Individual states charter nonstock corporations for their stated philanthropic purposes. This is a particular form of a corporate charter in which no stock is issued. There is no ownership in the traditional sense. Rather, the community at large owns the corporation. It has limited liability by definition. Such organizations may be licensed to do business by more than one state.

Foundations

Foundations may be created by a specific NFP or by an independent entity, such as an individual or a for-profit entity. Such foundations are organized to receive and manage assets and to make grants to the sponsoring organization or, if independent, to qualifying organizations or individuals. Foundations generally do not provide direct services. Foundations are governed by boards of trustees that have a fiduciary obligation for the assets under their control. They also have a moral, if not legal, obligation to follow the intent of the donor(s).

Charitable Trusts
Individuals generally establish charitable trusts to carry out some philanthropic intent. Charitable trusts are complicated entities that play a major role in estate planning as well as serving as vehicles for giving money to charity. The terms of the trust are specified in the trust agreement, and one or more trustees administer the resulting trust.

Associations
Associations are created by groups of individuals or corporations that have some interest in common. The most recognized examples are clubs and trade associations with a variety of purposes, as we mentioned earlier. Associations generally are membership organizations, although some member organizations can take a corporate form.

Governance Absent a Market Test
John Carver, a consultant on governance, suggests that the essential difference between not-for-profit and for-profit organizations is the presence or lack of a market test. Carver calls the environment lacking of this mechanism "life in the muted market." He notes that from a governance perspective the relevant factor that sets most not-for-profit and public organizations apart from for-profit organizations "with profound effects" is that "most nonprofit and public organizations lack a behavioral process to aggregate the many individual evaluations of product and cost. The organization is missing the foundation that would enable it to define success and failure, to know what is worth doing, and in the largest sense, even to recognize good performance." [3]

This concept is based on economic theory, specifically the notion that a product or service is offered in a competitive marketplace at a price that should reflect its cost *and* provide a profit. If the marketplace rejects the product at a given price, or if the organization does not make a profit, it has very compelling indicators of its effectiveness. To the degree that NFPs are in a competitive marketplace and provide a product or service at a fee, they do have the indication of market response. Frequently, they subsidize the product or service from endowment income, grants, and/or contributions so that they can offer a below-cost or free product or service. In such instances, they lose the market test for their services as an indicator of effectiveness. They do, however, confront a market test from contributors. This can be a powerful indicator of their marketing efforts and general market image.

In any case, managers of NFPs do not have the concept of profit to discipline their thinking. The substitute for this is the need to balance their budgets. As with for-profits, though, they do compete for resources. In 1997, the nonprofit sector had total revenues of $664.8 billion, representing 13.6 percent of national income. When health services were excluded, the total revenues were $338.5 billion, broken down by source as shown in Exhibit 12-2.

These data indicate that on average at least 63 percent of the income of NFPs must be acquired from donors or clients in competition with other organizations. Perhaps the government portion has competitive aspects as well, given the multiplicity of interests in competition for finite public revenues.

TYPES OF BOARDS

In the book *Boards That Make a Difference*, author John Carver writes about different types of boards, based on the activities of the organization.[4] Not-for-profit boards tend to function somewhat differently from for-profit boards. The following discussion is based on Carver's descriptions.

The Governing Board

The governing board provides the ultimate board function in terms of authority and accountability. It rests at the top of the governing pyramid. It is found in larger, more mature organizations that have a full-time, competent staff. Its role is very similar to that of the corporate board.

E x h i b i t   1 2 - 2

Sources of Contributions: 1997

Sector	Amount ($ Billions)	Percent of Total
Private contributions	$119.1	35
Private payments (fees)	$ 96.0	28
Government	$ 70.1	21
Other income (investment)	$ 53.3	16
TOTAL	$338.5	100

Source: Urban Institute, The New Nonprofit Almanac and Desk Reference (San Francisco: Jossey-Bass, 2002), pp. 13 and 91.

The Advisory Board

The function of the advisory board is to give counsel, not to govern. Examples of such advisory councils are parent, student, and alumni groups in educational organizations and residents in public housing or group homes. Advisory boards often are used to get prominent leaders to "lend their names" and to have some interest in an organization, particularly for fund-raising purposes. There are a few instances in which a sponsoring organization desires to retain all governance powers while using an advisory board to help it set policy and raise funds. A prominent example of this is the Salvation Army. All its local boards are advisory. Another example is that of separate schools (for example, medical, law, business, engineering, education) within individual state universities. The governance function is performed by a state-appointed board at the university level, but at the school level there is an advisory board or council that works closely with the dean.

The Workgroup Board

The workgroup type of board is found in small organizations with little or no staff. The board members must govern and serve as the workforce as well, a practical outcome given the limited resources and highly specific objectives of small NFPs. The line between board and management is necessarily blurred in these situations, often creating some difficult dynamics.

DIFFERENCES IN GOVERNANCE PRACTICES

As with for-profit corporations, the size and governance complexities vary widely in NFPs. Some NFPs are established and managed by individuals, and their governance issues are not unlike those of a small owner-managed enterprise, except that they must conform to the laws applicable to tax-exempt organizations. It is in this type of organization that we commonly find the workgroup boards. Our interest here, though, is in the larger, more complex organizations which involve an active and diverse governing board and a full-time management staff and which perform services for and solicit funds from the public. We choose to concentrate on how these larger NFPs differ in governance practices from public for-profit corporations.

Volunteers

One major distinction between the for-profit board and the not-for-profit board is that the latter is usually composed exclusively of volunteers.

Dedicated and competent volunteers are the body and soul of most NFPs at both the board and operating levels. The volunteers are committed because of interests and beliefs, not compensation. Volunteer boards, however, must be managed differently from compensated boards. For example, it is awkward at best for the volunteer board to enforce attendance and performance standards on its members. Often, a volunteer's efforts must give way to the competing demands of family and professional work. Such rebalancing of the volunteer's time commitments is a common phenomenon.

Imagine the negative impact on the performance of not-for-profit boards if the standards required of for-profit boards were applied to them. High performance for not-for-profit boards results from the combination of the members' belief in and commitment to the NFP's objectives and from the caliber of the board's leadership. By definition, there is a community of interest among the volunteer board members. How well they are led—not just collectively, but also individually—determines the level of board performance. The chair of a not-for-profit board must invest substantially more personal energy into this leadership position than the chair of a typical for-profit board, who has the tools of monetary leverage at hand. The not-for-profit board chair has little leverage over board members, other than the members' commitment to the not-for-profit mission and the powers of personal persuasion.

The Legal Obligations of NFP Directors

The legal obligations of directors or trustees of NFPs are not markedly different from those of for-profit directors. A primary obligation is the duty of loyalty, which chiefly means to avoid conflicts of interest. There may be a stronger emphasis on fiduciary obligations when a large amount of property or an endowment is involved, as is frequently the case with trusts and foundations. Conflicts arise most frequently when there is a property or service transaction between a trustee and the organization, and because there is no ready market, perceptions of values may be quite subjective. An example of such a transaction would be a trustee serving as the lawyer for the trust or foundation and charging fees for services rendered. Such situations must be approached with an abundance of caution, and the duty of loyalty should be applied rigorously.

A second obligation of the NFP director is the duty of care. In part, this duty requires ensuring that fiscal and program controls are in place to guarantee that performance standards are met and that all potential risks to clients are recognized and protected against. Effective internal controls require that the board exercise due care in its oversight responsibilities, that is, that it remain knowledgeable of the organization's situation and activities. Discharging this responsibility requires a specific level of expertise on the board or, at least, that the board is highly confident that such expertise exists within management.

The internal control function is just as important in NFPs as in for-profit organizations. NFPs, however, often tend to be more lax with regard to business practices either because of size or because of an atmosphere of informality. Unfortunately, it is not uncommon for an accountant, bookkeeper, or even a senior officer to embezzle from an NFP. The perpetrators of such acts frequently mask their activities with the appearance of limited competence and confusion. They also take advantage of the atmosphere that encourages a focus on the institution's mission to the exclusion of more practical issues, such as an ordinary inspection of the organization's accounts.

The most difficult issue for not-for-profit boards is to maintain control over the operating director of the organization, who, hopefully, is dynamic, charismatic, and action-oriented. These are the very attributes that complicate the board's control task. The charisma, drive, and dominance that characterize the hard-charging leader may turn toward less savory pursuits. This is especially true when the leader of an NFP has been in place for many years—perhaps since even before all current members of the board—and has been instrumental in growing the organization. In such situations, the director may become a bit arrogant and feel that he or she is the person key to the organization's success. When members of the board hear rumors of improper conduct in such a situation, they tend to fall back on their long-established confidence in the director and give him or her the benefit of the doubt.

The drift of some organizations into what seems later to be an unthinkable situation can best be described as the *inevitability of gradualism*. The executive director of an organization does not suddenly arrive at receiving a level of compensation more appropriate for the chief executive officer (CEO) of a large for-profit company. The out-of-control situation more than likely developed slowly and gradually over a long period of time. To begin with, it is logical for directors to convince themselves that they must provide a competitive compensation structure if they are to attract the most competent candidates for the job of executive director of the organization. It is also not difficult to slide into a pattern of providing annual increases in compensation, consistent with those of for-profit companies. When the board does not meet very often and does not have access to the details, the travel and other expenses being charged to the organization may escalate beyond reason because they are never challenged. Board members may realize at some point that the executive director's compensation and perquisites are out of control without quite realizing how the situation evolved. While many directors join not-for-profit boards because they are interested in the organization's mission, they nevertheless must remain conscious of their duties, similar to directors of for-profit companies.

STAKEHOLDER THEORY

All organizations have multiple stakeholders whose needs must be considered to achieve sustainable success. The needs of the stakeholders can be viewed as a hierarchy, and there are some revealing differences between those of not-for-profit and for-profit organizations.

The First Level—The Client

The first level in the hierarchy of stakeholder needs is the customer, or client, who is the recipient of the benefits of the goods or services provided by the organization. NFPs differ from for-profit companies in that they have two types of customers—clients as well as donors. The NFP acts on its mission by meeting the needs of the clients, and as in the case of for-profit businesses, the best NFPs exhibit a strong desire to be distinctive in ways that are meaningful to their clients.

We tend to think of NFPs as providers of free services, and this is frequently the case. In many cases, however, as we have already discussed, the goods or services are provided on some sort of fee basis. If fees are charged, the NFPs usually are competing for clients with both other NFPs and for-profit companies. NFPs are always competing for donors' contributions. The concept of competition is, consequently, applicable to NFPs, even though many of them do not recognize this competitive reality of their existence.

The Second Level—The Employee

The second level in the hierarchy of stakeholder needs is the employee. Given that employees in a service environment are instrumental in the task of meeting client needs, fulfilling employees' expectations is crucial to a firm's success. Employees are entitled to a return on their time in the form of salaries or wages and benefits. They also want job security, acceptable working conditions, and job satisfaction.

The key difference between NFPs and for-profits with regard to employees is that NFP employees frequently work for wages that are much less than they could obtain in the commercial market. This is so because they are motivated to serve others. Whether this approach to compensation is a good practice is open to debate. Clearly, there are many dedicated individuals who make personal sacrifices to serve others and are not deterred by low compensation. Low compensation, however, is often a barrier to attracting competent people in sufficient numbers. Thus, while the practices may vary between the two types of organizations, the issue of attracting and retaining competent people is very similar. It is no simple task to weed out those willing to work for below-market wages due to a lack of ability from those competent people who accept the wage scale because of an opportunity to serve others.

This is also the level where one should consider the volunteer. A critical skill of many NFPs is the ability to attract and manage a large group of volunteers. An excellent example of this is the group known as Court Appointed Special Advocates (CASA). These volunteers are people who, at the direction of juvenile and domestic relations court judges, accept responsibility for a number of teenagers who have no place to turn, save a return to the wretched circumstances that brought them to the courts to begin with. The volunteer leverage, the ratio of volunteers to staff, in these situations is tremendous, almost 40:1 from a national perspective. CASA is obviously an outstanding example of the leveraged power inherent in the army of volunteers who are willing to support nonprofit causes.

The Third Level—Suppliers and Creditors

The third level of stakeholders whose needs must be considered consists of suppliers and creditors. Since NFPs are generally service organizations, they rarely need substantial raw materials. Suppliers of tangible goods, therefore, characteristically are not major players in the NFP arena. There are exceptions to this, however, such as food banks, which are very dependent on suppliers for the food they distribute. When NFPs do need goods or services, they often can look to suppliers for in-kind donations. Some organizations become very skilled at this and actually build sustained alliances with supportive suppliers.

The Fourth Level—The Community

The fourth level of stakeholders is the community. Both types of organizations provide benefits to the community with their goods or services and by creating jobs. In addition, for-profit organizations pay taxes, and they often play a major role in philanthropic and economic development in a community. The difference is that the purpose of NFPs is to benefit the community, whereas for-profits provide benefits to the community that flow from the success of their commercial purposes.

The Fifth Level—Ownership

It is at the fifth level of stakeholders, ownership, that there are substantial differences between for-profit organizations and NFPs. The for-profit organization has owners. An important step toward meeting their financial needs is to do well at meeting the needs of all the other stakeholders. It is ideally a closed system in which the better the job the business does in meeting the needs of the other stakeholders, the more money the owners make, permitting the owners to reinvest in and share the rewards of the business, further improving their ability to meet the needs of the other stakeholders.

NFPs do not have owners in the sense that for-profit enterprises do. They do have sponsors, either an individual or a group, committed to creating and perpetuating the organization, and they have natural constituencies, the people who are interested in and committed to what the organization does. The sponsor, while it does not have conventional economic ownership, does indeed own the responsibility for the success of the organization. It has all the characteristics of ownership other than economic interests. In fact, the strength of the sponsorship in terms of financial resources, competence, and commitment is a critical ingredient for success. It is the foundation on which the NFP must build.

We often see very well-meaning and idealistic individuals who are devoted to a specific philanthropic cause form an NFP to address this passionate interest of theirs. If they do not have adequate financial resources, they make the same mistake that some for-profit startups make; they begin operations undercapitalized. Their other potentially fatal weakness is a lack of business acumen. Founders generally come from a professional background in the field and have little business training. They may, in fact, actually have negative attitudes about business in general, seeing it as materialistic with values that are not consistent with their purposes.

Other Committed Constituencies

The most organized of the natural constituencies are membership organizations. Members may function very much as shareholders do. In some organizations, they elect the trustees or directors. Educational institutions have strong constituencies in both the alumni and the parents of students. An excellent example of such constituency strength is the widely recognized organizational ability and political clout of the National Rifle Association, apparent to a degree far beyond that suggested by its numerical membership. In the event that there are no members, however, the owners in the narrow sense are the natural constituencies and in a broader sense the community or society at large. If they accumulate equity in property, it

is held by the organization for the benefit of its clients for as long as it operates. If the organization ever ceases to function and liquidates, any equity
in its property usually must go to some other nonprofit entity. Frequently,
grantors of significant property will designate where the property should
go upon liquidation or when the property no longer is used for the intended purpose. Otherwise, the articles of incorporation will specify the details
regarding disposal of the property.

Consider, for example, a nonprofit hospital that was sold to a for-
profit chain of hospitals. The proceeds of the sale were placed in a foundation from which grants were made to support health services in the
community. The nonprofit hospital had a self-perpetuating board that,
upon sale of the hospital's assets, became the board of the foundation.
This sequence of actions seems rather innocuous, but in fact, the boards in
place at the time of these conversions become some of the most powerful
people in the community. How they understand their responsibilities to
their communities is an ethical challenge.

BOARD SELECTION: LEADERSHIP

In for-profit organizations, the owners elect the directors. Directors of for-
profits generally are paid fees and are selected for their ability to contribute to the success of the firm and to provide effective oversight. Good
boards have a diversity of talent that, in total, meets the needs of the
organization. In NFPs, however, the directors or trustees are usually volunteers, selected for one or more of the "three Ws." These are wealth, wisdom, and work. Similarly to for-profit companies, good boards need a
diversity of talent that blends together to meet the needs of the organization. Only in very rare instances will directors or trustees of NFP entities
be paid a fee, and even in these cases it is generally quite modest. The
sponsoring group or organization should be the seedbed for the directors
of the organization. In a startup situation, this group is generally the
source of the organization's leadership. Over time, as the organization
matures and strengthens, the leadership becomes self-perpetuating.

Who Will Lead?

The actual leaders of the NFP board vary, sometimes coming from the volunteer side and sometimes from the staff side. The volunteer leadership
may be centered on one strong individual, often acting as the chairperson
of the board and serving for many years. Alternatively, leadership may be
found in a group of individuals who serve a limited number of terms and
rotate the board chair. The latter is more likely to be the case in larger,

more mature organizations. The leadership usually comes from one of two sources, the sponsoring organization if there is one or the natural constituency of the organization. All successful NFPs have a natural constituency. Schools have parents and alumni. Arts organizations have people interested in the particular art form. Social service organizations find professionals in the field as well as others who are interested in the particular service or cause.

How to Construct the Board?

In some cases, the boards of NFPs are appointed by the sponsoring organization. In most cases, they are self-perpetuating, selecting individuals from their natural constituencies. In the better-managed NFPs, there is usually an active nominating or governance committee that functions similarly to those of their for-profit counterparts. The committee members should have a clear understanding of the types of talent they need, work at identifying strong candidates, and conduct effective due diligence on possible board candidates. Unfortunately, a common mistake is for NFP boards not to take this nominating function seriously, resulting in board members who do not bring the range of talents needed or lack a meaningful commitment to the organization. If the NFPs are membership organizations, the board members can be elected by the membership from their ranks, using criteria that are very similar to those of for-profit organizations.

Passion versus Savvy

Successful organizations demonstrate a passion for what they do. NFPs are almost always started by people with a passion, but passion is not enough to guarantee success. People who care deeply about the programs of the organization and intend to make their contributions to the organization through hard work frequently start NFPs. Naturally, they are the prime candidates for board membership. As General George C. Marshall of World War II fame said, however, "Do not feel deeply and think poorly." Organizations must go beyond passion to be effective. They must not let their passion cloud their reasoning. If these organizers have limited organizational experience, their best intentions may not produce an effective organization. They must understand the inextricable link between mission, competence, and funding.

In NFPs, board members frequently face the need to bring more practical and experienced administrators or businesspeople onto the board. Bringing on individuals with such competence, however, frequently will set up a conflict between those whose focus is on the mission and those who are more concerned about the economics. In effective organizations, there is a balanced meeting of these minds. The passionate people understand and care about meeting the mission effectively. The important question is who will provide the business acumen and financial savvy needed to augment the fervor for the mission provided by the passionate volunteers.

Businesspeople Bring Key Skills

A forceful marketing posture can energize an NFP to approach a wider range of constituencies, create more effective products and services, and become more competitive for the attention and support of the larger public. These realities support the premise that NFP boards should seek out businesspeople for membership. The businessman or businesswoman brings to the board an understanding of market forces, the need to compete, recognition of the dire need for profitable operations, and important financial, marketing, and/or operational expertise. Directors with business backgrounds instinctively look to assess the organization's assets and its strategic positioning, move to keep the organization focused on its primary mission (avoiding mission creep), and bring a structured approach to helping the enterprise meet its goals.

The Role of Clients

In some venues, particularly in educational and social service organizations, there are people who think that it is beneficial to have clients on the board in order to be more inclusive. This is a compelling argument, in theory, but often not very practical. Clearly understanding clients and their needs and being responsive to their views are important for every organization. Clients, however, rarely have the education and/or the experience to participate in resolving governance issues. There is the added risk of the client's presence inhibiting frank discussion of critical issues for fear of offending the client. The organization and its client base are poorly served in such circumstances, even though the motivation is commendable.

BOARD SIZE AND TERMS

The size of NFP boards varies widely, usually reflecting the scale and complexity of the organization. Small NFPs will tend to have small, closely knit boards, usually consisting of fewer than 10 or 12 members. These boards function similarly to for-profit boards, but generally the NFP boards are larger than those of for-profit companies. Typically, we find NFP boards in the range of 15 to 20 board members, which tends to be the ideal size for most organizations. The largest boards, however, may be more honorary in nature and may include 40 or more members. In these cases, there is usually an executive committee that actually performs the work and wields the organization's power as a matter of efficiency and effectiveness.

Maximum terms of board service are used widely by NFPs, whereas for-profit firms rarely employ term limits. Terms are usually 3 or 4 years, and directors are limited to two or three terms. Once a director has served the maximum allowed term, he or she must then leave the board but is often eligible for reelection after being off the board for 1 or 2 years. The stronger the organization, the more likely there is to be a meaningful board rotation process. The stronger organizations have a deeper pool of potential directors from which to draw, and there may be more prestige associated with serving as a director or trustee. The benefit of term limits is to keep new talent and experience coming into the organization.

Occasionally, an unusual individual will select an organization as his or her primary philanthropic interest and stay meaningfully involved for a long period of time. If the individual has a powerful, controlling personality, however, this is not always a positive factor. The organization may become too dependent on him or her and also may be limited by his or her interests or point of view. Sometimes such an individual will be a discouragement for others to become involved. Most people seem to want to be deeply involved for a few years and then move on to other things as their life situation and/or their interests evolve. By rotating board members, the organization retains a fresh point of view. Rotation also creates the collateral benefit of building a team of board alumni who act as advocates for the organization in the larger community.

BOARD ORGANIZATION: COMMITTEES

A central issue in board organization is the degree to which the board members are actually involved in the operation of the enterprise. In many NFPs, the board members are much more involved than the typical for-profit board. When the NFP has limited resources, greater board involvement may be crucial. Conversely, if the organization has a professional management team in place, such involvement frequently causes problems. Well-intentioned or not, trustees or directors can cross the line separating board responsibilities and management prerogatives. Because so many NFPs are acutely dependent on the active involvement of board members, one cannot make unbendable rules about how they should behave. In any given case, the involved parties must understand the needs of the situation and work out mutually agreeable roles for the members of the board and for management.

Most boards organize their work through the formation of committees. The committee structure generally reflects the size of the organization and the size of its board. Smaller boards may function largely without committees, being in effect a committee of the whole. The typical NFP board, however, works through a committee structure much as the for-profits do, with most having between three and five standing committees. Organizations have different names for their committees, but the major committees reflect the primary functions of the organization. They are

- Governance or nominating
- Operations, program, or personnel
- Finance, budget, or audit
- Development or fund-raising

The committee structure should mirror the management organizational structure, meaning that the board should organize its functional committees to reflect the organization of operating management. The appropriate manager with matching responsibility can staff each committee. There is frequently an executive committee, particularly when the board is large. The duties of the executive committee vary widely. Sometimes it uses its powers only as an expedient to act quickly in the absence of a formal board meeting. At the other end of the spectrum, it serves as the actual decision-making body, bringing its actions to the board after the fact. The middle-of-the-road function is for the executive committee to coordinate the activities of the other committees and to make recommendations to the full board. While an active and powerful executive committee can provide an efficient method of governing, its approach is not democratic by definition. Other members of the board rightfully may consider themselves as less important. Because support for an NFP is rooted in involvement, anything that lessens this sense of involvement actually poses a danger to the strength of the organization.

FREQUENCY OF MEETINGS

The frequency of meetings of NFP boards usually reflects how the board has chosen to operate its committees. When an NFP operates through its committees, it might meet only two to four times a year. On the other hand, if the full board is where the essential work is conducted, it might meet monthly, perhaps dropping off a meeting in the summer or during holiday seasons. It should be noted that we are describing a governing board. A workgroup board might meet monthly or more frequently, with key members involved even daily.

There are three other variables that affect the frequency of meetings:

- *Geographic dispersion of the board membership.* If the members all live in the same area, there can be more frequent, shorter meetings. When the members have to travel long distances, there tend to be less frequent meetings, but they may last somewhat longer, usually 1 or 2 days.
- *The issues faced by the organization.* When a mature organization is functioning well with minimum change, the board does not need to meet very often. When there are major issues or projects, however, the board or its committees must meet more frequently. Sometimes a major project or problem will require certain members of the board to be involved almost daily for some period of time.
- *The strength of management.* When there is a full-time professional staff to which the board has delegated the management of the organization, it is not as necessary for the board to meet frequently. When part-time volunteers, including board members, do much of the work, however, the board has to be more active.

POLITICS

Politics can be present in any organization, and NFPs are no exception. Politics arise from several causes; personality clashes, individual ambitions, different agendas for the future of the organization, and protecting staff members are just some of the causes. It takes effective leadership to work through the politics when they occur in order to build consensus and teamwork. There is no single way of managing politics, but we do need to recognize that the personal chemistry of the board members with each other and with management is of vital importance. When this chemistry is poisoned for any reason, the situation should be addressed promptly.

SENIOR MANAGEMENT SELECTION, PERFORMANCE, AND APPRAISAL

Traditionally, the head of the staff of an NFP has been seen as an executive director or administrator, with the senior board leader having the title of president. A workable arrangement may exist if there is a strong and active person in the president's role and the senior manager's role is more that of the operating officer. The larger and more successful NFPs, however, tend toward the corporate model of seeing the head of the staff as a CEO. The title is frequently president, with the volunteer leader serving as chairperson of the board. The choice here is a function of role definition. Is the senior manager going to function primarily as a CEO, with all the responsibilities that role entails, or is he or she going to be an operating officer, with the broader CEO responsibilities carried out at the board level?

In any case, selection of the senior full-time manager is one of the most critical decisions that the board makes in both for-profit and NFP organizations. The goal for both groups is to get the "right person." With the right person in the top position, many problems never arise; however, with the wrong person, a varied set of problems is likely to be introduced. The process of selecting the senior executive should be very similar within the two types of organizations, with clarity about the role or job definition and the characteristics essential for success in fulfilling the role important to effective completion of the task. Paradoxically, once the CEO is selected, the roles, in a sense, are reversed. Certainly, the CEO continues to work for the board, but an effective CEO plays a major role in the effectiveness of the board. An experienced and very successful CEO of an NFP museum has said that "the CEO gets the board he or she deserves." This clearly puts a leadership burden on the CEO, even though he or she is technically subordinate to the board.

CEO AND SENIOR MANAGEMENT COMPENSATION

Compensation in the NFP arena is somewhat different from that in for-profit organizations because there is little room for incentive compensation, particularly as it relates to profitability. Some organizations may pay bonuses based on subjective evaluations or some performance targets, but these tend to be the exception. An effective compensation strategy is nevertheless still very important. The organization must be competitive in compensation to attract and retain the people it wants. In many smaller organizations and faith-based organizations, we find good people working at sacrificial levels of compensation. The larger, more complex organizations generally pay much better and often quite well. In these cases, compensation is a "package" inclusive of salary, fringe benefits, and retirement benefits.

THE BOTTOM LINE: ACCOUNTABILITY

As with for-profit organizations, NFP enterprises are accountable for meeting the needs of their stakeholders. An organization's failure to perform in a competitive market for resources may result in important stakeholders' withdrawing their support and looking elsewhere for the gratification of their respective priorities. The for-profit entity has the discipline of profit that provides an obvious measure of economic performance. The accountability flows from management to the board to the shareholders. In the NFP organization, the flow of accountability is similar, but because there are no shareholders, the question becomes, "To whom is the board accountable?" The answer is that the board is accountable to its stakeholders—but particularly to its funding sources, on whom it depends for survival. These contributors or funding sources "invest" their funds to support the mission of the organization, and their continued support depends on their perception of the effectiveness of the organization.

The issue of accountability has two key elements, the first of which is how the board measures the success of the organization. The board and management must agree on the drivers of success, as well as on how to identify and measure the appropriate outcomes. The truly effective NFPs learn to do this very well. Most NFPs, however, probably could improve in this area. The other element in accountability is public relations. Because the support of its donors is critical, the NFP must have an effective way of communicating to its constituencies its efficiency in making a positive impact on the community. Many avenues exist for these communications, and NFPs should constantly seek to expand and improve their capabilities in this area.

REVIEW QUESTIONS

1. What is the importance of the term *not for profit* as compared with *nonprofit*?
2. What are the primary roles of not-for-profit organizations in our economic system?
3. What are the characteristic differences in governance between not-for-profit and for-profit organizations?
4. What are the various types of not-for-profit boards?
5. Who are the stakeholders of a typical not-for-profit organization?

CHAPTER 13

Final Thoughts

We compose our final thoughts on the topic of corporate governance in an atmosphere of heightened awareness and distrust of the American model of corporate reporting and corporate governance itself. A handful of appalling abuses of the public's trust have launched a period of previously unthinkable bankruptcies, high-profile indictments, and rancorous congressional hearings. In response, market averages have fallen, and investors remain wary. In the spotlight of the critical public eye, American corporations are cautiously examining their governance processes while panels of experts are debating proposed revised standards.

On reflection, we find ourselves still committed to touting the basic duties of every director—the fiduciary duty, the duty of loyalty, and the duty of care. Further, we recognize the profound import of the faithful execution of these duties. American democracy was built on the principle of an educated populace, and under the umbrella of democracy, America's capitalistic economy has flourished, at least when compared with other political economies in recent history and around the globe. True capitalism, however, presumes the free flow of information—accurate information—that discriminating consumers use to make enlightened choices in the marketplace. Thus it is that we extol integrity, honesty, and the resulting trust as the cornerstones of the American free market economy. When we find ourselves in a period of skepticism and doubt about the veracity of these cornerstones, as we do now, we must take stock of the situation and determine a corrective course of action.

Going forward, then, we offer our reflections on the substantive issues presented in this book as well as those before the American investing public today. We remain committed to the ideal—the virtuous underpinnings of corporate governance in the United States—while fully aware of the real—the flawed reality of our current system and of human nature itself. It is with a spirit of balancing these two views that we submit our final thoughts.

A RESTLESSNESS

As we described in our Preface, corporate America is experiencing a series of ethical and legal lapses. We find ourselves wondering if these problems are caused simply by a few corporate offenders, or whether they are indicative of systemic weaknesses in the scheme of corporate American operations. Most likely it is a combination of both. Regardless, we do know that these questions are shaking the investing public's confidence in corporations and, as a result, in the markets that comprise the stocks of publicly traded corporations. Before an appropriate response can be fashioned, we must first understand what has happened and why. We should be very conscious, however, of the reality that inaccurate diagnoses and inappropriate remedies will not solve the problem but could bring their own set of new troubles.

ATTEMPTS AT REGULATION OFTEN LEAD TO UNINTENDED CONSEQUENCES

Well-meaning attempts to regulate business activities perceived to be unsavory often lead to serious unintended consequences. We remind the readers of the explosion in the levels of total compensation of chief executive officers (CEOs) that resulted in part from attempts by the federal government to set limits on the tax deductibility of corporate salaries. The result, after 10 years of experience, is that the compensation of CEOs has skyrocketed, with total compensation now equal to many times the former levels. This result seems to be diametrically opposite to that sought by those writing the law. In complex situations, it is often difficult to forecast the outcome of any regulatory action. Those affected will, in the process of acting in their own self-interest, bring into play alternatives not thought through sufficiently by those initiating the change.

We therefore suggest caution as many call for increased regulation and changes to the laws to tighten controls on public corporations. The current laws are adequate, for the most part, from our perspective. What is needed is stricter enforcement and serious penalties for the dishonest and illegal acts of directors, CEOs, and senior managers.

As the rules are tightened and the burdens of being a public corporation become more onerous, we can expect an increase in the trend of companies "going private." This trend would be enhanced by the large sources of private debt and equity available and the consistent and ludicrous demands of financial analysts and large institutional investors for relentless quarter-to-quarter favorable financial results. Many investors, boards, and managers are finding the private arena more conducive to good business operations, where the emphasis properly can be given to cash flow and wealth creation rather than quarterly increases in earnings per share. Would a massive shift to private companies, though, be in the best interests of the economy and investors in general?

The danger, of course, is that in an effort to curb the abuses of the few, we create burdens for the majority that deter economic growth and access by the average investor to good equity investments.

THE TRANSGRESSIONS

Perhaps the best way to begin thinking about current trends in American business is to look at the types of transgressions that have violated or skirted the rules. They include for the most part

- Executive compensation grossly disproportionate to corporate results
- Stock promotion that has gone to an extreme in the creation of very questionable or unproven business concepts. These concepts have been hyped in initial public offerings (IPOs) and stock run-ups to the profit of the investment bankers, market makers, and insiders and at the expense of the average investor. It is difficult to discern how much of this activity has resulted from poor economic judgment and how much from unethical behavior.
- The misuse of corporate funds
- Trading on insider information, particularly by managers exercising stock options that have rewarded short-term thinking
- Disclosure problems that have misrepresented the true earnings and financial condition of too many companies
- Obstruction of justice by concealing activities or destroying evidence

There is little that can be done to the system of business regulation to protect investors from bad economic judgment. It remains one of the risks of business itself. The moral lapses and the intolerable ethics, however, can and should be dealt with. We note that many transgressions on the part of corporate executives in the early 2000s violate existing laws, and we hope that judicial responses will encompass aggressive prosecution of what amounts to criminal behavior. American business and the investing population are in need of a signal that white-collar crime is as reprehensible as any other type of dishonesty and that violators will forfeit their ill-gotten gains and serve meaningful time in prison. Such a response has not occurred consistently in the past. Going forward, it seems essential that the violators be rooted out of the system and that punishment be made severe enough to deter others if its integrity is to be preserved.

HAS SOMETHING HAPPENED TO AMERICAN VALUES?

The long list of ongoing corporate misconduct leads some to question our sense of values as a society. In too many prominent settings it appears that unethical and dishonest behavior is tolerated—and even admired—if it results in winning or making large sums of money. Some politicians seem to have no trouble misrepresenting the facts for their political gain. They call it *spin*, but this is often a socially acceptable word for bias, if not lying. Hollywood and the media celebrate antiheroes and their glamorous and decadent lifestyles. We also have become accustomed to seeing people who have chosen to serve—religious leaders, labor leaders, or other activists—violate their fiduciary responsibilities and even flaunt their hypocrisy. We are left to wonder whether our society truly values integrity, or whether we have become tolerant of a looser standard of behavior. Has our increasingly permissive society encouraged the corporate malfeasance that is eroding investor confidence?

INTEGRITY MATTERS

During the heyday of the dot-com mania, many investors and employees made substantial sums of money on new economy stocks. Later, the stocks tumbled, companies collapsed, and many workers were left unemployed and sorely disappointed with only worthless stock options to show for their efforts. Was there guilt to assign to the people promoting the stocks or to the greedy and gullible investors who were looking for the easy buck? Some investors chose to pass on new economy stocks, including Warren Buffett, CEO of Berkshire Hathaway, who claimed he could not quantitatively justify the investments. He was not alone. Frank Batten of Landmark Communications describes a very different value system when he talks about whether or not the Weather Channel should have "gone public."

> In 2000, we dodged a bullet. At that time, we faced strong internal pressure to make an initial public offering and offer stock options to members of our weather.com unit. At the height of the dot.com frenzy in the stock market, weather.com's managers were finding it difficult to recruit and retain excellent people. We were experiencing extraordinarily high turnover, which was

disrupting operations and hurting sales. Many of our good people were lured away with promises of stock options and the prospect of "getting rich quick" through a subsequent IPO.

We debated this issue very seriously, and we ultimately decided against an IPO and options. Instead, we installed a long-term performance incentive plan for weather.com staffers. A few months later that decision was validated when the dot.com market came tumbling down.

I have been asked why I objected to an IPO when the dot.com market was on a crazy high. Why not take the cash-in at a fantastic price? Actually we might have made an extraordinary return if we could have pulled off a stunt like that. But I had two problems with the idea—one practical and the other a question of ethics and fairness.

The practical problem was that the odds of pulling it off would have been low. That's clear in the wake of the Nasdaq meltdown, but it seemed to me a big problem even before the crash. Let's assume the "market value," on paper, of weather.com had been bid up into the billions of dollars after an IPO. Securities and Exchange Commission rules would have locked up the equity positions of Landmark and its employees for some months. After the lock-up period, *if* the value had still been high, Landmark would still have been limited to dribbling stock sales into the market in small lots. The market for those stocks would have been so thin that any sizable sale would have killed the price. So, Landmark would have cashed in a big bundle only if the stock had stayed dramatically overpriced for a long time.

The ethical problem was that it didn't feel right to engage in the equivalent of "tulip mania." Some dot.com prices had no relationship to any return most of these companies could make in decades. Companies like Amazon and Yahoo! were wildly overpriced, let alone what I call the "smoke.coms" (smoke, mirrors, and little else). I could not justify selling a new stock knowing that, in all probability, a few Wall Street insiders would make a small killing on the IPO while many "widows and orphans" would get ripped off. A business strategy of making investments with the goal of making quick bucks in crazy markets would be akin to shooting craps in Las Vegas. Over the long term, the odds would be better at the craps table.

And, finally, there was the one telling question to which I never got a satisfactory answer: "What does the next generation of good people at weather.com get, after the value of the company has been handed out to this generation?" As long as I lacked a good answer to that question, I felt an IPO would be hard to justify.[1]

This story makes several important points. First, there are still Frank Battens out there—a lot of them—who value integrity and are concerned with how they make their money. We are certain that they are in the majority—those very decent, hard-working people who are trying to do the right thing run most businesses. The excesses of recent years have been readily apparent to many observers who chose not to participate, for ethical and perhaps legal reasons.

Despite the majority of principled individuals, the sad events of corporate crime have happened on a large, if not unprecedented, scale. Many people have become caught up in the easy-buck, anything-goes culture, which must come to a quick end if corporate America is to regain the public's confidence. This confidence is essential to the smooth functioning of our capital markets.

TRANSGRESSORS

To begin to fix the problem, we need to have some perspective as to what went wrong. Let's examine the following players in the drama and, subsequently, the role of each group:

- CEOs and senior management
- Investment bankers
- Market makers
- Investment analysts
- Public accounting firms
- Regulators
- Boards of directors

CEOs and Senior Management

Clearly, some CEOs and senior managers developed grandiose strategies that were either flawed or poorly executed. They may or may not have been sincere in their beliefs about the potential of the strategies, but they were very clever in two respects—they knew how to promote their strategies to the investment community, and they knew how to design compensation plans that paid off handsomely from the resulting stock appreciation. How much of this movement was ego and hype, how much was incompetence, and how much was pure greed and dishonesty is very difficult to say. In many cases, some or all of these circumstances were in play.

One of the more curious explanations by some CEOs is that they were not aware of what was going on inside their own organizations. Clearly, a CEO must delegate and cannot know every detail of activity within the firm. Nonetheless, a truly involved CEO accepts the responsibility of being accountable for corporate activities and recognizes the importance of having effective controls in place to keep himself or herself informed. Most important, the CEO sets a tone of integrity at the top of the organization that works to govern the behavior of subordinates. Failure to establish this culture of honesty and accountability can have dire consequences for the organization.

Investment Bankers, Market Makers, and Analysts

Investment bankers, market makers, and analysts have had a major role in creating the problems of corporate America in that they have created the temptations to which CEOs and boards have succumbed. Investment bankers are transaction-driven—they make huge fees from transactions such as mergers, acquisitions, and divestitures—and therefore have a bias toward making them happen—something that they do very well. Investment bankers make their fees without regard to what happens to investors' money once a transaction has occurred. Of course, there is the longer-term cost of lost reputation, but this has not seemed to be a huge deterrent. Short memories abound in this arena, a perfect reflection of its short-term thinking.

Market makers, likewise, are transaction-driven. They depend on people buying and selling to earn fees or spreads on the transactions. Logically, they promote stocks. Both investment bankers and market makers (frequently the same firms) do this by having analysts provide recommendations. Analysts are often paid on the volume of shares moved in the stocks they follow. The evidence here is painfully clear—buy recommendations drastically outnumber sell recommendations. The imbalance is simply stunning.

What is being described is a system that is fraught with inherent conflicts of interest among the investment industry, the issuing companies, and investors. Those with the most at risk—investors—are the least well informed, a perverse twist of the ideal situation. There is no practical way to close this information gap completely, but a drive for greater corporate transparency and disconnection of the analyst from the underwriter would help.

Public Accounting Firms

The traditional role of the auditors has been to ensure that the information provided to investors is accurate—in an effort to overcome their information deficit. There are a number of reasons that this has not worked well in recent cases. One is that the accounting rules have become so complicated that the layperson has difficulty understanding what is being reported. More sophisticated investors can cut through the rules to the underlying economics, but others are left dependent on what analysts tell them, assuming that their reporting is accurate and unbiased.

Auditing also has been seen as a commodity, and auditors have been under tremendous pressure to be price competitive. This pressure, in turn, made it more difficult to do a thorough job, which costs more. This is a vicious circle, broken only if fundamentally high standards exist within the audit firm. Ironically, the organization that they are auditing is also paying the bill. Thus, when auditors find a problem or get in a dispute with a client, they are under threat of losing the account. Add to this the fact that many accounting firms also act as consultants for very large fees and have numerous incentives to keep their customers happy. Under the existing system, auditors cannot be truly independent. The selection of independent auditors for publicly held companies typically is voted on at annual shareholder meetings. The choice of which firm to promote to the ballot, however, is usually made by the board well in advance of the meeting. The shareholder vote is almost always a purely pro forma proceeding, whereas the actual selection responsibility lies with the board.

Regulators

Regulators understand all of these problems and have attempted to write regulations to address them. The regulations to date, though, have not dealt with the systemic economic conflicts of interest that are at the core of the problem. Regulators have two responsibilities—prevention and prosecution. The regulations give honest people rules to play by, and they work for most people. Greedy, unethical, and dishonest parties, however, are not going to play by the rules. For the errant, there must be consequences for violations—and these have not always been pursued with vigor for a variety of reasons, including lack of staff, political considerations, and incompetence, among others.

Boards of Directors

Boards of directors fulfilled many responsibilities within failed and beleaguered firms, yet they somehow were unsuccessful in preventing or halting the demise of their organizations. They hired the CEOs and top managers, they created the incentive plans, they approved the business plans, and they oversaw the execution. In most cases, they also approved relevant transactions with investment bankers.

Why, then, did the directors fail in their duties? There are probably as many explanations as there are situations. Generally, though, the reasons include some combination of well-meaning incompetence, lack of industry expertise, demanding schedules, lack of large enough stakes to motivate careful attention, lack of independence from management, lack of information, collusion for personal gain, and painfully poor governance processes.

WHAT SHOULD BE DONE?

Because there are multiple causes of America's business dilemmas, no single solution will suffice to resolve them. As this is written, the political process is in high gear to devise new laws and regulations to help correct the problems. We refrain from suggesting what these revised regulations should be, except to make a few general observations, because the revisions may or may not have been passed well before the reader sees this book. Rather than propose revisions ourselves, we want to summarize how we think regulation should assist boards in ensuring that their companies measure up to high standards of governance. Our general comments are straightforward. Regulators (writers of the rules) should

- Vigorously enforce existing laws and regulations and levy penalties that are severe and uniformly applied.
- Carefully create new regulations and practices that will ensure that the system functions more effectively. The New York Stock Exchange recommendations are a major step in this direction.[2]
- Rethink and restructure the existing relationships and incentives that drive unethical behavior, addressing, for example:
  - How the bargaining power of the client and the external auditor could be equalized
  - How investment bankers, market makers, and directors could share more of the risk borne by the shareholder
  - How securities analysts could be decoupled entirely from underwriting and market making activities
  - The need for a national campaign on behalf of investor groups and the public exchanges to raise the standards of all boards to meet the new definitions of independence of action and competency.

THE RIGHT BOARD, THE RIGHT CEO, AND THE RIGHT STRATEGY

We follow the admonitions just listed with the some practical advice to board members. We have drawn on the material presented in the preceding chapters of this book, hoping to provide a road map for more effective corporate governance—and we hope the path will be well traveled.

The Dream of Every Shareholder: An Effective Board

The strength of any board correlates with the aggregate abilities of the directors and with their individual capacities for independent action. The latter is difficult to quantify, whereas the former is generally apparent, based on the director's career experience and specific skills. The more diverse the backgrounds and skill sets of directors, the greater is the likelihood of effective aggregate ability.

It is necessary to understand and deal with tradeoffs that will have to be made to fit the individual directors to the larger purpose of the organization. First and foremost, candidates for the board must have unquestioned integrity. Because shareholders entrust directors with complete authority to act on their behalf, shareholders must be confident that the candidates are of the highest character and adhere to lofty ethical standards. Individual directors should bring needed expertise to the board, which could be related to the industry, customers, financial matters, or general management skills and experience. The stronger the individual members of the board, the stronger the board will be. Finally, it is essential that individual directors, regardless of their other attributes, be capable of functioning effectively on a team and of engaging in no-fault confrontation, and be willing to express contrary views when they are called for.

The Buck Stops with the Board

The shareholders can credit or blame the board for the success or failure of the organization, but the board has no one else to whom it can shift the credit or blame. The directors must recognize their role and be willing to take responsibility for the results of their actions or inactions. When things are going well, it is easy for directors and shareholders to become complacent. Even then, there must be a watchful eye for potential problems. When there is a crisis, the board usually mobilizes itself, unfortunately often with more passion than reason. It is when an organization is in gradual, perhaps almost imperceptible decline that a board can be lulled into undue self-satisfaction. The board must be aware of the ever-changing situation of the firm and be ready to intervene when it is necessary.

Successful organizations have a passion for their mission, but they must go beyond passion to operate effectively. They must understand the inextricable link between mission, competence, and finances. They must not let their passion cloud their reasoning.

Integrity Is Not Negotiable

A culture of integrity begins with the board of any organization. It is reflected in the decisions and behavior of the directors, collectively and individually; in whom they hire and promote; and in the actions they tolerate. Integrity includes both the substance of decisions and actions of the board and the resulting reputation, which is a matter of perception. Unpleasant surprises naturally will arise. If the board and the company have a reputation for forthright and prompt disclosures and actions, they will build credibility with their constituents. As a result, the constituents are more likely to give them the benefit of any doubt.

The converse is also true: a lack of integrity will cause constituents to overreact to bad news, believing the worst, regardless of what is reported.

Constructing the Board: Integrity Is Not Enough

Conscientious persons understand the serious fiduciary responsibilities of directors and will undertake to fulfill them to the best of their abilities. Effective representation, however, requires more than integrity; it also requires the competence to make sound decisions. Good directors know their limits and turn to more expert advisers when their judgment so dictates.

A primary rule for directors is to know well those with whom they are associating as a director. If senior board members and senior management are not forthright and trustworthy, there is a high potential for problems to arise. The board is totally dependent on the CEO for full, accurate, and timely information. The integrity and the diligence with which a board approaches its duties are severely tested when dilemmas present themselves. These are the times when a director is thankful that he or she was thoughtful in deciding whether or not to join the board or to remain with the board after a change in leadership.

The Fallout from Poor Board Selection

The boards of most U.S. public corporations bear little resemblance to the ideal vision of board composition—small in size with a clear majority of outside, professional, keenly committed directors whose incentives and compensation are related to the company's long-term performance. Many boards are too large and too often consist of insiders who are beholden to the CEO, along with a group of outsiders chosen for their loyalty, connections, diversity, or public stature. These pivotal outside board members sometimes make their livings as professional board members and may serve on as many as 12 or more major boards. The number of boards that such directors sit on makes it next to impossible for them to have the knowledge of or even sufficient interest in their companies' activities that a director's duty of care requires.

Directors Need a Stake in the Game

There is a growing view that directors need to own significant amounts of equity to motivate them to become fully engaged. Competent directors are usually very busy people with many demands on their time. The allocation of their time and their financial resources is likely to be aligned. Thus, unless they are willing to make substantial investments relative to their net worth in a business, they are implicitly saying that they are allocating their resources elsewhere. It seems that directors would be more likely, then, to put their time and energies where their personal funds are invested.

Avenues by Which CEOs Have or Gain Control of the Board

CEOs may gradually gain control over their boards by a process of ensuring the election of friends or supporters as openings occur. In these situations, the less-than-desirable level of CEO control can persist for long periods of time, to the detriment of helpless shareholders. Under the governance system in place in the United States, it is perfectly legal for such a situation to continue indefinitely because there is no simple method to displace enough directors to effect change. The only mechanisms available for dealing with this phenomenon are shareholder lawsuits or hostile takeover bids in the event that the firm's market value drops to levels attractive to potential investors. As we described in Chapter 3, various "poison pill" measures have virtually eliminated the ability of outsiders to effect hostile takeovers, but such tactics require shareholder approval before they can be implemented. These realities leave the unhappy shareholder with the nonnegotiable option to sell his or her shares.

Important Board Decisions

The single most important decision that a board makes is selection of the CEO, particularly when there is a difficult situation. The right leader solves problems; the wrong one creates them. Getting the right leader means first having a profound understanding of the job so that there can be a clear focus on the characteristics needed for success. Success begins with a good "fit" between the person (CEO) and the situation.

Selecting or confirming the business or businesses in which the firm will operate is second in importance only to selection of the CEO. An effective management team may become ineffective by perpetually fighting against a poor market position, a poor labor environment, foreign competitors that enjoy cost advantages, and/or extensive regulatory burdens. A board should recognize that strong management should find a way to exit from bad businesses and eventually deploy the firm's resources in a better way.

The CEO Must Mesh with the Board

In a very positive sense, it is important for the CEO to "manage" the board. When the CEO clearly fails to establish a close working relationship with the board, the board will find it difficult to have a lot of confidence in the CEO. A CEO should always presell the board on all key transactions, especially prior to involving the press. The CEO must inform board members of any major actions early on and keep them involved and apprised throughout the process in order to secure their support and ensure alignment of their philosophy and espoused strategic direction with the proposed course of action. Finally, the CEO must be astute enough to identify the figurative and practical leadership of the board, whose support must be established and maintained in order for the CEO to succeed.

The board and the CEO must work together to

- Clearly identify the businesses in which they want to operate and why
- Hire the right people in terms of both their ability and their values
- Align the interests of the board and management with those of the shareholders
- Develop mutually agreeable goals, policies, and standards of performance
- Carefully evaluate the plans to achieve those goals
- Clearly understand the situation of the firm and evaluate the results
- React appropriately to the results by holding management accountable and rewarding or intervening as necessary

The Meaning of an Arm's-Length Relationship

A board that crosses the line by interfering or micromanaging the organization can undermine the effectiveness of the CEO and will find it difficult to hold the CEO accountable for things they have actually had a part in promulgating. On the other hand, a board that is too detached from what is happening or too passive in carrying out its responsibilities may in fact be abdicating its role in governance of the organization. Directors must find a way to balance these two extremes—avoiding crossing the line but yet staying proactive in carrying out their responsibilities.

Politics

Politics can be present in any organization and arise from several causes; personality clashes, individual ambitions, different agendas for the future of the organization, and protecting staff members are just some of the causes. Effective leadership is required to work through the politics when they occur to build consensus and teamwork. There is no single way of managing politics, but we do need to recognize that the personal chemistry of board members with each other and with management is of vital importance. When this chemistry is tainted for any reason, the situation should be addressed promptly.

Attracting and Retaining Talent

After a talented team has been put into place, the board must manage its collective affairs based on a few simple principles. The board has a highly important responsibility to attract and retain talented managers and hold them accountable for executing the company's agreed-upon strategy and for achieving outstanding results compared with peer companies. The directors should tie their own compensation, as well as that of the managers they attract, directly to the performance of the firm to the most practical degree possible.

The board should strive to put in place an effective compensation scheme. Talent does indeed make a difference, and outstanding talent generally costs more than mediocre talent. Thus, if the board desires outstanding results, it should be prepared to pay for a strong management team. An important objective of compensation is to appropriately and fairly match rewards to results. In the corporate setting, this translates to aligning the compensation so as to reward and motivate increases in shareholder value. As with most significant initiatives, this is easier to describe than to accomplish. Ideally, the CEO should participate in the downside risk as well as the upside profitability. Few compensation plans do this well. Furthermore, boards should beware that the wide use of comparison processes relative to executive pay generally has served to support the gradual rise of the prevailing levels of CEO compensation regardless of firm performance.

The board also should consider enhancing the likelihood of achieving its overall strategies by providing financial incentives for all levels in the organization. The entire workforce thus will become change agents rather than resisters of change. Performance should not be judged quarter by quarter but should, instead, be linked to appreciation of the company's value (market value or capitalization) over a longer time frame at a rate that exceeds the market in general. In order to judge the performance of the leadership team adequately, the board should meet regularly without the inside board members to evaluate performance.

WHEN TROUBLE ARISES

Trouble can take many forms for a board of directors, with prominent causes occurring when the corporation fails to produce acceptable results, perhaps placing it in fiscal jeopardy, or violates the civil or criminal law and is sued or prosecuted for its actions. Directors can get into trouble, individually and collectively, from the actions they did not take but should have, as well as from the action they did take and should not have. What makes being a director even more perilous is that often it is not the action or inaction itself that defines trouble but instead the outcomes or results of the conduct.

There are many ways in which a board, collectively, can get into trouble. The following are among the most common:

- Conspiring in or tolerating legal violations
- Poor results that bring about the wrath of shareholders
- Lack of board leadership
- Internal political or personality conflict problems
- Ineffective board organization and processes
- Securities violations
- Undercapitalization

CHARACTERISTICS OF EFFECTIVE BOARDS

We summarize here a few attributes that characterize boards that tend to be effective and successful.

Knowledge of the Law

Effective boards understand the law and their legal obligations in terms of their duties. The major duties are

- The fiduciary duty
- The duty of loyalty and the duty of fair dealing
- The duty of care
- The duty not to entrench
- The duty of supervision

The Willingness to Act Decisively

There are instances a board will face when time is of the essence. The CEO may be killed in an accident or die suddenly from an illness. There may be some scandal involving the company, or the CEO may be accused of, or found guilty of, some indiscretion that triggers a clause in his or her contract that allows removal for cause. There could be some external event, such as the CEO's leading an attempt at a leveraged buyout (LBO) of the firm. There are many such events that require the board to move with what the Navy terms "all deliberate speed," meaning that all processes must move forward as fast as prudently possible. Boards must have a capacity for rapid response in critical situations as crises test the independence of the board and its willingness to act. The survival of the company and the best interests of shareholders are often at stake.

A Strong Board Admits Its Mistakes and Takes Action

Boards, because they consist of human beings, will make mistakes. The important lesson is that the earlier the board realizes and admits to itself that a mistake has been made and takes the necessary action, the less will be the damage to the company and its shareholders. Thus humility is an important attribute for board members and is critical to the long-term success of an organization.

Boards Must Change, Adjust, and Adapt over Time

We noted in the vignette in Chapter 4 the continuous evolution of a high-technology company's board and its strategies as the firm grew steadily from a small startup with a strong technology base to a huge international technology company. It was essential for the board to adapt and restructure itself to meet the needs of the growing concern. As time went on, the talents brought to the board by certain directors were no longer needed, and they had to be replaced with new directors whose talents, skills, and experience more closely reflected the needs of the firm going forward.

We must remind ourselves of the very long time frame within which corporations function. Many continue on for decades, requiring an orderly series of transitions in both boards and CEOs. It is therefore important to take an equally long-term view regarding the governance processes described in this book. The fact that a board is especially effective at one point in time does not mean that shareholders can relax and expect continuity. Boards do not suddenly become exceptional or troubled. Lists of the 10 worst boards and the 10 best boards are published regularly in the business press. The movement of these boards to excellence or ridicule took place gradually over an extended period of time, hardly overnight. As terms expired, the relative effectiveness of the entire board was shaped by the sequential selection of replacement directors.

SOME FINAL THOUGHTS

Ignorance Is No Excuse

The most likely barrier to conducting an effective board meeting is the basic asymmetry in the amount of information to which management has access as opposed to that to which the board has access. All discussions are therefore one-sided unless an effort is made to close this gap and get all the directors on a more equal information footing with management. Furthermore, the board must keep itself informed about all important aspects of the company's operations. If the directors lack confidence that the CEO is candid or that he or she understands the situation, they must take the necessary steps to inform themselves. When instinct raises suspicions, they must press the point. The more resistant management is in explaining current activities, the more insistent directors should be in seeking answers. The shareholders deserve nothing less.

A Successful Organization Is Clear about Its Purpose

Just as a board needs to be future-oriented, it also must avoid too much emphasis on the administrative and the trivial. Some of this administrative work is legally necessary, but too frequently boards will deliberately allow it to distract them from their more difficult appointed tasks. Finding the right balance of emphasis greatly enhances the board's effectiveness and is an excellent indicator of the quality of its leadership.

Defining the purpose of an organization or carrying out the intent of the organizers is the responsibility of its board. If there is confusion or ambiguity about whom the organization is trying to serve, what it is trying to do, or the direction it is trying to take, all other decisions that are derived from the purpose will be equally confused and ambiguous. The boards of successful organizations have focus, centered on the purpose for which they were formed. They understand which efforts are consistent with their goals and which lead them astray. In this sense, they have disciplined thought and action.

Bylaws and Charters Are Important

Too often we think of the bylaws and corporate charter as sterile legal documents. We give them little thought, and most directors and CEOs do not even know what is in them. They are the rules of governance, however, and all directors have a responsibility to be aware of and understand them. In certain delicate situations, the finer points of the bylaws and charter may be critical in determining the outcome of the issue at hand. Many a victor in bitter confrontation owes his or her success to a better understanding of the rules, and the clever use of them in challenging circumstances.

Manage Consultants Carefully

There is a place for using consultants in a corporate environment. Getting one's company's money's worth, however, requires skill on the part of the board and the CEO. Both the board and the CEO must be particularly clear and direct about what expertise the company needs, the scope of the consulting project, and the product or service to be delivered. Unfortunately, too often consultants are used as a substitute for management, which is a sign of weakness in the organization.

LOOKING AHEAD

Our entire economic system, the most productive and wealth-creating ever devised, is vulnerable and at risk if effective governance practices are not in place across the broad spectrum of publicly held companies. There is no alternative going forward. Absent widespread effective governance, capital markets will operate inefficiently in an atmosphere of distrust and with continued erosion of investor confidence, especially on the part of individuals. Without access to these markets, economic growth and our rising standard of living will inexorably falter as creativity and aggressive growth strategies starve for lack of fresh capital.

There is, in fact, a national security issue here as well. As the only superpower, the world relies on the United States as the primary engine of worldwide economic growth and as a global peacekeeper, notwithstanding the jealous protests of many of our allies who are yet to take full responsibility for their own national security. Such a worldwide role cannot be sustained without the strong economic base underlying its support. Winning wars and keeping the peace are built on industrial power as much as on military power.

This economic base, in turn, cannot continue in the absence of effective governance practices. We cannot rely exclusively on new and ever more restrictive legislation out of the Congress, nor can we rely exclusively on the various regulatory agencies to eliminate corporate malfeasance through more stringent enforcement of existing and new regulations, as necessary as these are. Surely, the current imperative for greater management accountability and corporate transparency will help to restore investor confidence, but these legal and regulatory strictures also come at some cost to the good corporate citizens who compose the overwhelming majority of publicly held companies.

We are convinced that these companies must transform their boards into effective instruments of sound governance. There are many companies whose shareholders already enjoy the fruits of good governance. There are, however, far too many who do not; whose boards are servants of the CEO rather than of the shareholders, and who woefully lack the competence and independence of thought and action absolutely essential to positive board performance. There must be a higher standard for board membership that reflects this unceasing need for independent judgment. Many CEOs will reflexively resist the nomination of such independent thinkers, viewing them as natural adversaries or, at best, wild cards in what historically has been a stacked deck, as evidenced by those CEOs who have been lavishly rewarded for failures. The irony, of course, is that the stronger the board, the greater are the chances of superior policy decisions and the value-creating results that follow them, both for shareholders and for management.

Acquiring and perpetuating an independent and competent board of directors must become a primary goal of every publicly held corporation. We are increasingly optimistic that the coming years will see a gradual shift toward this goal as institutional investors combine and exert more power, the public exchanges require it, and individual investors take their proxy statements more seriously.

Morality and ethics cannot be legislated or even mandated, as history has proven time and again. Even the harshest penalties fail to eliminate all violators. Rather, we see the burden for responsible and effective governance ultimately falling on existing boards and the integrity of their nominating processes. We are hopeful that a serious and sustained migration in this direction has begun and with it the restoration of investor confidence.

It should be apparent at this point that the functioning of a company's board of directors is somewhat indescribable in that it draws on the unique amalgamation of the skills, experiences, and motivations of the individual directors. The effectiveness of the board as a whole is circumscribed by the board's ability to organize itself and rise to the challenging occasions that surely will confront its business. Among the most important of these challenges is the choosing of a CEO, which does not happen often enough for most directors to gain significant experience in such decisions. The result is that the most important decisions often must be made based on instinct and values rather than experience. We are hopeful that policy, too, plays a role in process of CEO selection. Directors should recognize their role in governance: to direct the making and administration of policies—policies that address the selection of the CEO, as well as the other important decisions of the board and hence the firm.

We salute the thousands of directors who struggle to make our system perform. Our hope is that this work contributes to the ongoing debate.

REVIEW QUESTIONS

1. How would you characterize the current climate regarding corporate governance in the United States?
2. Do you think there has been a deterioration in American values?
3. What are the principal transgressions with which boards are faced?
4. What is the role of integrity in the governance process?
5. Who are the major players in the corporate governance game?
6. What are your final thoughts with regard to corporate governance?

Notes

PREFACE

[1] Wessel, David, "Venal Sins: Why the Bad Guys of the Boardroom Emerged en Masse," *Wall Street Journal*, June 20, 2002, p. A1.

CHAPTER 1

[1] Smith, Adam, *An Inquiry Into the Nature and Causes of the Wealth of Nations* (New York: Random House/Modern Library, 1994).

[2] Shi, David E., *The Simple Life* (New York: Oxford University Press, 1985), p. 8.

[3] Beatty, Jack (ed.), *Colossus: How the Corporation Changed America* (New York: Broadway Books, 2000), p. 6.

[4] Johnson, Paul, *A History of the American People* (New York: Harper Perennial, 1997), p. 560.

[5] *Abstract of the Census of Manufactures* (Washington: U.S. Government Printing Office, 1919) Table 195, p. 340.

[6] Johnson, Paul, *A History of the American People* (New York: Harper Perennial, 1997), pp. 559–560.

CHAPTER 2

[1] Lorsch, Jay W., *Pawns or Potentates: The Reality of America's Corporate Boards* (Boston: Harvard Business School Press, 1989), p. 7.

[2] *The Principles of Corporate Governance: Analysis and Recommendations* (St. Paul, MN: American Law Institute, 1994), p. 61.

[3] Drucker, Peter F., *Managing in Turbulent Times* (New York: Harper & Row, 1980), p. 29.

[4] *Managerial Duties and Business Law* (Boston: Harvard Business School Press, 1995), p. 4.

[5] *The Principles of Corporate Governance: Analysis and Recommendations* (St. Paul, MN: American Law Institute, 1994), pp. 283–285.

[6] *Ibid.*, pp. 300–301.

[7] *Ibid.*, pp. 138–139.

[8] *Ibid.*, p. 405.

CHAPTER 3

[1] Lorsch, Jay W., *Pawns or Potentates: The Reality of America's Corporate Boards* (Boston: Harvard Business School Press, 1989), p. 7.

[2] *Ibid.*, p. 7.

[3] This material has drawn on *Audit Committees: Best Practices for Protecting Shareholder Interests* (New York: Price Waterhouse Coopers, 1999). Additional sources of this material include "Report of the NACD Blue Ribbon Commission on Audit Committees, A Practical Guide," National Association of Corporate Directors and The Center for Board Leadership, New York, 2000; "Report and Recommendations of the Blue Ribbon Committee on Improving the Effectiveness of Corporate Audit Committees," sponsored by the New York Stock Exchange, the National Association of Securities Dealers, and the Securities and Exchange Commission, *http://www.nyse.com/pdfs/blueribb.pdf*, accessed February 19, 2001; "SEC Will Place Greater Emphasis on Corporate Governance, Levitt Says," *Investor Relations Business*, January 8, 2001, pp. 4–5; "Final Rule: Revision of the Commission's Auditor Independence Requirements," Securities and Exchange Commission; 17 CFR Parts 210 and 240, *http://www.sec.gov/rules/final/33-7919.htm*, accessed February 18, 2001; Stephen Barlas, "Corporate Audit Committee Must Gear Up," *Strategic Finance* 82(7):23–24, January 2001; Mark S. Beasley et al., "Fraudulent Financial Reporting: Consideration of Industry Traits and Corporate Governance Mechanisms," *Accounting Horizons*, December 2000, pp. 441-454 (this study focused on the technology, health care, and financial services industries; the companies generally were small market capitalization companies listed on the Nasdaq or OTC markets; sample included 200 companies with SEC enforcement actions); Mark S. Beasley et al., "Preventing Fraudulent Financial Reporting," *The CPA Journal*, December 2000 (*http://www.nysscpa.org/cpajournal/2000/1200/features/f121400a.htm*) accessed February 19, 2000.

CHAPTER 4

[1] Hambrick, Donald C., and Eric M. Johnson, "Outsider Directors with a Stake: The Linchpin in Improving Governance," *California Management Review* 42(4):108-127, 2000.

CHAPTER 7

[1] Murphy, Kevin J., and Jay Dial, "General Dynamics: Compensation and Strategy (A)," Harvard Business School case study, Harvard Business School, Boston (9-494-048), revised December 3, 1997.

[2] Jefferson, David A., and Andy Pasztor, "Pentagon Audits Show Contractors Owe U.S. Hundreds of Millions in A-12 Job," *Wall Street Journal*, December 19, 1990, p. A4.

[3] GD Proxy Statement, March 28, 1991.

[4] GD Proxy Statements, March 28, 1991, and December 29, 1991.

[5] Daily stock prices from Dow Jones News Retrieval and Compustat.

[6] General Dynamics' Annual Reports.

[7] Murphy, Kevin J., and Jay Dial, "General Dynamics: Compensation and Strategy (B)," Harvard Business School case study, Harvard Business School, Boston (9-494-049), revised December 3, 1997.

[8] General Dynamics' Annual Reports.

[9] "Business Brief: Warren Buffett Gives General Dynamics a Proxy to Vote Berkshire's 15% Stake," *Wall Street Journal*, September 18, 1992, p. B3. Buffett revised his grant of proxy to "as long as Mr. Anders remains as chairman of General Dynamics" in May 1993.

[10] Murphy, Kevin J., and Jay Dial, "General Dynamics: Compensation and Strategy (B)," Harvard Business School case study, Harvard Business School, Boston (9-494-049), revised December 3, 1997.

[11] *The Crystal Report on Executive Compensation* 4(8), October 1992.

CHAPTER 8

[1] PepsiCo Presentation to the MS Global Consumer Conference, November 7, 2001.

[2] Machiavelli, Niccolo, *The Prince* (1532), from *The Portable Machiavelli*, edited and translated by Peter Bondanella and Mark Musa (New York: Viking Penguin, 1979), p. 94.

CHAPTER 9

[1] Brans, H. W., *The First American: The Life and Times of Benjamin Franklin* (New York: Doubleday, 2000), pp. 40–41.

[2] DeBlasi, Michelle, "Stocking Up on Buybacks," *Bloomberg*, May 1999, p. 109.

[3] Brealey, Richard A., and Stewart C. Myers, *Principles of Corporate Finance* (New York: Irwin/McGraw-Hill, 2000), p. 442.

[4] *Ibid.*, p. 443.

[5] *Ibid.*, p. 442.

[6] *Ibid.*, p. 487.

[7] *Ibid.*, pp. 441–442.

[8] *Ibid.*, pp. 442, 446.

[9] Lie, Erik, and Heidi J. Lei, "The Role of Personal Taxes in Corporate Decisions: An Empirical Analysis of Share Repurchases and Dividends," *Journal of Finance and Quantitative Analysis* (December 1999), p. 542.

[10] Brealey, Richard A., and Stewart C. Myers, *Principles of Corporate Finance* (New York: Irwin/McGraw-Hill, 2000), p. 441.

CHAPTER 11

[1] Berkshire Hathaway Annual Report, 1985, p. 9.

CHAPTER 12

[1] Abbott, Charles C., *Governance: A Guide for Trustees and Directors* (Boston: The Cheswick Center, 1979).

[2] Urban Institute, *The New Nonprofit Almanac and Desk Reference* (San Francisco: Jossey-Bass, 2002), pp. 4–5.

[3] Carver, John, *Boards That Make a Difference* (San Francisco: Jossey-Bass, 1990), pp. 6–7.

[4] *Ibid.*, pp. 2–3.

CHAPTER 13

[1] Batten, Frank, *The Weather Channel* (Boston: Harvard Business School Press, 2002), pp. 232–234.

[2] New York Stock Exchange, "Report of the Corporate Accountability and Listing Standards Committee," June 6, 2002.

INDEX

AA bond rating, 158
Accountability:
   criteria for board, 201–202
   of management, 196
   in not-for-profit organizations, 225–226
Accounting firms, 233–234
Acquisitions, 145, 165–166, 178
Activism, 175–177
Adaptation, 242
Advisers, 13
Advisory boards, 212, 213
Africa, 5
Agendas, 36, 88, 89
Agent, registered, 35
Ages:
   of candidates, 100
   mandatory retirement, 63
Aggressive investors, 174
Allocation of risk/income/control, 157–159
Amazon, 231
American Law Institute, 14, 16
American revolution, 3, 4
American Stock Exchange, 151
Analysts, 233
Anders, William, 115–119
Annual shareholders' meetings, 37–38
Antitrust laws, 11
Arm's-length relationship, 137, 163, 239
Aronson v. Lewis, 26–27
Articles of Confederation, 4
Articles of incorporation, 34–36
Assessment, outside, 105–106
Associations, not-for-profit, 211
Attendance records, 202
Attracting talent, 240
Audit committees, 45–46, 48–53
   charter of, 49
   control function of, 25
   failure of, 53
   guiding principles for, 48–49
   independence of, 200
   membership of, 50–51
   mission of, 49
   organization/actions of, 50–53
   policies/practices of, 52–53
   roles/responsibilities of, 51

Auditors, 233–234
Authorized capital stock, 35–36

Bankers, 233
Banks, 13, 70–73
Base salaries, 122, 123
Batten, Frank, 230–231
Benchmarking with peers, 105
Berkshire Hathaway, 76, 118, 193, 230
Bill of Rights, 4
Black-market opportunities, 8
Black Monday, 168
Board-management relationship, 15–16,
    133–148
   and corporate strategy, 135–148
   and intervention, 146–147
   and oversight responsibility, 145–146
   as part of solution, 239
   and sustainable competitive advantage,
    141–142
Board meetings, 83–90
   agenda for, 88, 89
   attendees at, 87–88
   efficiency/formality of, 87
   frequency of, 36, 86, 88, 90, 223–224
   mechanics of, 86–87
   minutes of, 88
   preparation for, 85–86
   scheduling of, 88, 90
   teamwork in, 86
Board(s) of directors, 11, 55–79
   adaptation of, 242
   and articles of incorporation, 36
   attributes of, 200–202
   the best, 202–204
   CEO control over, 76–78, 238
   committees of, 44–46, 195
   control and power of, 78–79
   corporate strategy function of, 137–138
   and dominant personalities, 75–76
   effective, 236, 241–242
   failures of (*see* Failures, board)
   important decisions by, 238–239
   integrity of, 236–237
   intervention by, 146–147
   leadership of, 193–194

Board(s) of directors (*Cont.*):
  legal knowledge of, 241
  long-term effectiveness of, 73–74
  of mature vs. growth companies, 74–75
  mistakes admitted to by, 242
  nominating committee for, 63–70
  of not-for-profit organizations, 212–213,
    219–222
  organization of, 57–61
  performance evaluation role of, 107
  profile of, 64–65
  quality of, 201
  reelection of incumbent, 62–63
  representative, 57, 80–82
  results of poor selection of, 237
  retiring CEO on, 62
  selection of new members for, 63–65,
    67–68, 220–221
  size of, 56–58, 178, 221–222
  and stock ownership, 61–62, 238
  structure of, 56–57, 78, 237
  structuring new (case study), 70–73
  and taking responsibility, 236
  as transgressors, 234
  and willingness to act decisively, 241–242
  (*See also* Directors)
Boards That Make a Difference (John Carver),
  212
Bonds, corporate, 158, 159
Bonuses, 110, 111, 116, 123–125
Brand recognition, 135
Brehm v. Eisner, 27
Buffett, Warren, 76, 118, 127, 193, 230
Business judgment rule, 14, 26–28
BusinessWeek, 200, 203
Buyback (of shares), 180
Bylaws, 36–42
  in articles of incorporation, 36
  considerations for, 38–40
  defensive measures in, 40–42
  disputes regarding (case study), 39–40
  importance of, 243–244

C Corporations, 10, 150, 152
Campbell Soup, 202
Capital, investment, 2
Capital gains, 125, 126
Capital stock, authorized, 35–36
Capital structure, 155–161
  allocation of risk/income/control in,
    157–159
  and corporate structure, 161–163
  and cost, 160–161
  and off-balance-sheet financing, 159–160
Capitalism, 1–2, 6
Care, duty of, 22–24, 28–30, 34, 191, 214–215
Carver, John, 211, 212
CASA (Court Appointed Special
  Advocates), 217

Cash compensation, 112, 113
Cause for removal, 36–37, 62, 70, 128
Caveat emptor, 190
CEO compensation, 109–131
  to attract/retain talent, 240
  building a plan for, 121–122
  components of, 122–127
  consequences of regulation on, 228–229
  and employment contracts, 127–128
  full disclosure about, 176
  General Dynamics strategy (case study),
    114–119
  goal of, 112
  golden parachutes as, 128–129
  issues in, 120–121
  norms for, 110–113
  in not-for-profits, 215
  for outside candidate, 97–98
  and outstanding options triggers,
    129–130
  transgressions with, 229
CEO succession, 91–108
  insider vs. outsider candidates for, 92–98
  as major board task, 193, 238
  normal process of, 100–103
  outsider selection (case study), 96–98
  and performance evaluation of new
    CEO, 103–107
  role of CEO in, 91–92
  sudden need for, 98–100
  and unimpressive candidates, 103
CEOs (*see* Chief executive officers)
CFOs (chief financial officers), 45
Chairman of the board, 43
Change of control, 130
Charitable trusts, 211
Charters of incorporation, 9
  importance of, 243–244
  state grants of, 13
Chief executive officers (CEOs), 11
  boards controlled by, 76–78, 238
  as chairman of the board, 43
  compensation of (*see* CEO compensation)
  dominant personality of, 75–76
  and employment contracts, 127–128
  of not-for-profit organizations, 224–225
  performance evaluation of new, 103–107
  performance evaluation role of, 107
  retiring, 62
  selection of (*see* CEO succession)
  as transgressors, 232
Chief financial officers (CFOs), 45
Chief operating officers (COOs), 72
Citicorp, 167, 168
Citigroup, 74
Civil rights movement, 5
Civil system, 7
Civil War, 11
Class A common stock, 35

Class-action lawsuits, 174, 177, 198, 199
Class B common stock, 35
Classes:
  of directors, 42
  social, 3
Clients, not-for-profit, 216, 221
Coca Cola, 76
Colonial rule, 5
Commerce Bank, 70, 71
Commercial sector, 208
Committee(s):
  for boards, 44–46, 195
  importance of, 85–86
  in not-for-profit organizations, 222–223
  of outside directors, 44
Common good, 8
Common stock, 35
Community, 217
Community banks, 70–73
Compaq Corporation, 177
Compensation:
  bylaws regarding, 37
  CEO (see CEO compensation)
  director, 57, 59
  and not-for-profit organizations, 215–217, 225
  volunteers vs., 213–214
Compensation committees, 45, 201
Competence, 13, 189
Competition, 1, 2
  with the corporation, 21–22
  and not-for-profits, 216
  trusts and reduced, 11
Competitive advantage, sustainable, 141–142
Comptroller of the Currency, 186
Compustat database, 80
Confidence, 168–169
Conflicts, political and personality, 194–195
Conflicts of interest, 13
  as cause for removal, 62
  director, 190–192
  in not-for-profits, 214
  of outside candidate, 97–98
Conspiracies, 192
Constitution of the United States, 4–5
Consultants, 244
Contingency plans, 99
Contracts, 7, 127–128
Contributions, not-for-profit, 212
Control:
  of boards by CEOs, 76–78, 238
  in capital structure, 157–159
COOs (chief operating officers), 72
Corporate bonds, 158, 159
Corporate governance, 2
  evolution of, 9–10
  role of, 11–12
Corporate name, 34

Corporate officers, 43–44
Corporate opportunities, 21
Corporate strategy, 135–148
  board function in, 137–138
  crisis-handling (case study), 139–140
  ever-changing nature of, 142–145
  formulation vs. implementation of, 140–141
  PepsiCo restructuring (case study), 135–137
  restructuring via acquisitions/divestitures, 145
  and sustainable competitive advantage, 141–142
Corporate structure, 150–155
  diversified, 163–170
  and financial structure, 161–163
  private vs. public ownership, 153
  public, 153–155
  selection of, 151–153
  types of, 150–151
Corporations:
  definition of, 10
  nonbusiness, 9
  not-for-profit, 210
  objective/conduct of, 16–18
Cost (of capital), 160–161
Court Appointed Special Advocates (CASA), 217
Courts, 8
Creditors, 217
Criminal system, 7
Crises, 139–140, 175
Cross-directorships, 200

Dartmouth College v. Woodward, 10
Debt, 157–159, 168
Decapitalization, 168
Decentralization (see Diversification and decentralization)
Decision making, 192–193, 238–239
Declaration of Independence, 4, 5
Defense, national, 7
Defense industry, 115
Defensive measures, 40–42, 182
Delaware:
  business judgment rule in, 26–28
  director-related laws of, 13–14, 15
  duty of care rules in, 28–29
  as state of incorporation, 34
Delegation, 15
Deliberative process (of succession planning), 100–103
Democracy, 4
Democratic governance, 4–5
Development, economic and social, 6
Digital technology, 3
Directors, 13–31
  duties of (see Duties, director)

Directors (*Cont.*):
  governing role of, 14–16
  indemnification of, 30
  independence of, 59–61
  lead, 43
  motivation of, 188
  on multiple boards, 174
  number of, 36, 37
  review of, 62–63
  standards for, 26–28
  state laws related to, 13–14
  trustees vs., 34
Directors and officers indemnification
    (DOI) insurance, 30, 199
Disclosure problems, 229
Disney, 76
Dissident shareholders, 174
Distributions, 118
Diversification and decentralization,
    142–143, 161–170
  acquiring businesses to achieve, 165–166
  and repurchase of shares, 166–169
  restructuring strategies for, 164
  selling businesses to achieve, 164–165
  and selling entire business, 165
  spinning off businesses to achieve, 165
Diversity (of board membership), 55–56, 75
Divestitures, 117, 145
Dividends, 117, 118, 152
Divisibility of ownership, 10
Documents, governing (*see* Governing
    documents)
DOI insurance (*see* Directors' and officers'
    indemnification insurance)
Dominant personalities, 75–76, 215
Donations, 217
Donors, 226
Dot-com mania, 230–233
"Double dip," 98
Double taxation, 152
Dow-Jones Industrials Index, 57–61, 80–81,
    105, 110, 112
Drivers of success, 226
Drucker, Peter, 17, 208
Due diligence, 68–70, 188–189
Dun and Bradstreet, 158
Duration, 36
Duties, director, 16–26
  care, duty of, 22–24, 28–30, 34, 191,
    214–215
  fiduciary duties, 16–20, 214
  of hostile takeover offers, dealing with,
    25–26
  loyalty/fair dealing, 20–22, 30, 34, 214
  not to entrench, 24
  supervision, 24–25

Earnings-per-share (EPS), 169–170
East India Company, 9

Economic development, 6
Economic unions, 7
EDS (Electronic Data Services), 195
Education, 3
Eisner, Michael, 76
Election(s):
  bylaws regarding, 36
  of directors, 69–73
  of incumbent directors, 62–63
Electronic Data Services (EDS), 195
Elizabeth I, queen of England, 9
Embarrassment to the firm, 62
Embezzlement, 215
Emergency situations, 98–100
Emotional quotient (EQ), 102
Employment circumstances, change in, 63
Employment contracts, 127–128
Enforcement, 8, 228–230
English common law, 4
English rule of law, 4
Enron, 176
Entire fairness, 28
Entrench, duty not to, 24
Entrenchment:
  board, 173–174
  and defensive measures, 40–42
  quasi-public companies produced by, 77
Environmental Protection Agency (EPA),
    186
EPS (*see* Earnings-per-share)
EQ (emotional quotient), 102
Equity, 158, 218–219
Ethics, 25, 189–190, 192
Excess funds, 152, 153, 167–168
Executive board, 43, 44
Executive committees, 44–45, 94, 100, 223
Executive search firms, 94
Exercising options, 126
Experience (of candidates), 100
External parity, 122
External pressures, 173–186
  board reaction to outside events, 177–178
  friendly mergers vs. hostile takeovers,
    178–185
  hostile takeover bid (case study), 179–181
  regulatory agencies, 185–186
  shareholder activism, 175–177

Failures, board, 187–205
  and audit committees, 53
  collective problems leading to, 192–198
  and good vs. bad boards, 200–204
  individual problems leading to, 189–192
  and legal concerns/indemnification,
    198–199
  out-of-touch board leading to (case
    study), 196–198
  preventing, 188–189, 199–200
  types of, 241

Fair dealing, duty of, 20–22
Fairness, entire, 28
Federal Communications Commission, 186
Federal laws, 14
Federal Reserve Bank, 186
Federal Trade Commission (FTC), 185–186
Federalism, 4
Fees (of not-for-profits), 216
Fiduciary duty, 16–20, 214
405(c)(3) organizations, 209
405(c)(4) organizations, 209
405(c)(6) organizations, 209
Focus, pressure to, 143
Food and Drug Administration, 175
Fortune 500, 74
Fortune.com, 74
Foundational decisions, 193
Foundations, not-for-profit, 210–211
Fraud, 185
Free enterprise, 1, 2
Free-market economic system, 6
French revolution, 3
Friendly mergers, 173, 178–185
Fringe benefits, 123–124
FTC (see Federal Trade Commission)
"Fulfilling their obligations," 13
Full disclosure, 16, 176–177
    duty of loyalty rules for, 30
    laws regarding, 14
    and lawsuits, 199

The "Game," 6–9
GD (see General Dynamics)
GDP (gross domestic product), 209
GE (see General Electric)
General Dynamics (GD), 114–119
General Electric (GE), 76, 96, 115, 122, 202
General Motors (GM), 74, 195
General partners, 150
Genghis Khan, 141
Geographic dispersion (of board member-
    ship), 224
Germany, 5
Gerstner, Lou, 96
Gettysburg Address (Abraham Lincoln), 4
GM (see General Motors)
"Going private," 228
"Going public," 230–231
Goizueta, Roberto, 76
Golden parachutes, 128–129, 180
"Goods and goodness," balance of, 6
Governance, 2–12
    and capitalism, 6
    corporate, 2
    democratic, 4–5
    evolution of, 2–4, 9–10
    and the "Game," 6–9
    need for, 2
    not-for-profit, 210–216

Governance (Cont.):
    peace and prosperity achieved with, 5
    role of corporate, 11–12
    and trusts, 10–11
Governance committees, 46
Governance model, 134
Governing boards, not-for-profit, 212
Governing documents, 33–47
    articles of incorporation, 34–36
    bylaws, 36–42
    procedure guidelines, 42–46
    and state of incorporation, 33–34
Government sector, 208
Grants, stock, 127
Greeks, ancient, 4, 141
Greenmail, 174, 184–185
Gross domestic product (GDP), 209
Growth companies, 74–75
Gutenberg, Johannes, 3

Hambrick, Donald, 61
Headhunters, 94
Hewlett-Packard Corporation, 74, 177
High-tech company (case study), 65–67
High-yield bonds, 158
A History of the American People (Paul
    Johnson), 10
Hostile takeovers, 173
    benefits of, 182–183
    case study of, 179–181
    defensive measures against, 40–42
    directors' duties in dealing with, 25–26
    friendly mergers vs., 178–185
    share repurchasing to deter, 169
Human resources (HR) committees, 94, 100

IBM, 74, 202
Ignorance, 191, 243
Illegal acts, 62, 139
Immediate family members, 59
Implementation (of corporate strategy),
    140–141
Implementers, 141
"In the money," 126
Incentive plans, 116–119
Income, 157–159
Incorporation:
    articles of, 34–36
    state of, 33–34
Indemnification, 30, 198–199
Independence, 43, 59–61, 64, 134, 200–201
Individuals, potential problems with, 189–192
Inevitability of gradualism, 215
Information:
    availability of, 83, 85
    gathering and disseminating, 3
Informed business decisions, 28
Initial public offerings (IPOs), 65, 66, 153,
    196, 229

Inside candidates, 92–98, 102–103
Inside directors, 43, 59–61, 201
Insider information, 229
Insider trading, 16, 199
    full disclosure about, 176
    laws regarding, 14
Integrity, 13, 56, 189–190, 230–232, 236–237
Intel, 202
Interest rates, 158, 159
Interim CEOs, 99
Interlocking directorships, 201
Internal Revenue Service, 10, 151, 185, 208, 209
Investment bankers, 233
Investment capital, 2
Investors, aggressive, 174
"Invisible hand of self-interest," 1, 6
Involuntary termination, 99
IPOs (see Initial public offerings)

J. P. Stevens & Co. Shareholders Litigation, 26
Japan, 5
Johnson, Eric, 61
Johnson, Paul, 10
Johnson & Johnson, 202
Junk bonds, 40, 158
Justice Department, 139
Justice system, 185

Kentucky Fried Chicken, 136
Knowledge of law, 199, 241

Labor relations, 175–176
Landmark Communications, 230, 231
Law, knowledge of, 199, 241
Lawsuits, 174, 177, 198–199
LBO (leveraged buyout), 99
Lead directors, 43
Leadership, board, 84, 193–194, 214, 219–220
Leasing, 158
Legal issues:
    for boards, 189, 198–199
    for NFP directors, 214–216
Legal system, 7
Leveraged buyout (LBO), 99
Liability (of directors), 30
"Life in the muted market," 211
Limitations:
    on directors, 189
    on special meetings, 41
Limited-liability corporations (LLCs), 10, 151
Limited liability (of owners), 10
Limited-liability partnerships (LLPs), 150
Limited partners, 150
Lincoln, Abraham, 4
Literacy, 3
LLCs (see Limited-liability corporations)
LLPs (limited-liability partnerships), 150
Location (of meetings), 86–87

London Company, 9
Long-term compensation, 111–114, 123–125
Long-term effectiveness (of boards), 73–74
Long view, 18
Lorsch, Jay, 33
Loss of confidence, 147
Loyalty, duty of, 20–22, 30, 34, 64, 214

Machiavelli, Nicolo, 142
Magna Carta, 4
Management, 224
Mandatory retirement ages, 63
Market makers, 233
Market reaction, 169–170
Market test, 211–212
Marshall, George C., 220
Marshall, John, 9–10
Mature companies, 74–75
Meetings:
    of annual shareholders, 37–38
    board (see Board meetings)
    not-for-profit, 223–224
    special shareholder, 38
Members, 151, 218–219
Mercury Interactive, 74
Mergers, 174, 178–185
Military, 7
Minority groups, rights of, 4
Minutes, board meeting, 87, 88
Mistakes, admitting, 242
Misuse of corporate funds, 229
Monopolies, 11
Moral conflict, 2
Morality, 8
Morgan, J. P., 10
Morgan Stanley Dean Witter, 167
Motivation, 188
Mountain Bank, 70–73
Movable type, 3
Muscovy Company, 9

Name, corporate, 34
Nasdaq, 105, 151, 231
National defense, 7
National Rifle Association, 218
"New economy," 143–144
The New Nonprofit Almanac and Desk
    Reference, 209
New York Stock Exchange (NYSE), 59, 151
New York Times Company, 210
NFP organizations (see Not-for-profit
    organizations)
Nominating committees, 46, 63–70, 100
    board profile created by, 64–65
    due diligence on candidates by, 68–70
    high-tech (case study), 65–67
    inside directors on, 201
    search/screening process of, 67–68
Nonbusiness corporations, 9

Noncompete agreements, 127–128
Nonprofit (term), 207
Nonqualifying stock options, 125
Nooyi, Indra, 136
Not-for-profit (NFP) organizations, 207–226
  accountability in, 225–226
  board for, 55–56, 212–213, 219–222
  categories/revenues of, 209
  committees for, 222–223
  and compensation, 225
  frequency of meetings for, 223–224
  governance of, 210–216
  and politics, 224
  role of, 208–209
  senior management for, 224–225
  stakeholders in, 216–219
  as tax-exempt organizations, 209–210
  as term, 207–208
NYSE (see New York Stock Exchange)

Obstruction of justice, 229
OCC (see Office of the Comptroller of the
    Currency)
Off-balance-sheet financing, 159–160
Office, registered, 35
Office of the Comptroller of the Currency
    (OCC), 70, 72
Officers, corporate, 43–44
"Old economy, 143
Operating leases, 160
Opportunities, corporate, 21
Organization, board, 57–61
Organizers, 141
OTC (over-the-counter) trading, 151
Out-of-touch boards, 196–198
Outside assessment, 105–106
Outside candidates, 92–98
Outstanding options, triggers for, 129–130
Over-the-counter (OTC) trading, 151
Oversight responsibility, 23–25, 145–146
Ownership, stock, 61–62

P/E (see Price-earnings)
Parity, external, 122
Partnerships, 9, 150, 151
Passion, savvy vs., 220–221
Peace and prosperity, 5
Peers:
  benchmarking with, 105
  review by, 63, 194
Penalties, 228
PepsiCo, 135–137
PepsiCo Food Systems, 136
Performance criteria:
  for CEO compensation, 113–114, 119–121
  for CEO evaluation, 106–107
Performance evaluation, 103–107
  benchmarking with peers as criterion in,
    105

Performance evaluation (Cont.):
  outside assessments in, 105–106
  role of CEO/board in, 107
  strategy implementation as criterion in,
    104–105
Perot, Ross, 195
Perquisites (perks), 124, 198
Personal attributes (of candidates),
    101–102
Personal property rights, 7
Personalities, dominant, 75–76
Personality conflicts, 194–195
Perspective, board, 84
Pizza Hut, 136
Platinum parachutes, 129
Pluralistic society, 207
"Poison pill," 42, 77, 183
Police powers, 8
Politics, 194–195, 224, 240
Portfolio of businesses, 162–163
Portfolio theory, 142
Preemptive candidates, 99
Preferred stock, 158
Pressure to focus, 143
Presumption, 27
Price-earnings (P/E), 169–170
Principles of Corporate Governance (American
    Law Institute), 14, 16, 20–23, 25–27
Printing, 3
Privacy rights, 8
Private ownership, 11–12, 153
  of corporations, 150
  decision to change to, 228
Procedure guidelines, 42–46
Profile, board, 64–65
Profit, 17, 208, 212
Profitability, 11, 18
Property, equity in, 218–219
Proprietorships, 9, 150
Prosecution, 229–230
Prosperity, 8
Proxy fights, 174, 177
Proxy statements (proxies), 38,
    110, 174
Prudent man rule, 34
Public ownership, 11, 151, 153–155
Public relations, 226
Public safety, 7
Public Welfare Foundation, 210
Punishment, 230
Purpose:
  in articles of incorporation, 35
  clarity of, 243
  in test of effectiveness, 11

Quaker Oats, 136, 137
Qualified stock options, 126
Quasi-public companies, 77
Quorum, 39–40

Raiders, 40–42, 185
"Reasonable person" test, 29
Recruitment, director, 69, 72
Reelection (of incumbent directors), 62–63
Reference checks, 68
Registered office or agent, 35
Regulation(s), 14
    of CEO compensation, 228–229
    consequences of, 228–229
Regulatory agencies:
    external pressure from, 185–186
    as transgressors, 234
Reinemund, Steven S., 136
Representation, 13
Representative boards, 80–82
Representative government, 4
Repurchase of shares, 166–170
Responsibility, taking, 236
Restricted stock, 97–98, 116
Restructuring strategies, 164
Retention (of talent), 240
Retirement ages, mandatory, 63
Retiring CEOs, 62, 91–92
Retrenchment, 178 (See also Entrenchment)
Revenues, 111, 113
Review, director, 62–63
Revolutions, 3, 4, 9
Rights (of minority groups), 4
Risk/risk management, 46, 157–159
Romans, ancient, 4, 141
Rome, 9
Rotation of board members, 222
Russia, 5

S Corporation, 151
Salaries, 109–111, 116, 122, 123
Salton, 74
Salvation Army, 213
Savvy, passion vs., 220–221
Scheduling, board-meeting, 88, 90
Search firms, executive, 94
SEC (see Securities and Exchange
    Commission)
Secretaries, 87, 88
Section 501(c), 209
Securities and Exchange Commission (SEC),
    16, 45, 151, 153, 184, 185, 199, 231
Securities manipulation, 139
Segregation, 5
Self-governance, 5
Self-interest, 1, 6, 13
Selling businesses, 164–165
Senior management:
    board conflicts with, 16
    day-to-day decisions made by, 15
    of not-for-profit organizations, 224–225
    as transgressors, 232
September 11, 2001, terrorist attacks, 80
Severance packages, 127–128, 180

Share-repurchase plans, 117, 166–170
Shareholder activism, 173, 175–177
Shareholder value, 11, 170
Shareholders, 13
    control of corporation by, 15
    social obligations vs. responsibility to,
        18–20
Short–term bonuses, 123, 124
Siebel Systems, 74
SIPs (stock investment plans), 116
Slavery, 4, 5
Small capitalization stocks, 155
Smith, Adam, 1, 6
Smith v. Van Gorkom, 28
Smith's Snackfoods Company (TSSC), 136
"Smoke.coms," 231
Socialistic systems, 8
Societies, 3
    development of, 6
    obligations of, 18–20
    revolutions in, 3, 4, 9
    values of, 230
Solutions:
    attracting/retaining talent as part of, 240
    board as part of, 235–242
    CEO-board relationship as part of, 239
    politics as part of, 240
    regulators as part of, 235
South America, 5
South Sea bubble, 154
South Sea Company, 154
S&P 500 Index (see Standard & Poor's 500
    Index)
Spanish Company, 9
Special committees, 46, 94, 100
Special shareholder meetings, 38, 41
"Spin," 230
Spinning off businesses, 165
Sponsors, 218
Staff work, 85
Staggered terms, 41–42
Stakeholders:
    board members as, 238
    in not-for-profit organizations, 216–219
Standard & Poor's (S&P) 500 Index, 57–61,
    74, 80–82, 105, 110, 112, 113, 155, 156,
    158, 159, 203, 204
Standards (for directors), 26–28
Standing committees, 44, 46
State laws, director-related, 13–15
Stericycle, 74
Stock, 35–36
    directors' ownership of, 61–62, 238
    grants of, 127
    promotion of, 229
    runups of, 229
Stock exchanges, 16
Stock investment plans (SIPs), 116
Stock options, 97–98, 109, 116, 125–127

Stock purchase plans, 127
Stockholder gain, 18
Stockholders, 151
Strategy, corporate (*see* Corporate strategy)
Strategy implementation, 104–105
Structure:
  of boards, 56–57, 78
  capital, 155–161
  corporate, 150–155
Subchapter S, 10
Subjective good faith standard, 29
Supervision, duty of, 24–25
Supervisory board, 43–44
Suppliers, 217
"Survival of the fittest," 1
Sustainable competitive advantage, 141–142
Synergy, 179

Taco Bell, 136
Tariffs, 11
Tax considerations, 10
  for CEO compensation, 109
  for not-for-profits, 208
  for organization forms, 152
  for stock options, 125–127
  for stock-repurchase plans, 168
Tax-exempt organizations, 209–210
Teamwork, 86
Technology, 2–3
Teleconference meetings, 87
10-Q form, 45
Term limits, 24, 63
Termination:
  dates of (for corporation), 36
  involuntary, 99
Terms, 69–70
  of board service, 222
  staggered, 41–42
The Smith's Snackfoods Company (TSSC),
  136
Time Warner, 167
Toleration of legal violations, 192
Totalitarian regimes, 5
Training, board, 194
Transfer of ownership, 10
Transgressions, 232–235
Transistors, 3
Transportation, 7
Tricon Global Restaurants, 136
Tropicana Food Products, 136

Trust (characteristic), 190
Trustees, 34
Trusts (organizational form), 10–11, 211
TSSC (The Smith's Snackfoods Company),
  136
"Tulip mania," 231

UBI (unrelated business income), 210
Underground economy, 8
Underinvested directors, 202
"Underwater" stocks, 116, 126
Unions:
  economic, 7
  labor, 175–176
United States, 4
  enforcement in, 8
  game's rules in, 7
Universal education, 3
Universities, 213
Unlimited life, 10
Unocal Corp. (case), 27
Unrelated business income (UBI), 210
U.S. Supreme Court, 9–10

Values:
  of candidates, 101
  societal, 230
Vesting, 125–126, 129–130
Virginia:
  business judgment rule in, 28
  director-related laws of, 14, 15
  duty of care rule in, 29
  model corporate code of, 34
Virginia Code Annotated, 14
Virginia Company of London, 9
Volunteers, 213–214, 217

Wal-Mart, 74
Wealth, 3
Wealth of Nations (Adam Smith), 6
Weather Channel, 230–231
Welch, Jack, 76, 96, 122
Welfare programs, 8–9
Welfare Reform Act of 1996, 8–9
White knights, 184
Willingness to act decisively, 241–242
WLR Foods (case), 29
Workgroup boards, 213, 223

Yahoo!, 231

ABOUT THE AUTHORS

John L. Colley, Jr., D.B.A., is the Almand R. Coleman Professor of Business Administration at the University of Virginia's Darden Graduate School of Business Administration. He has served as Chief of Operations and System Analysis for Hughes Aircraft Company and as a director for numerous corporations.

Jacqueline L. Doyle, Ph.D., is a Visiting Assistant Professor of Business Administration and former General Motors Post-Doctoral Fellow at Darden, where she teaches MBA and executive education courses in corporate strategy, operations, and service operations strategy. Her board service has been in the nonprofit sector.

George W. Logan is a Visiting Lecturer in Business Administration at Darden as well as Instituto Centroamericano de Administracion de Empresas (INCAE) in Costa Rica and Nicaragua. He has served on the boards of a variety of companies and foundations.

Wallace Stettinius is a Visiting Lecturer in Business Administration at Darden and Senior Executive Fellow at Virginia Commonwealth University. He teaches MBA and executive education-level courses in corporate governance, management, and executive development and has served on numerous boards both as chairman and as director.